LEASIDE

LEASIDE

JANE PITFIELD
EDITOR

NATURAL HERITAGE BOOKS
TORONTO

Published by Natural Heritage/Natural History Inc.
P.O. Box 95, Station O, Toronto, Ontario M4A 2M8

Front cover illustration: painting of "Leaside," William Lea's octagonal
home by artist David Peacock. *Collection of the Pitfield family.*

Design by Blanche Hamill, Norton Hamill Design
Printed and bound in Canada by Hignell Printing Limited

Canadian Cataloguing in Publication Data

Leaside

Includes bibliographical references and index.
ISBN 1-896219-54-3

1. Leaside (Toronto, Ont.)—History.   I. Pitfield, Jane.

FC3099.L43L43 1999   971.3'541   C99-930516-6
F1059.5.L43L43 1999

THE CANADA COUNCIL | LE CONSEIL DES ARTS
FOR THE ARTS | DU CANADA
SINCE 1957 | DEPUIS 1957

Natural Heritage/Natural History Inc. acknowledges the support received for its
publishing program from the Canada Council Block Grant Program. We also
acknowledge with gratitude the assistance of the Association for the Export of
Canadian Books, Ottawa.

This book is dedicated to the residents of Leaside, past, present and future. May our community of Leaside continue to grow and prosper in the years to come.

CONTENTS

INTRODUCTION

I~N THE~ spring of 1997, I realized that there was a need for a book about our community "Leaside." Being much aware of the amalgamation with Toronto looming later in the year, I was struck by the fact that Leaside had previously been amalgamated with the Borough of East York in 1967, and yet had managed to retain its unique character. I felt it was very important to provide a comprehensive account of the development of the town of Leaside so that its residents, especially those new to the area, could understand the fascinating chain of events that have taken place over the years.

Fortunately, there were some previously published materials to provide background material. John Scott wrote a book titled *The Story of Leaside* for the Leaside Council in 1931. Charles Clay wrote *The Leaside Story* in 1958 on the occasion of the town's 45th anniversary. In 1982, Jack Rempel's book, *The Town of Leaside: A Brief History*, was published by the East York Historical Society. All of these publications are out-of-print and no longer readily available.

Many months after beginning to compile this book, I read J. I. Rempel's last words from his publication: "...my only intention here was to show the contribution of the Lea family to the early development of this area. Someone else will have to amplify other aspects of municipal, industrial, religious or recreational developments."

In the spring of 1997, I met with a small group of Leasiders who had expressed interest in being involved with this project. This book is the result of the contribution of many people, all of whom are acknowledged under our list of contributors. Their contributions have taken many forms, from being interviewed to researching and writing, and to the provision of photographs, maps and other memorabilia.

Ultimately, it was recognized that we needed a structure for our inclusive approach, a book that is largely historical, yet designed to recognize and celebrate the people, places and events that have combined to make Leaside unique. While the main focus is on the period from 1913 to 1967, emphasizing the years that Leaside existed as its own town, we chose to begin with pre-settlement times and the early geological formation, to set the stage for what ultimately became Leaside. As well, there is inclusion of some happenings beyond 1967. As a result of these decisions, the overall approach is largely thematic, within a general chronological framework.

It is our hope that all readers will not only enjoy *Leaside* but will develop an appreciation for the rich heritage of our community, and that a new sense of pride will result.

While every effort has been made to ensure the accuracy of the information in this publication, we (the Editor and the Publisher) would gratefully receive any corrections which will be incorporated into future editions.

Jane Pitfield, Editor
1999

1

FROM PRE-SETTLEMENT
TO SETTLEMENT

CERTAIN PHYSICAL and topographical characteristics of what became the Leaside area attracted Aboriginal peoples first and, eventually, in the early 19th century, European settlement. Once the primeval forest was cleared by the early pioneers, the quality of the soil enabled agriculture to flourish and give sustenance to the original settlers, and to the generations which followed.

Some 80 years later, in the late 19th century, the topography of the plateau overlooking the valley of the Don attracted the railway companies which eventually converted the rich agricultural lands into the urban centre called Leaside.

What were the forces in pre-history and pre-settlement times which formed the land?

Thousands of years ago, the Leaside area was affected by a series of ancient Ice Ages. The land, part of the Lake Ontario basin, was covered by a succession of glaciers and large lakes. At least two major glaciations moved across the area in the Pleistocene Epoch. Between the two advances of the glaciers, a period of temperate climate occured, somewhat warmer than today's climate, as indicated by warm climate fossils from the old Don Valley Brick Works. Cold climate fossils found in the Scarborough Bluffs (deposits of Lake Coleman and Lake Scarborough) indicate the return of the glaciers which covered what today is Toronto.

Pollen grains from these deposits identify the flora which existed. During the period of Lake Coleman, deciduous trees, indicators of a warm period, included oak, elm, ironwood, maple, hickory, beech, basswood and sweet gum. Then, as the larger Lake Scarborough formed, pollen samples of conifers such as spruce, pine, balsam, hemlock, larch which grow in lower temperatures, increased, indicating a cooler climate.

On top of these lake deposits were the glacial deposits from which the Leaside area was formed.

Some 48,000 years ago, as temperatures rose, the glaciers which covered most of Canada began to melt. They receded in this area to create Lake Ontario, a body of water much larger than the lake which we now know.

Once again, about 35,000 years ago, the glaciers began building, with glacial waters depositing river sand and mud into a lake, called Lake Thorncliffe by some. The glacier continued to grow until it covered all of what is now Ontario, as well as the northern United States, some 18,000 to 20,000 years ago.

Geologists tell us another warm period occurred about 13,500 years ago. This temperature increase caused the great body of frozen water to slowly melt back, allowing a land mass, part of what is today's Ontario (an area defined by present day London, Guelph and Orangeville), to emerge from the ice.

A further 2,000 years passed before the glaciers receded from north of present day Toronto. The melting glaciers created a very large "Lake Ontario" called Lake Iroquois. The northern shore of Lake Iroquois ran along a line several hundred yards north of present day Eglinton Avenue. What is now the City of Toronto would have been under the water of this lake which was some 180 feet above the level of present day Lake Ontario.

Submerged for thousands of years (when not frozen solid) under a succession of lakes, the Leaside lands were shaped by erosion and sedimentary deposits. Silt, sand and boulders were washed into the expanded Lake Iroquois where wave action and gravity smoothed the edges of the lake bottom, ultimately creating a plateau. Leaside, Oakville, Burlington and Hamilton are all part of this so-called "Iroquois Plain."

As temperatures rose, water levels gradually fell and Lake Iroquois, once dammed by ice at Cornwall, began to flow eastward and drain into the St. Lawrence basin. Gradually, the lake was reduced in size to that of present day Lake Ontario.

As the lake receded, the plateau-like Leaside lands emerged, high and dry. Centuries of spring run-offs carried by the branches of the Don carved the deep valleys which surround the relatively flat Leaside land on three sides.

The flora and fauna native to Leaside migrated to this area less than 11,000 years ago, however, fossils of the earlier temporary warm periods have been unearthed. As well, about 120,000 years ago this area was

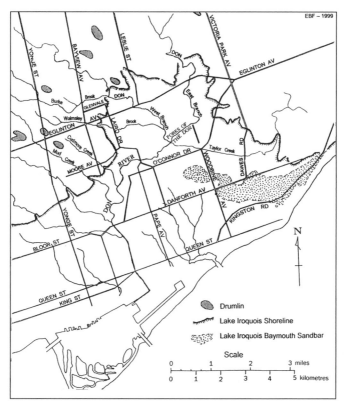

Map showing extent of the waters of Lake Iroquois. *Mapwork by Ed Freeman.*

home to a variety of wildlife: the giant beaver and white tailed deer (fossils found in Don Valley Brick Yards); bison, bear, stag-moose, and mammoth or possibly mastodon (found near present day Shaw Street at Ossington Avenue); and Tundra musk-oxen (found by the Scarborough Bluffs). Fossils of species inhabiting the area since the last Ice Age include an 11,700 year old brown bear; and a 11,300 year old caribou-sized deer called Torontoceras (found during the Etobicoke Station subway excavation in the 1980s).

The earliest humans, Paleo-Indians, arrived in this area from the south about 9,000 years ago.[1] "The first known humans in the Toronto area were the Laurentian peoples—stone workers, who lived just east of present day Toronto, from 3,000 to 1,000 B.C."[2] By the time that Native people appeared, the western portion of this area would have been ice-free. Native farming of corn, beans and squash was known to have occurred in the area bounded by Bathurst, Eglinton, Duplex and

Strathallen streets circa 1645 A.D. However, reliable evidence points to human habitation at least 200 years earlier in North Toronto. The Huron had a settlement here for about 25 years, now called the Quantat Village, with traditional long houses grouped near an artesian spring, and surrounded by corn fields. This discovery, made during the basement excavation of Franklin Jackes' Castlefield house in 1887, was identified by Toronto's first professional archeologist, David Boyle.[3]

The short duration of the Quantat site was typical and attributed to the fact that the Native population did not practise crop rotation. Corn, very destructive of soil, probably failed after a few decades of continuous planting. The Natives would also have gathered berries and nuts and hunted the local deer, but seemingly they did not hunt wolves which were also plentiful. According to Elizabeth Simcoe's diary, dated January 14, 1794: "The Indians do not kill wolves, they seldom take trouble that does not answer to them, & the Wolves are not good to eat & their skins are of little value."[4]

Étienne Brûle, interpreter for Champlain and an explorer in his own right, is believed to have seen the environs of the Don and the Leaside lands in the early 1600s. At that time, the main Native settlement was at the mouth of the Humber River, a few miles to the west. There, they spent the winter months sheltered by the dense forest that covered the area.

By the 1780s, under the pressures of the American Revolution, survey parties had penetrated far into the endless forests. With the arrival of Lieutenant-Governor John Graves Simcoe in 1793, the village of York was established and, by 1800, permanently settled on the layers of fertile, often muddy, sediment deposited by ancient Lake Iroquois. Beyond the village limits, well up into the hills, scattered settlements were forming across the countryside.

Large numbers of slaves from the United States, following the famed "Underground Railway," sought shelter in Ontario, from the 1850s up to 1865 when the American Civil War ended. More than 1,500 of the estimated 40,000 settled in Toronto where they contributed to economic and political life of the area.[5] "For a time the population of what is now Leaside was largely augmented by the influx of negroes escaping from the bondage of slavery prevalent in the United States at that period."[6]

Forty-one years prior to this, however, the arrival in Canada of a British immigrant and his subsequent purchase of land in York Township, marks the true beginning of the Leaside we know.

2

THE LEA FAMILY

THE HISTORY of the Lea family is at the heart of the history of Lea-side. In no other part of the Toronto area has a family been more closely associated to the development of a community than the Leas were in Leaside.

The Lea name appears in mid-15th century Spain. A Ferdinando Lea emigrated from Spain to England. In succeeding generations, one branch of the family anglicized the surname to "Leigh," the other branch retained the "Lea" spelling. Both branches prospered and many rose to nobility. In the mid-1500s, Sir Thomas Leigh became Lord Mayor of London.[1]

John Lea was born in Lancashire in 1773. He married Mary Hutchi-son from Cumberland. On May 28, 1814, their first child, William Lea, was born in Lancaster. Four years later they left England for the United States.

In the spring of 1818, John and Mary Lea, with their son, sailed from Liverpool in a barque commanded by Captain Birkett. After tossing on the Atlantic for three months, they arrived in Philadelphia. There they remained for only a short time, then travelled by stagecoach over the Alleghany Mountains to Pittsburgh, where they stayed for a year. Either not liking the country or the people of their new home, or possibly concerned about the lingering anti-British sentiment, John Lea decided not to stay in America. Leaving his family to follow when he was resettled, he went to Canada in search of a suitable place for a home. Once John Lea had found a location to his liking in the Township of York, he informed Mary of his purchase of Lot 13, Concession 3, situated three concessions north from the Toronto bay. She and William were to join him.

Mary Lea, with her young son, travelled east along the shore of Lake Erie, crossed the Niagara River at Black Rock and went on past the Falls, the sound of which William remembered hearing. The sight of the more familiar British soldiers in their scarlet uniforms at Niagara on the British side of the river gave Mary courage.

With William, who was about five years old, Mary crossed Lake Ontario in a schooner belonging to a person named Garside. The year was 1819. Upon arrival at York, at that time a town consisting of 1,174 people (including children), 91 one-storey houses, 68 two-storey ones and a total of 21 shops,[2] they proceeded to the newly-acquired farm, a small log house with a few cleared acres. The rest of the two hundred acre property was heavily timbered. Records indicate that the log home was located where Laird Drive and Lea Avenue meet. Over the ten years that they lived there, John Lea Jr. was born (1823) and later, a daughter, Mary Margaret, was added to the family.

John Lea had chosen York because the price of land there was inexpensive as compared with other parts of Upper Canada. He desired land that was fertile and easily drained for the crops he planned to grow. "Leaside stands about 150 feet above lake level on land that is high and dry."[3] With close proximity to Yonge Street (the only main road at the time) and close to a good market to sell his produce, he found Lot 13 in the third concession a perfect match for his ambitions. The 200 acres were purchased from Alexander McDonnell for two hundred guineas. This transaction was recorded on January 20, 1820. (According to family tradition, he paid one guinea per acre for the land which was expensive for the time but, the cleared land and the completed log home probably contributed to the higher price)[4] While it seemed expensive for property in this area, it had in its favour woodlands that could be cleared quickly, with a portion of this tough, back-breaking labour already completed.

John Lea was a successful farmer. In time, he bought cows and kept a dairy as well as planting an orchard of Northern Spy apples.[5] In 1829, only ten years after his initial purchase, he was able to erect a larger brick home, in the same vicinity as the original log cabin. It is claimed that this was the first brick house to be built in York Township.[6] The house resembled an English country home and, with its four chimneys, was considered to be unique. At that time, homes were taxed according to the number of fireplaces they contained, however one fireplace was tax-free. This home may, in fact, have had five, as one (the middle) chimney was purported to be double-sized, perhaps to accommodate the construction of two back-to-back fireplaces.

The home of John Lea Sr. Built in 1829 and believed to be the first brick home in York County, it would have stood in the vicinity of the juncture of Lea and Laird. *Collection of the Lea Family. Courtesy Ted and Barbara Lea.*

Behind the home was a large pond into which the "Leaside Creek" flowed from the vicinity of today's Bayview and Eglinton. From here the pond would have connected to the Don River. Access to the Lea farm was by way of Williams Street which came across from Yonge Street at what is now Glebe Road.

"Little is recorded of the early period of John's pioneering days. These must have been days of hard work and loneliness for a young English farmer, but he apparently prospered through his toil as the area became known for its high productivity. There are stories that at one time negro slaves escaping from the United States took up residence in the area. It is possible they assisted with land clearing, and were, for the most part, employed as farm help."[7]

John Sr. died in 1854 at the age of 81 years.[8] His wife, Mary Hutchison, had predeceased him in 1846, at the age of 55 years. They are buried in the cemetery of St. John's Anglican Church, York Mills. Upon his death, the farm was divided and each son received about 100 acres of land. The brick home and one hundred and ten acres (this included the house, orchard and all the out-buildings) were left to his son, John Jr.

John Jr. had married Sarah Charles, daughter of James Charles, a well-known Toronto dry goods businessman. Their daughter, Mary, and son,

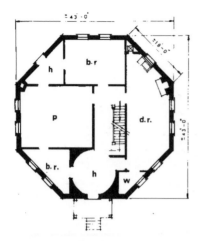

Plan of the William Lea house. Sketched as the late Estella M. Lamb (daughter of Charles Lea) remembered it. She was born in this house and she approved the final drawing as being correct. *From* The Town of Leaside *by J.I. Rempel, 1982.*

James, were born there. In its final years, this brick house was left vacant and subsequently burnt down about 1912.[9]

John Sr. had left ninety acres of the old homestead, part of Lot 13, Concession 3 to his eldest son William. In 1841, he bought additional land, 130 acres, just to the south of his father's farm. When William Lea founded the Village of Leaside, somewhere between 1851 and 1854, he built an odd-looking house with eight gables that reminded one of the old toll house. This strange-looking octagonal structure, two storeys high with an additional much smaller storey added on top, he named "Leaside."[10]

Octagonal houses had been a trend in the United States. The book which may have inspired William Lea was *A Home For All, or the Gravel Wall and Octagon Mode of Building* by Orson S. Fowler. In 1973, Fowler's book was republished under the title *The Octagon House, a home for all.*[11] During this period, it was also the trend for many churches, barns and schools to be built in an octagonal style. Lea's house, the first octagonal home in the Toronto area, and perhaps in Ontario, was located close to where Leaside Memorial Gardens now stands. The octagonal home, "Leaside," is pictured on the front cover of this book.

William justified his choice of the octagonal shape as he said, "...like a bee's cell, it enclosed the greatest amount of space within the least amount of wall."[12] The house doubled as a court house, the only court house east of Yonge Street, once William became a Magistrate for the County of York. In fact, not only was his octagonal house distinctive, it also served as a residence, a post office and a town hall, as well as a court house.

Considered an eccentric by many, William's long beard seemed to symbolize his unique appearance and range of interests. In his career, he

Residence of Orson S. Fowler of Fishkill, New York. This designer of octagonal homes influenced William Lea in his decision to build "Leaside." *Taken from* The Octagonal House, a home for all *by Orson Fowler, 1973.*

demonstrated his intelligence, along with a home-grown scientific curiosity. In religion, he was Anglican and in his politics, a Conservative. A poet who loved nature and tried to preserve it, William was an early environmentalist. "He was also a painter and an antiquitarian."[13] An historian, William wrote extensively on the Don River. His historical address on the early settlement of the Don River delivered to the Canadian Institute was published in the *Toronto Evening Telegram* of January 17, 1881 and February 4, 1881.[14]

Much of William's land was planted as an apple orchard, extending over what would later become the Gatineau Power Station property and the Thorncliffe Racetrack. "Other early farms had extensive orchards and there is a story that the Murrays (on the farm just south of William Lea) grew apples for export and experimented with a yellow crabapple which, owing to its colour did not market well."[15] As tomatoes also proved to be a profitable crop, William built a tomato cannery beside his home, and became the supplier of tomatoes for the old Queen's Hotel (located where the Royal York is today). His tomato crops stretched to the part of the property which later became the "Leaside Aerodrome" (at Wicksteed). Over the years, William carried on farming, fruit growing and farm gardening with his sons.

A laneway called William Lea's Lane connected the house to Yonge Street, the main thoroughfare. In 1881, William sold a parcel of land to

William Lea (1814-1893), son of John Lea Sr., donated land for the original St. Cuthbert's Church in 1890. The octagonal house, "Leaside," was William Lea's home. *S. Walter Stewart Library, Elmore Gray collection.*

the Canadian Pacific Railway (CPR) as a place for the railway to build a train station. As well, he generously gave a half-acre of land to the Anglican Church of England, for the purpose of building the original wooden St. Cuthbert's on the Government Road (as Bayview was called then). The Leas of Leaside quite frequently had attended St. Barnabas Church, across the Don River around Danforth and Broadview (near the Playter Estate). The Playter and Lea families were closely associated by marriage, Mary Margaret having married John Playter.

"William Lea had been educated at boarding school in York."[16]. In 1841, William married Mary Ann Taylor, the first of what would become three wives. Mary Anne was the second daughter of James Taylor who had emigrated from Tadington, Derbyshire, England and settled on the east side of the Don River. William and Mary had two daughters, both of whom died in infancy. Their mother soon followed, dying within three years of her marriage.

In 1848, William married Elizabeth Davids, eldest daughter of Charles Kendrick Davids from Dartford, Kent. They had seven children (three sons and four daughters): Joseph, Charles, James David, Lillian, Mary Alice, Jessie and Fannie. Elizabeth died in 1867, at the age of 52 years. Three years later, William married his third wife Sophia Blogg. She was the sister of Elizabeth Davids and the widow of John L. Blogg, remembered by many Torontonians of the time as the fashionable bootmaker. Blogg's shop was on King Street.

William died in 1893, at 78 years of age. Both William and his second wife, Elizabeth, are buried at St. John's Anglican Church, York Mills, with William's parents. Sophia Blogg died in 1903.

Lea Lane with tomato cannery on right. Date of photograph is unknown. *S. Walter Stewart Library, Elmore Gray collection.*

Two years after his second marriage, William Lea was elected to the office of Township Councillor and would hold office for seven years. During Lord Elgin's period of government, William was appointed a Justice of the Peace, a prestigious position, possibly a political reward for his support of the Conservative party.

William increased his original land holdings of 90 acres, left to him by his father. Over the years he purchased additional land until he had a total of 250 acres. This land, along with the adjoining farm of his brother John Jr., the Murray farm to the south and the Elgie and Beatty farms to the north, ultimately became the Town of Leaside.

Upon William's death in 1893, his eldest son Joseph, took over the tomato cannery and lived in the octagonal home until 1903. In 1913 the house, having been abandoned for ten years, was demolished by the Canadian Northern Railway. Having been left unprotected for this span of time, the house was in bad shape. Much of the interior had been ruined by the boys of the neighbourhood who had broken the panes of glass, wrenched away the stair rails and thrown about the magazines from the attic.[17]

The CNoR purposely set fire to the old landmark as part of the clearing of land for the company's proposed new sidings and townsite. It is said that it took all day to burn the magnificent pine woodwork. There was not a single knot in it. Today, such wood trim would be worth a great deal.

The William Lea home, showing the original porch of the octagonal house. The man with the dog is Mr. Blogg. The man with folded arms is Joseph Lea, William's oldest son. The young woman dressed in black in the background is his niece, Estella Mary (Mrs. Canon Lamb). *From the Archives at Todmorden Mills Museum.*

William Lea's Lane looking east. The house on the left is the farm home of Charles, William's second son. *From the Archives at Todmorden Mills Museum.*

St. Cuthbert's Road, looking west from Bessborough Drive to St. Cuthbert's Church on the left. The home of John Lea Jr. is on the right. *Photograph taken in February 1938 by the late Stuart L. Thompson.*

Home built by John Lea Jr., across from St. Cuthbert's Church. Eventually the site was occupied by Humphrey Funeral Home. *Leaside Public Library Collection.*

"Leaside," William Lea's octagonal house, burning in 1913. *S. Walter Stewart Library, Elmore Gray collection.*

The flames also consumed a fine collection of old engravings and pho-tographs, including many pictures of both Queen Victoria and King Edward VII. The travels in Canada on the occasion of the King's first visit were recorded and illustrated in both the *Star* and the *Globe.* All were devoured by the fire.

The scorched remains of this burnt building stood sadly until 1918. The planned sidings and townsite had not materialized and the Canadian Northern Railway, in bankruptcy, was taken over by the federal govern-ment as part of the Canadian National Railways. The gutted shell of William Lea's "Leaside" was later torn down. Today, all that remains to remind us of this once exceptional building is a plaque, erected by the East York Historical Society, located outside on the wall of the Leaside Memorial Gardens.

John Lea Jr., William's younger brother, left the original Lea brick house in 1870 and built a home across from St. Cuthbert's Church, fur-ther east on Bayview (where Humphrey's Funeral Home presently stands). As an area farmer, he was well-known as a cattle breeder.

John Lea and his wife, Sarah, had two sons and one daughter. James Lea, their first son, built what is now 201 Sutherland Drive around 1909. Today, it does not front on Sutherland, but rather was constructed to face James Lea Lane which came in from Bayview at the time. Edgar Lea, son of James Lea, the great grandson of John Sr., was the last member of the

The photograph is believed to be Charles Lea with his wife
Charlotte (Playter). Daughter Estella Mary (later to become
Mrs. P. M. Lamb) is sitting on her mother's knee. *Leaside
Public Library Collection*

family to live in the house.

The Sutherland Drive house became a nursery school run by Mrs.
Eve Procunier from 1939 to the late 1950s. It was affectionately called
"The Wendy House" after Wendy in the story of Peter Pan. Today, the
house still stands as a residence and is owned by the Rutherford family.
The porch was added to the original home and the present owners have
renovated the attic, creating additional living space.

3

THE RAILWAYS OF LEASIDE JUNCTION

"THERE WAS a time in this fair land when the railway did not run...."[1] that was 1880. In 1881, the railway began to run in Leaside and has continued to do so for over 118 years. Today, few residents would think of their Leaside community as a "railway town." But railway town it was.

Leaside is the child of the railway, more correctly the child of three railways.—

THE FIRST RAILWAY—THE ONTARIO AND QUEBEC RAILWAY

In the 1870s, a "railway mania" swept North America. For a period of 20 years there was a feverish race to build railway lines into every region of the continent, into as many cities, towns and villages as possible. The elusive goal of large and certain profit drove the scramble for routes and real estate.

As part of that railway mania, in the late 1870s, the Ontario and Quebec Railway was incorporated to build a railway line from West Toronto along the city's northern limits in an easterly direction through Peterborough, Perth and Ottawa to Montreal.

Because high and long railway trestles were very expensive to build, the surveyors for the Ontario and Quebec Railway chose, as the location to build their bridge across the Don River, a spot where its valley was as narrow and shallow as possible. This decision caused the right-of-way to curve northward and pass through the southeast corner of the Third Concession, the farm of William Lea. Consequently, a few acres of his property were purchased by the Ontario and Quebec Railway for its proposed Toronto to Peterborough line. The payment was generous, and as well, there was an inherent belief that the coming of the railway meant prosperity and progress.

The railway company laid track as far east as Perth and, once there, ran into financial difficulty as did many lines during the "mania." As a result, the Ontario and Quebec Railway was forced to cede the line to the Canadian Pacific Railway (CPR) in 1884, on a 999 year lease. While the rail line through Leaside appears to be that of the Canadian Pacific Railway, the right-of-way, however, is leased from the Ontario and Quebec Railway which continues to exist as a corporate entity. (The lease has 884 years to run!)

The Ontario and Quebec Railway line showing the "right-of-way" through the farm of William Lea.[2] *Adapted by Jim Hannah. From* The Toronto World, *March 1912.*

In 1996, the shareholders of the Ontario and Quebec Railway, after very lengthy negotiations, finally reached an agreement with developers to allow a bridge from Nesbitt Drive to cross above its rail line. Construction of the bridge that would provide access to the new community of Governor's Bridge Estates finally began in November 1998.

Thus, a long forgotten railway company[3] emerged from the past to determine how and when a new residential community would be built in the Leaside area.

THE SECOND RAILWAY—THE CANADIAN PACIFIC RAILWAY

In 1884, the Canadian Pacific Railway, now operating the line, needed a level site on its North Toronto subdivision for maintenance shops, rail sidings for assembling trains and for the establishment of a connection to the downtown centre of a growing Toronto. The corner of the Third Concession met all of the criteria. A junction was constructed in 1892 and a line (the Don Branch)[4] was built heading south, following the Don River to the original Union Station on Toronto's waterfront.

To control the rail activity at the junction, a station was needed. In September 1894, the Canadian Pacific opened its station and named it Leaside Junction, in honour of the owner of the land, William Lea, who called his unique octagonal home, "Leaside." Thus, Leaside became a name and a location on the map.

The Canadian Pacific Station at Leaside Junction, looking west towards Toronto. Date: May 1899. *Canadian Pacific Archives.*

Canadian Pacific's "new" Leaside Station, looking towards Agincourt. Date: November 1946. *Canadian Pacific Archives.*

The term "Junction" gradually disappeared from the name and the Leaside Station served as a busy stop for Canadian Pacific passenger trains for about 100 years.

In the 1940s, fire caused irreparable damage to the Leaside Station. It was rebuilt in 1946.

The many trains (30 per day) which we do see and hear today are Canadian Pacific Railway freight trains. The trains no longer stop on their way through Leaside along CP Rail's busy trans-Canada line.

The Leaside sidings, now largely without activity, and the abandoned railway yards present a windswept landscape of broken concrete, shattered glass and weeds. They are a silent reminder of the 80 years of smoke, steam, steel and the iron men who created the railway age.

Keep in mind, however, during the period of the early 1900s, the name, Leaside, applied only to the station and its rail yards. The surrounding countryside was open farmland overlooking the valley of the Don and was considered to be part of North Toronto. With urban development stopped far to the south on the east side of the Don Valley, there was no such entity as the community of Leaside.

THE THIRD RAILWAY—THE CANADIAN NORTHERN RAILWAY

In the early 1900s, Donald Mann and William Mackenzie, principal shareholders[5] of the Canadian Northern Railway built two successful (that is, very profitable) model towns; one in British Columbia, the other in Quebec. There were fortunes to be amassed in real estate.

At this time in Toronto, the Canadian Northern was planning massive capital expenditures to upgrade its facilities: remove the steep grade from its Ottawa line's entry into Toronto; build a prestigous station which befitted its status as a transcontinental railway; establish extensive repair facilities, marshalling yards and build employee housing. Ambitious and hugely expensive plans, indeed!

The Canadian Northern and Canadian Pacific both saw Toronto's development and growth moving north along the Yonge Street corridor. Cooperatively, they planned to build a truly grand North Toronto "union" station where the Canadian Pacific's Leaside line crosses Yonge Street at Summerhill Avenue. The Canadian Northern would link[6] its transcontinental main line into the Canadian Pacific line at Leaside and pay trackage fees for using the line to enter North Toronto.

William Mackenzie and Donald Mann chose the level farmland directly north of the Leaside Junction station as the site for the massive new railway repair and marshalling facilities.

To finance this large capital project, Mackenzie and Mann[7] would use the profits from a new model town much like their very profitable towns of Port Mann (Vancouver) and Mount Royal (Montreal). And thus, Leaside with all its railway connections would come into being.

The original Leaside Station of 1894 and its 1946 replacement operated as one of Toronto's busiest stations for over 75 years. At least ten daily passenger trains on the busy Toronto-Ottawa-Montreal triangle stopped at the station along with 40 or so freight trains, many of which paused briefly after their climb up the Don Branch.

With the elimination of passenger trains by the Canadian Pacific, the station closed in 1970. Ten years later, the station was re-opened by CP Hotels as the Village Station Restaurant with a caboose and three classic railway dining cars. In 1985 the restaurant closed and the cars were removed.

BACK TO THE FUTURE—SOME PREDICTIONS ABOUT THE RAILWAY

The three railways in sequence then, chose the location, selected the name, and literally drew the map of Leaside.

What does the future hold for the railway? In 2000, there are an estimated 2.4 million automobiles in the Greater Toronto Area. By the year 2010, that number will grow to 3.5 million. We simply cannot lay enough asphalt to accommodate those cars.

Means other than the automobile must be found to move large numbers of people into and out of Toronto. Ultimately, the railway lines, built over 100 years ago and which radiate out from the city core to all of the suburbs will carry those people. The future of railway passenger service lies in carrying suburban commuters to and from the city.

Canadian Pacific's North Toronto Station circa 1949. The once busy terminal served the Canadian Pacific and briefly the Canadian Northern Railway. Those trains travelled the Leaside main line. The building became Toronto's busiest LCBO outlet. Now in private hands, the station is slated for restoration. *City of Toronto Archives.*

Leaside's railway line provides a ready-made, cross-town transportation corridor. The line connects the Toronto suburbs with Union Station; it intersects all north/south arterial roads and it crosses both of the north/south subway lines. The railway line through Leaside may play a pivotal role in the future transportation plans for Toronto.

The old 1916 North Toronto[8] Canadian Pacific Railway Station (once a liquor store) could become an important connection with the Yonge Street subway's Summerhill Station.

The trip by train from Leaside Junction to the heart of downtown Toronto takes just 12 minutes. That could be 21st century convenience delivered by a 19th century railway line.

4

FROM THE YORK LAND COMPANY
TO FREDERICK TODD TO LEASIDE

THE HISTORY of Leaside has many connections with the railway. Once the Canadian Northern chose the land north and west of the Leaside Junction station for the location of its new real estate project, William Mackenzie and Donald Mann established the York Land Company as Canadian Northern's development arm. Quietly, the Company began assembling property in the area. Prices varied from $900.00 to $4000.00 an acre. The total CNoR purchase exceeded two million dollars. By 1912, the Company had accumulated over 1,000 acres bounded on the south by the Canadian Pacific tracks, on the west by Bayview Avenue, on the east by Leslie Street and, on the north, three farms above Eglinton Avenue.

This massive land purchase was made public in *The Toronto World* March 1912. The purchase of land in York Township was described under the headline of "Toronto's largest land deal." The acquisition included: Lea property (300 acres); Pugsley Farm (100 acres); Hunt (Junior) Farm (100 acres); odd lots (50 acres); Dr. Norman Allen (135 acres); Atkinson Farm (100 acres): a total of 900 acres. All of the owners were required to vacate the land by August 1912.[1]

In April 1912, the Canadian Northern Railway announced its intentions to build a large residential community in what was known as North Toronto. Canadian Northern's plans for the project did not include railway service to the community immediately, but the Railway did build the planned extensive repair facilities adjacent to the Canadian Pacific's Leaside yards and main line.

Mackenzie and Mann engaged Frederick Todd,[2] the town planner and landscape architect from Montreal, to lay out the plan for a "model town." Leaside was intended to be the new upper class residential area

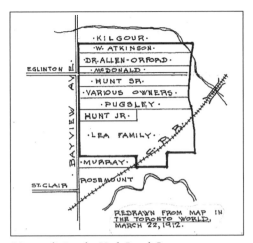

Map outlining the York Land Company property.
Redrawn by J. Rempel (1931) from map in The
Toronto World[3] *March 22, 1912.*

of Toronto, the "new Rosedale." The detailed street and lot plan of the
community was completed in late April, 1913 and the project was named
and incorporated as the Town of Leaside. The project was innovative for
its time – a pre-planned town, laid out fully before a building existed.
The railway service to be provided by the CNoR was intended not only
to foster residential growth but to attract industrial activities.

But, the anticipated residential development of the new town did not
happen. A global recession, the outbreak of the First World War, the
bankruptcy of the Canadian Northern Railway and Leaside's isolated location, all combined to prevent the project from proceeding. However,
extensive industrial development did grow along the Canadian Pacific
Railway corridor, accelerated by the First World War munitions factories.

The wide and steep-sided valley of the Don posed a major physical
barrier to convenient access from the south to the Leaside open land.
Without a road connection which spanned the valley, the undeveloped
land would remain that way. As well, Millwood Road, the route to the
south, dead-ended at the Leaside (north) side of the CPR tracks.

Two major construction projects were required to connect the open
land of Leaside to Toronto in the south. In October 1927, both projects
were completed—a high level bridge across the Don Valley (now called
the Leaside Viaduct) and an underpass.

Leaside's open land was now readily accessible by car although many still
considered the area to be in "the middle of nowhere." Growth was slow for
that reason, coupled with the onset of the Great Depression in 1929.

Building the Millwood CPR Underpass; date circa 1926. Looking northwest under the Canadian Pacific main line from what would become Millwood Road and the southern entrance into Leaside. What would you see today if you looked northwest from this spot? *City of Toronto Archives.*

The residential Leaside community with which we are familiar, began taking form in the late 1930s as the economy emerged from the Depression. Streets, sewers and water mains could not be built for the entire area of Leaside all at once. Construction took place as sections of Leaside became populated. Its development continued through the 1950s, finally with the completion of North Leaside. There is no neatly defined "completion" of Leaside. The community today continues to change and grow with new development.

A RETROSPECTIVE VIEW OF FREDERICK TODD'S TOWN PLAN FOR LEASIDE

"The Factories" (The Industrial Zone)

Todd's[4] original 1912 concept for the Town, called for a separation of the residential area from the zoned industrial section. This was Canada's first planned industrial development park and the concept has become the model for most new communities.

The industrial area was defined by Laird Drive on the west, Wicksteed Avenue on the north and the Canadian Pacific mainline on the south and east. This zone represented about one quarter of the Town's acreage. The remaining land to the west and north was designated for residential use.

Aerial view of Leaside, 1929. This view shows the sprawling yards of the Canadian Northern[5] Railway's Leaside repair shops. The steam locomotive, its passenger coaches and freight cars required massive maintenance and repair facilities. Can you pick out Laird Drive? the Durant Motors car factory? Beyond Laird Drive lies mainly open land. *City of Toronto Archives.*

The relatively large industrial area was established with the intent of using its property tax assessment to maintain low property taxes for the homeowners. The industrial zone became a highly utilized area almost immediately. This was some 30 years before the residential area began to take form. In 1912, Leaside had only 43 residents and many acres of open, undeveloped farm land for housing.

In 1913, the Canada Wire and Cable Company became the first industry to locate in Leaside, on a large tract of land running east from Laird Drive and south of Wicksteed Avenue. With the opening of World War I, the Leaside Munitions Company (a subsidiary of Canada Wire and Cable) built a large factory directly south of the Canada Wire site. In 1922, the Durant Motor Company purchased the Leaside Munitions factory which had closed at the end of the war.

In the pre-war period, the Canadian Northern Railway constructed its massive repair facilities and marshalling yards off what is now Esandar Drive. This was industry at its heaviest and smokiest.

In 1917, the need for an airfield to train pilots for the Royal Flying Corps caused Todd's industrial area to be expanded well north of

The Leaside industrial area, looking southeast. Dated circa 1930. The aerodrome is gone. Eglinton Avenue (which dead-ends at the edge of the West Don Valley) is now the northern border of the busy industrial area. The open land of the residential area still awaited development. *Canada Wire and Cable Collection.*

Wicksteed Avenue to accommodate the field. After the war, the airfield closed and Eglinton Avenue replaced Wicksteed as the northern boundary of the industrial area.

In the 1920s, a host of regional, national and international industries settled in this desirable part of Leaside, drawn by the cheap land, low taxes, access to the Toronto market and the excellent service of two railways. In 1931, Leaside's industrial zone was home to 29 companies and, by 1939, this number had grown to 52. All of this simply to say, the industrial zone was a thriving area of employment and manufacturing activity long before the houses appeared in the residential area. However, in attracting labour to the town, this industrialization became the impetus for the urbanization process.

When residential development did begin in the late 1930s, Todd's rationale of a large, industrial assessment used to subsidize residential property taxes did, in fact, take place. From the 1940s through to 1967, Leaside residents were envied for their modest property taxes—well below those of the surrounding municipalities. Leasiders were very happy with "the factories" as the area was called.

In 1967, with amalgamation with neighbouring East York, Leaside property taxes jumped abruptly over five years. Leaside residents had angrily opposed that amalgamation, citing increased taxes and loss of the Leaside identity as the inevitable outcomes.

Today, the so-called "factory area" has undergone significant change. Much of the heavy industry and manufacturing which had been its hallmark has gone, being replaced by light industrial and commercial businesses. Since the late 1990s there has been some re-zoning to introduce retail and residential use into the old industrial area. However, many successful enterprises do remain and the area has been re-named the Leaside Business Park, to reflect the new purposes for which the empty land will be used.

Looking back, Frederick Todd's industrial urban plan for Leaside functioned well for about 80 years. That's not bad in a century which has witnessed tumultuous change in the industrial and transportation sectors.

The Unintended Consequences—The Coming of Traffic

When Frederick Todd laid out Leaside's town plan in 1912, both the adjacent townships of Scarborough and North York were sparsely populated open and productive farmland. Cut off by the Don Valley and distant from downtown, the Leaside lands were truly isolated. The train provided the only easy access from North Toronto.

Leaside's location and the nature of the plan for the town combined to cause Leaside to function as a giant urban cul de sac. Well into the 1950s, Eglinton Avenue stopped at the western brink of the Don Valley and became a dirt path leading down to the west branch of the Don. Bayview Avenue was unpaved at Moore Avenue and still a dirt country road beyond Eglinton into the 1940s. McRae Drive led into the industrial area and stopped there. Millwood Road dead-ended at the north side of the CPR tracks until 1927.

With the automobile and the bus in their infancy, the railway and street railway were the only means of transportation. Mackenzie and Mann had planned to run a streetcar line into the Leaside area. It never happened. If a person entered the Leaside lands from the west, there was no easy and direct way out to the north, to the east or to the south and, added to that, there was no particular destination to go to in any of those directions.

Innovative for its time, the Leaside town plan contained many of the elements of present day subdivisions – curving streets, crescents, cul de sacs, no through roads, zoned commercial/retail areas and industry separated from the residential area.

Leaside Transportation Company, 1925. *From the Archives at Todmorden Mills Museum.*

Photograph of early bus is entitled "Smashed up 1925. Burnt up 6 months later."
The man shown is identified as Albert Pilcher. *From the Archives at Todmorden Mills Museum.*

The newly-opened Leaside Viaduct. Date: April 1928. Looking south from the unde-veloped Leaside lands, across the viaduct towards the Township of East York. By 1928, Leaside had many factories, but the homes were yet to come. The bridge was widened to six lanes in the 1960s. *City of Toronto Archives.*

In 1912, Todd could have no inkling of what impact the automobile would have on North America generally, or on Leaside specifically. Rather, Leaside's early problem was a total lack of traffic. People could not get there and, as a result, the residential lots lay empty throughout the 1920s and the 1930s.

The first attempt to create traffic into Leaside came in 1927 with the construction of the Leaside Viaduct[6] across the Don Valley and the opening of the Millwood underpass which carried the road under the CPR mainline and south to the new viaduct.

There was now a road from Leaside that led somewhere—to east end Toronto. There was now a road *through* Leaside, from Moore Avenue to Southvale Drive to Millwood Road.

The two aspects of the automobile which Frederick Todd could not have imagined were its numbers and the mobility which it created. The automobile resulted in the massive development of distant dormitory suburbs from which thousands of residents each day made the double trip by car from their homes to their place of work downtown. In trav-elling from home to work (and back again), the commuters had to go around or get through the ring of old inner suburbs of Leaside, North Toronto, Weston, Swansea and Mimico.

Side view of the Leaside Viaduct. Date: November 1928. Looking east along the Don Valley from the North Toronto Sewage Treatment Plant (under construction). *City of Toronto Archives.*

In 1956, the most dramatic change came for Leaside and the growth of traffic. Eglinton Avenue was extended eastward across the west branch of the Don River and out to the growing suburbs of Don Mills and Scarborough. Eglinton Avenue, a residential street, instantly became a high volume, high speed arterial road running through the heart of Leaside.

Laird Drive which had served only to give access to the factories, now connected into arterial Eglinton. Southvale and Moore would never be the same again. McRae Drive, once dead-ending in the factories, now gave a direct connection to busy Eglinton. McRae, too, would never be the same.

Paving Bayview Avenue north of Eglinton in the 1940s converted a neighbourhood shopping street into a busy arterial road which led to the expanding suburbs of North York. Bayview's extension south in the late 1950s made it possible for commuters to get downtown directly. However, it simply added more traffic to a stop-and-go Bayview.

When busy arterial roads get clogged, commuters flow into the adjacent residential streets looking for a way around the tie-up. The first attempt in Leaside to control such infiltration was the use of the ubiquitous stop signs. Leaside became famous for its stop signs! These stop signs were soon followed by the many no-turns-during-rush hour signs.

In the bigger picture, Eglinton Avenue is the source of the traffic problem. Costly plans have been proposed which are designed to draw commuter traffic away from Eglinton and divert it around Leaside, plans such as the Leslie Street Extension and the Redway Road Extension, plans which to date have not materialized.

One wonders how Frederick Todd might have responded to Leaside's traffic issues today.

THE DEVELOPMENT OF LEASIDE'S RESIDENTIAL AREA

Toronto's growth in the early 1900s was north along the Yonge Street corridor. By 1912, this made the Leaside location potentially one of the most attractive areas in the city for residential development. Todd's town plan for Leaside was made public in 1913. A glance at the original 1913 plan reveals some salient features.

Outside of the large industrial area, the town plan was an absolute myriad of thousands of housing lots. The farmland gathered by the York Land Company represented an investment of over $2,000,000.

Each open acre of land by the design standards of the day, could be subdivided into four residential lots. In Todd's plan, however, probably more than four lots were created on average for each acre. Mackenzie and Mann, always operating at the financial edge, needed to re-coup huge profits from the Leaside project to fund the major capital improvements being made to their Canadian Northern Railway. The imperative was clear for Frederick Todd – load as many residential lots into the plan as possible.

Today when visitors from the suburbs see Leaside, they are struck by how close the houses are. The use of many attached houses and smaller bungalows also enabled smaller lots to be used. In general, land use was quite different from nearby Rosedale to which Leaside had compared itself in the early marketing campaigns.

In the 1913 plan, there were no areas designated for schools, parks, stores, library, fire hall, churches or some form of municipal town centre. If the town council, which would eventually govern Leaside, wanted those amenities, the council would have to buy the property from the York Land Company (The Canadian Northern Railway). Mackenzie, Mann and colleagues knew how to make a dollar!

Even before the formal plan was made public, the York Land Company began selling land to developers and industries. In May 1912, Winnipeg real estate investor, J. F. Hansen, purchased 1.5 million dollars worth of the planned Leaside lots. Later that year, in December, the

CNoR announced that more than two acres of land secured by a Montreal firm would be for the construction of a brass foundry. It was to employ 3,000 to 4,000 men.

In February 1913, the Bayview Land Company purchased $340,000 worth of land (300 odd lots) in the residential and business sections. Finally, in March of that year, Neelys Limited purchased land for a cost totalling one million dollars. They formed a syndicate to build 125 homes on their lots in the spring of 1913.

In summary, by March 1913, the York Land Company had sold over three million dollars worth of land to developers and industries (about half the land available in the new suburbs).[7]

By March 1914, with the spring construction around the corner, Leaside was soon to become a physical reality.

"What an orgy of construction, what a hammering of nails and tearing of saws there will be when Leaside wakes up for the season and the will of the giants is fulfilled... A few years from now the 'Tally-ho' man will be bawling thru his megaphone as he shows visitors to Toronto the prosperous homes at Leaside."[8]

The CNoR had felt Leaside should be annexed to an existing municipality to add prestige and to provide costly streets, sewers, water and public transportation. Consequently, in June 1912, they had approached the Town of North Toronto only to be refused. The following month, North Toronto became annexed to the City of Toronto.[9]

As another option, the York Land Company, under the direction of Colonel Davidson and Randolph McRae, initiated, in March 1913, the procedure whereby Leaside would be incorporated into a municipality by an act of the Provincial Legislature. At the same time, the York Land Company approached the City of Toronto to request annexation of Leaside. The City of Toronto also rejected this request and, on April 23, 1913, Bill No. 55 of the Provincial Legislature incorporated the CNoR property into the Town of Leaside. Leaside was "on its own."

When incorporated, Leaside had a population of 43 and an area encompassing 1,025 acres of surveyed land. On May 8, 1913, Leaside's voting citizens met to nominate a Town Council. Five CNoR employees were acclaimed. To provide a certain degree of stability, the Mayor, Randolph McRae, and the four Councillors, Harvey Fitzsimmons, Laurence Boulton, George Saunders, and Archibald McRae, were to serve a term of two and a half years. Thereafter, elections would be held each year.

Leaside had no money in the bank, and no source of revenue for 1913. Any money would have to be raised by municipal debentures. By April

South Leaside, looking north. Date: circa 1948. South Leaside's curving streets show well, with Hanna Road winding graciously through the centre of the photo. Only a magnifying glass reveals it, but all of South Leaside has its new trees. For some reason, homes on Leacrest Avenue have yet to get theirs. *City of Toronto Archives.*

1914, the town had acquired over $150,000.00 in debentures to be spent on the supply of services. Throughout the war years, Leaside would experience financial problems.

By the end of 1917, Leaside's financial situation had reached catastrophic proportions. The York Land Company was the major culprit, having accumulated a string of unpaid taxes. However, they still owned half of Leaside. By the end of 1919, the Council threatened to sell off the York Land holdings.

Although the first sale of home sites was advertised in *The Toronto World* on June 12, 1913, construction, however, had ceased with the outbreak of the war. Few of these houses were ever built.[10]

Under the auspices of the 1919 Ontario Housing Act, the newly formed Leaside Housing Company received a provincial loan of $100,000.00 to build working-class houses.

North Leaside was developed without having a park area designated. The schoolyard of Northlea School has served as the community park. Early in Leaside's growth, the town fathers saw the need for parkland and ensured that each Leaside school (Bessborough and St. Anselm's excepted) had a large park-like schoolyard.

Perhaps the most striking feature of Todd's plan, as with Mount Royal, was the curving street plan, most prominent in South Leaside; striking because town planning of the day relied mainly on a grid pattern. Adjacent Toronto reflected that grid pattern. This imposed some restrictions on Todd, because his Leaside streets would emerge to the west and should meet the streets from Toronto. A glance at a map will show that he missed on a few!

Most residential streets were to be 66 feet wide. Twenty foot lanes were included on the blocks that had deep lots. Three streets were to provide direct and efficient access through Leaside. With a width of 80 feet, Soudan Avenue (now Parkhurst) and not Eglinton Avenue was intended to be the major east/west street.

Two grand boulevards or diagonals were included: Edith Avenue (now Bessborough) 110 feet wide and McRae Drive (120 feet wide). Streets having widths of more than 80 feet were intended to accommodate heavier traffic flows.[11]

The pleasing curved streets resulted, to some degree, from the south to north-east curvature of the Canadian Pacific Railway line and the location of the industrial area. As in our modern suburbs, the curving streets of Leaside continue to confuse many drivers who happen into South Leaside.

Other than a sprinkling of houses built close to the industrial area for the workers (68 houses by 1929), most of Leaside's residential lots lay vacant for about 25 years. The late 1930s saw Leaside's housing growth begin (328 houses by 1938). The surge of building began in 1939 and by 1941 the population had jumped to 6,183.

Leaside's housing design was somewhat repetitive with about four plans being most prominent – the two-storey side hall, the single storey bungalow, the attached home pair and the centre hall plan.

In its urban history the homes of Leaside have experienced three distinct demographic transitions, each one re-newing Leaside in its unique way. Those transitions have been:

—the original owners—purchased a new home in Leaside in the 1930s, 1940s.

—the second wave—purchased a home in Leaside in the 1960s. This group usually re-decorated their home, added a deck or patio and made only minor changes to the house and landscaping.

—the third wave—purchased in the 1980s and 1990s. This group has authored a construction boom which rivals the original building of Leaside. With their renovations, knock-downs, add-ons, infills and

Two Leaside classics take shape. Date: 1949. Looking north at a pair of two-storey side entrance homes being built at 458 and 462 Broadway Avenue. Attached garages will be added to complete the construction. *Metro Toronto Reference Library, Salmon Collection.*

garage conversions, this group has changed the nature and appearance of housing in Leaside. Hundreds of sub-contractors and many architects have been kept busy for a decade on these projects.

These expensive projects have been completed with full confidence that the real estate values in Leaside will continue to climb. House prices in Leaside may have plateaued once or twice, but otherwise values have climbed steadily for 60 years. More importantly, these demographic transitions have regularly infused Leaside with new ideas, new energy and a new generation of young families. The schools of Leaside have remained full and vital with strong parental involvement, the key to a thriving community.

The young parents have provided the new volunteers to ensure that the recreational programs of figure skating, hockey, ballet, baseball, swimming and soccer continue to thrive. The changing population has also provided a new market which has resulted in the revitalization of Leaside's various retail areas.

The new 90s residents of Leaside do face one challenge. There are three Leaside icons—curving streets, stop signs and its trees. To a person, the visitor or the resident is impressed by the mature canopy of trees. Its trees are a key factor to the community's character. The large trees soften the effect of the repetitive housing design and small lots; they hide the tangle of overhead wires and they give Leaside its pleasing human scale. The early town fathers are to be admired for their foresight in systematically planting Leaside's trees in the 1940s. At the rate at which trees are being taken down, Leaside's green canopy will

Leaside, circa 1950. Photographer unknown. And you thought Leaside was always leafy and green! Can you identify the location?[12] *The Toronto Star Archives.*

have massive gaps within two or three years. To prevent those large gaps, the new 90s residents will have to work to replace their lost trees, soon.

Returning to yesteryear briefly, a few words about the original Leaside home buyers and their houses. Those new residents had grown up in the Great Depression, an event which deeply imprinted all who had experienced it. Some of the older males had served in the First World War; many of the younger men and women had seen service in World War II. Generally they were conservative; they had gained some financial security as they joined the growing middle class. They sought the peace and simplicity which Leaside seemed to offer.

Their children would become the first mass teen culture with sufficient numbers, time and money to dominate the airwaves with its music and to create its own self-imposed dress code. In the basement of the house, the coal bin and laundry room were complemented by a "rec room" for the use of the teens. The "finished basement" entered housing lexicon.

The bathroom shower made its appearance as did the living room fireplace which was used not for heating but for its ambiance on special occasions.

Modest housing of the day featured the verandah as can still be seen in many areas of Toronto. Upscale housing such as Rosedale, did not have verandahs. Thus, Leaside would not have verandahs, the simple small entrance stoop would replace it.

Many Leaside houses had a private drive and a garage, small by today's standards, to accommodate only one car. At the time the Leaside house designs were coming off the drawing board, many people did not own cars and, because of the 1939-45 war effort, the automobile was not available in quantity until the mid 1950s. But when the car did become available in numbers, it grew wider, longer, lower and sprouted massive fins. It no longer fitted in its Leaside garage! The small, junk-filled-garage-as-storage-space has become another Leaside icon.

So, once completely built and populated in the 1950s, what did Leaside become in people's minds?

Leaside was seen to be affluent, to have a strong sense of community as the Town of Leaside. People recognized the excellent recreational facilities and programs for the young people of the town, although North Leasiders had to travel south of Eglinton Avenue where the rink, pool, parks, tennis courts, library, ball diamonds and the high school were located. Leaside became known for its strong baseball teams and hockey teams. In retrospect, however, there were few recreational programs for girls.

There was good shopping, some of it walk-to. Leaside was close to downtown and good bus service to the subway made the trip to jobs in the city core convenient. The town had a solid industrial base, excellent schools and a full range of churches. The trees were a Leaside hallmark because most new housing in the expanding suburbs through the 1950s and 1960s remained without trees for many years.

Leaside's population was homogeneous and upwardly mobile. It was assumed that the offspring would attend university. There was a certain smugness or cachet in being a Leasider. It wasn't Rosedale or Moore Park or Lawrence Park, but it was very good. For some, the Leaside house served as a "starter home" for those who aspired to Rosedale style.

Since much of the Leaside residential lands lay empty for some 25 years, the final stages of North Leaside's construction would be carried into the 1950s. The land development company fell on hard times. Long before the 50s, the Canadian Northern Railway, in bankruptcy, had been absorbed by the Canadian National Railway. The York Land Company, the development arm of the Canadian Northern and owner

of most of Leaside's available land, had defaulted on its tax obligations
to the Town. Movers and shakers, Sir Donald Mann and Sir William
Mackenzie had long since disappeared from the scene. However, Frederick Todd's basic town plan of 1913 persisted and came to define what
Leaside would look like today. It had all worked out fairly well.

5

FACTORIES COME TO LEASIDE

THE PROVISION of low-cost, dependable hydro power to industrial communities created the impetus needed for the growth and development of manufacturing in Ontario. Many businessmen recognized the great opportunities inherent in this upsurge of industrial life and hastened to take advantage of this unique situation.

It was in 1913, when the Town was incorporated, that Leaside changed from being a strictly agricultural area. The genesis of its subsequent remarkable industrial development was on the horizon. That same year, under the guiding genius of H. H. Horsfall, the Canada Wire and Cable Company recognized, from an industrial perspective, the undisputed advantages being offered by Leaside. This Canada Wire and Cable executive had sixty homes built in the town shortly after the war; these formed the nucleus of the present residential district. Once these steps were taken, Leaside was well on its way to municipal stability and prosperity.

The remarkable industrial growth of Leaside and its concomitant residential development can be ascribed to the general stability of the municipality, an inviting site for the economical manufacture and distribution of factory products. It is a safe assumption that the executives of Leaside's varied industries satisfied themselves by comparing Leaside with other potential locations. It would seem that the superior advantages being offered by this town led them to select Leaside as the site of their respective plants.

CANADA WIRE AND CABLE (CWC)

At the turn of the century, the generating of electricity was very limited in scope, and Ontario's coal supply, for generations, had been coming primarily

Canada Wire and Cable office building with plant behind. Date: 1922. *Collection of the Bailey family.*

By 1941–43, the homes intended for Canada Wire and Cable employees have sprung up on Randolph Road, Sutherland Drive and Airdrie Road. The industrial area is booming. *Collection of the Bailey family.*

from Pennsylvania.[1] However, with three privately-owned hydro generating plants on the Canadian side of Niagara Falls, it was believed that hydro power could be produced much less expensively than thermal power.

In 1906, the Hydro Electric Power Commission of Ontario was formed as a public utilities commission by the Province of Ontario, in response to the need for low-cost, dependable hydro power to be supplied to industrial communities. Correspondingly, a tremendous demand developed for both primary and secondary distribution cable needed to carry hydro.

Herbert Horsfall, a superintendent with Dominion Wire Manufacturing in Montreal, was approached by Roderick J. Parke of the Toronto firm, Parke and Leith. Together they met with Emil A. Wallberg, a well-known contractor, asking him for financial backing. In February 1911, the Canada Wire and Cable Company Limited was incorporated with offices at Yonge and Richmond streets. Wallberg became President, Parke the Managing Director and Horsfall was appointed Secretary/Treasurer.[2] Their first factory space, owned by the Farmers Feed Company, was located on the banks of the Don River near Richmond Street. The new company also leased a portion of a plant at 1170 Dundas Street West. It was the Canadian General Electric Company who, at that time,

Canada Wire and Cable on Laird Drive with water tower. Date: 1922. *Collection of the Bailey family of Leaside*

supplied Canada Wire with weatherproof wires and rubber covered wires.

In November 1912, on behalf of Canada Wire and Cable, Emil Wallberg purchased sixteen acres in Leaside at the southeast corner of Wicksteed and Laird. He intended to erect a wire and cable factory, as well as build one hundred houses in 1914 to accommodate future employees. These semi-detached houses were to be located on Airdrie, Sutherland and Rumsey and were to be rented at a reasonable rate of approximately $12.00 per month. Some were also available for purchase for $2500.00. Sixty houses were to be built in 1914 and forty more in 1915. However, in 1914, the economic scene was becoming less favourable as international tension mounted. Although the walls of the factory buildings were up in Leaside, the Company suspended this operation and continued to work from the Dundas Street location.

World War I, however, created a new international need. The Directors at Canada Wire and Cable, led by their new President F. J. Bell, recognized an opportunity to utilize the empty Leaside buildings profitably. On June 28, 1916, they incorporated and became owners of the Leaside Munitions Company Limited, a wholly-owned subsidiary of Canada Wire and Cable Company Limited. Six-inch shells were produced rapidly and efficiently. The Munitions Board was so pleased by both the lower price (they had formerly paid $35.00 each) and delivery that further contracts were awarded. Near the end of the war, this Leaside plant was the largest producer of this type of ammunition in North America.[3]

In early 1919, while the premises on Laird were being vacated by the Leaside Munitions Company Limited, a fire occurred at the Dundas Street plant of Canada Wire and Cable, closing down that operation. A decision was made to move the wire and cable business to Leaside. Their newly occupied buildings fronted on Laird Drive, with the office buildings, which had been built in 1918, being the three-storey and one-storey buildings located along Wicksteed Avenue. The other buildings on the south side of the property near Commercial Street, which had also been used by the Munitions Company, were sold to Durant Motors of Canada Limited.

In 1918, a 117 ft. water tower was built by Canada Wire and Cable. Located in the centre of the property close to Laird Drive and just south of the Canada Wire buildings, the tank for the tower was 22 ft. in diameter and 19 ft. high, with a capacity of 75,000 gallons. For years the tower was a Leaside landmark, until its removal in 1956.

The Canada Wire and Cable Company adopted a somewhat paternalistic policy towards the struggling municipality. In November 1918,

Men "taking a break" at Canada Wire and Cable in Leaside in 1920. The man, second from the left with a patchwork pad on his knee, is Kenneth Farrows. At the time, the salary was $18.00 a week. *Courtesy the Farrows' family.*

the company volunteered to pay for the construction of a water main that would run along Soudan Avenue (now Parkhurst) to the Company's factory site. In return the company wanted to receive a fixed assessment rate. They were granted a fixed assessment of $1500.00 on their 28 acres of land for a period of ten years.

When a depression hit the economy in 1921, Canada Wire and Cable, in a move to keep its expenditures to a minimum, cut staff salaries by ten percent. "In 1920 they earned about $18.00 per week."[4] Despite the difficult times, however, Canada Wire and Cable were exporting to Brazil, New Zealand and Australia during these depression years. In August of 1921, F. J. Bell resigned as President, having served since 1914. Wallberg was elected President for the second time. However, by 1926, business recovered to more promising levels. Sales for that year totalled approximately 2.5 million, bringing them close to the peak year recorded by the company six years earlier. In 1929, Wallberg divested himself of his interests in Canada Wire and Cable and sold his entire holdings to Nesbitt Thomson and Company Limited, a Toronto financial house. This happened just one month before his sudden death on March 30, 1929.

Aerial view showing Laird and McRae Drive in 1922. The airfield is to the left, with Canada Wire and Cable and Durant Motors in the middle. *S. Walter Stewart Library, Elmore Gray Collection.*

A new building was erected south of the other buildings in 1927 to house the new enamel wire operation. Up to this time, magnetic wires had mostly been insulated with wrappings of cotton or silk. A year later an agreement also was made with Noranda Mines Limited to supply copper for copper rod to Canada Wire and Cable. Sales recorded for 1930 were $7,567,000.00, a drop of approximately 10% from the previous year. Sales continued to drop in the ensuring three years, reaching a low of close to $3,800,000.00 and earnings were recorded in the red. Measures were, once again, taken to reduce overhead through staff layoffs, salary reductions and cost trimming.[5]

In 1933, when the Dominion Motors Company (formerly Durant) ceased manufacturing cars and were selling their buildings and land, Canada Wire and Cable purchased 4.86 acres. The remaining 9.46 acres were sold to Frigidaire Canada Limited (a division of General Motors Corporation) the manufacturers of refrigerators and other appliances. The company moved into the Durant buildings on Commercial Road. Frigidaire remained in Leaside until 1958 when they decided to relocate and offered these buildings to Canada Wire and Cable at a favourable price.

Durant Motors had built an office building in 1928 across the street on the west side of Laird. When they stopped manufacturing cars, they offered it to Canada Wire and Cable for $75,000.00, but Canada Wire management "could not justify such an expenditure for pen pushers, preferring to spend their money for something materially more productive."[6]

In 1911, the Standard Underground Cable Company of Pittsburgh had established its Canadian subsidiary in Hamilton. By 1927, the stock of the Canadian operation was acquired by Nesbitt Thomson and, two years later, Standard Underground amalgamated with Canada Wire and Cable. The Hamilton plant continued operations until 1934 when the equipment was moved to Leaside and, by 1935, the company had moved into the Durant buildings on the east side of Laird.

As Canada Wire and Cable's sales and profits increased, new equipment was purchased. A new transformer station was installed in response to the need for greater power. During the Second World War, Canada Wire and Cable supplied aircraft wires, navy cables, degausser cable (for demagnetizing ships) and field telephone wires. As well, anti-submarine nets to protect coastal harbours were manufactured. Although over three hundred employees out of 1,200 personnel enlisted in the Armed Services, the company continued its regular business as well as responding to the war effort. At this time many women entered the workforce.

The remaining years of the 1930s saw a marked recovery in the general economy from the Depression years. By 1940, the company was returned to a state of momentum reminiscent of the late twenties.

With the end of the war in 1945, there was a demand for wire and cable in the building of houses. This boom led to the employment of 2,100 people, almost double their previous number. As a result the Leaside plant was rehabilitated, creating greater efficiency, increased production and improved working conditions.

However, in December of that year, a vote of all qualified hourly-paid employees was held at Leaside for the selection of a collective bargaining agent. As a result, Local 514 was certified and negotiations began. The year 1946 saw a breakdown in negotiations for the first agreement. A strike occurred from July until October 1946, leading to 110 production days being lost to the Leaside plant. Immeasurable sales and earnings were lost.

By 1951, a Wire Drawing Department building was erected on the northeast section of the holdings of CWC that faced Wicksteed Avenue. Expansion was in the air. In 1958, with the acquisition of 9.46 acres of property from Frigidaire, Canada Wire and Cable now owned twenty-five acres in the vicinity of Laird and Eglinton.

The vulcanizing extruder as it looked in 1998, amid the
debris of demolition. *Leaside Advertiser.*

In 1959, the vertical continuous vulcanizing extruder which allowed
the rubber around the cable to mold evenly as it was vertically dropped,
was installed to improve the quality of large size thermosetting insulated cables. This extruder is still standing on the site although everything
else was demolished in 1998. Well into the 1960s, Canada Wire and
Cable was continuing to expand across Canada, leading to reorganiza-
tion and development during the 1970s, with the updating of facilities
in full process.

The work force reached 2,700 employees by 1978, with annual sales of
100 million. About 1991, Canada Wire and Cable's property was purchased by Alcatel, a European firm. The property was sold when Alcatel
moved from Leaside to Markham in 1996. The site was purchased the following year by Mitchell Goldhar and will be developed into box stores
and a shopping mall. At the time of publication, the former buildings had
been demolished and the slow process of clearing and decommissioning
the soil has begun. Construction of the stores is slated for Spring 2000.

When the Canada Wire and Cable plant in Leaside was slated to be torn down, Alcatel, the owners, decided to let the people at the Todmorden Mills Museum remove whatever they wanted from the Canada Wire Archives. What was not taken by the museum was left for the employees working for the company at the time, to have whatever interested them. There was no record of who took what, so much of the Canada Wire memorabilia is now lost.

Ray Dade, a former employee and war veteran, wanted to know what had happened to the Roll of Honour that always hung in a hallway leading to the CWC reception area off Commercial Road. It not only contained his name, but also that of his brother, along with many of his childhood friends who were employees at Canada Wire and who had gone on to join the Services during the Second World War. The Roll contains some 287 names of those men and women. Some are bearing small crosses, signifying that they had made the ultimate sacrifice for King and Country.

After many phone calls, much tracking down of false leads and repeated visits to the almost flattened former building site, Ray came up empty-handed. No one knew who had liberated the Roll of Honour. His detective work finally paid off when, just on a whim, he went in to talk with someone at Branch 10, Todmorden Legion in East York. The search was over. Not only did the legion members know about the Honour Roll – it was hanging on their wall. Evidently, it had been found in a member's basement. Knowing that someone would think it was important, the individual had dropped it off at the only place he knew. That was at the legion hall.

Ray, along with the Legion President, Roy Gray, and Gene Wazny and others, felt that a formal unveiling ceremony should take place to celebrate the Roll of Honour's new-found home. This took place Sunday, October 25, 1998 at the Royal Canadian Legion Branch 10 on Pape Avenue, Toronto. Many former employees of Canada Wire and Cable and their families were invited to attend this historic event to commemorate the lives of those men and women. The Roll of Honour was presented to the Branch 10 Legion and can be found there today.

THE LEASIDE MUNITIONS COMPANY

The onset of World War I and Britain's need for shell production caused Canada Wire and Cable to suspend their Leaside operation and continue their production line on Dundas Street. The directors at Canada Wire saw an opportunity for the empty Leaside buildings and, on June 28,

View showing the extent of the Leaside Munitions works, taken from a drawing made in late 1918. *Originally in* The Red Reel, The Story of Canada Wire *by J. Harry Pryce.*

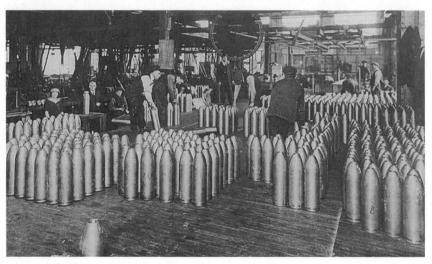

The 6″ shells, being produced by Leaside Munitions in 1917, being given final inspection. *Originally in* The Red Reel, The Story of Canada Wire.

1916, they incorporated to create and own the Leaside Munitions Company Ltd. The Imperial Munitions Board was set up in Ottawa to award contracts. Britain was in desperate need for shells and decided to utilize the industrial potential of its Dominions. The contract was awarded to Leaside in 1916 for the manufacture and assembly of 54,000 shells, all to be 9.2 inches in size. Workers, given bonuses after reaching a certain output level, were spurred on by huge clocks which recorded hourly production. Output was tremendous! Shells were turned out at a rate unheard of up to that time.

During this period, 4,000 people were employed at the plant. A 10-coach railway train operating every morning from Royce Avenue in the west end of Toronto, followed the CPR North Toronto line to the factory, bringing in the workers at a cost of $75.00 per day for the company. A fleet of buses running between Jackes Avenue and the Laird plant was

Looking south on Laird Drive, with a view of the Durant office building and the main bus terminal. *Originally in* The Story of Leaside *by John Scott.*

provided, at no charge, by James Bristow, Albert Mould and George Aldridge. From this service developed the Bristow Transportation Company for Leaside residents. (James Bristow also started a coal and fuel industry in Leaside). The Leaside Munitions Company subsidized the Leaside bus service, helped finance the first water mains, provided the first electrical power and built sixty homes (mostly the semi-detached houses on Airdrie, Sutherland and Rumsey).

Early in 1918, the US government awarded a contract for 50,000 12-inch naval shells and even financed an additional plant for this contract, a large single-storey brick building fronting on Laird Drive and extending along Commercial Road. Consequently, on May 31, 1918, eighteen acres were purchased east of Laird Drive and south of the existing plant along Commercial Road. Several buildings were erected to house the necessary forging presses, billet heating ovens and related equipment. However, after only two or three of these 12-inch shells had been produced, the Armistice was signed on November 11, 1918 and all production came to a standstill. The Americans gave the building to the Munitions Company in exchange for the cancelled contract. This marked the conclusion of the Leaside Munitions Company Ltd. The American building was left standing, but the other buildings were eventually demolished.

A fire occurring in April 1919 at the CWC Dundas Works closed down operations there. Work began immediately to move the wire manufacturing equipment to the Leaside plant. The buildings occupied were those fronting on Laird Drive, including the office buildings which had been built in 1918, the three-storey structure and the one-storey building extending east on Wicksteed Avenue. The other buildings, formerly occupied by the Leaside Munitions Company, were much too large and were sold to Durant Motors.

During the war years, the upper floor of the three-storey building provided barracks for the pilot trainees at the flying field located north of Wicksteed and east of Sutherland Drive. At the end of the war, three of the nine wooden hangars were purchased by Canada Wire and Cable for storage and carpentry shops. The last hangar was destroyed in 1971.

DURANT MOTORS

Durant Motors of Canada was incorporated September 3, 1921, the American "parent" being Durant Motors Inc. When Billy Durant, the American entrepreneur, lost control of General Motors in 1920, he decided to create a new empire for himself.[7] At this time, there were four other vehicle manufacturers in the Toronto area. They were: Willys Overland at Weston, Dodge Bros. of Canada making 40 cars a day on Dupont Avenue, the Ford Motor and assembly plant also on Dupont, and an obscure truck manufacturer Harmer-Knowles, located on Concord Avenue. After signing a 20-year contract with the American Durant firm granting Canadian rights, he was set to build and sell the low-priced Star and the medium-priced Durant motor car elsewhere. Accordingly, the factory site of the now defunct Leaside Munitions Company Ltd. was purchased from CWC and enlarged. The plant was built in three months. Temporary towers were built at each end of the site to monitor the construction and photographs were taken and rushed to New York to keep them apprised of the progress. Built to Durant specifications, the plant had the first depressed assembly line, that is, it was flush to the floor versus one foot above ground. When the Durant Motors of Canada Ltd. was established at Leaside in 1921, the company owned one building which covered a space of two acres. By 1931, they had purchased an additional eighteen acres and increased their plant size to eleven buildings. While retaining half the Canadian company's shares, Billy Durant was also to receive nearly half the profits.

The first Durant car manufactured in Canada was built March 1, 1922. "It is a Canadian automobile company, controlled by Canadian capital, directed and managed by a Canadian executive, which builds and merchandizes an outstanding line of passenger cars and commercial vehicles."[8]

Durant Motors. A partial view of the chassis line which had a capacity of up to 175 cars per day. *Originally in* The Story of Leaside *by John Scott.*

Building Durant motorcars and Rugby trucks in Leaside. *Originally in* The Story of Leaside *by John Scott.*

An interesting statement, with the American Billy Durant controlling half of the Canadian shares. Initially, mechanical parts were bought in the States, but soon the Leaside plant made its own car bodies. During the first two years of operation, the company manufactured 13,000 Stars and Durants, which were sold from coast to coast in Canada by 445 dealers.[9] The Flint car, however, although from an American Durant company car, was not built in Leaside.

The Durant Car made in Leaside. Date: 1930. *City of Toronto Archives, William James Collection.*

By 1924, Durant had become Canada's third largest domestic producer of automobiles. Both the production methods and models were being improved continuously and, by 1925, a Star Six and Road King speed truck were introduced to the public.

The Leaside plant was responsible for all of Durant's business in Britain. By the end of 1926, 5000 cars had been exported to the UK and Durant's profit was a quarter of a million dollars for the year.[10] While the US firm was beginning a gradual decline, Leaside was booming, with all previous deficits wiped out.

In 1926, Roy D. Kerby became President. Born in 1888 on a farm near Petrolia, Ontario, Kerby was a staunch Canadian who refused to let his wife buy anything on their trips to the United States. He had joined McLaughlin Motors in 1913 but left after the takeover by General Motors. Soon after joining Durant, Kerby became its first Canadian board member. His reputation for integrity gave him the name "Golden Rule Kerby," a strength he brought to Leaside. Under his leadership profits mounted the following year. Kerby kept his plant so busy with a new line of four and six-cylinder Durant and Rugby trucks that office space was turned into manufacturing space. Accordingly, a new administration building was begun as profits topped half a million.

Meanwhile the parent firm in Lansing, Michigan was experiencing increasing difficulties as competition had increased in their domestic marketplace. Their response was to create a new lineup in 1930, in the form of a low, racy, wire-wheeled Durant. This was the last major attempt to save the much-shrunken US empire. To finance the venture, the US firm borrowed $1,250,00.00 from the York Acceptance Corporation, a firm set up to finance sales from the Leaside factory, only to default on their loan, setting the stage for control to pass to the Canadian Company in Leaside. Full-page newspaper ads announced that Durant Motors was an all-Canadian company to meet Canadian needs.

By 1931, the Canadian Durant Motor Company had grown from one building (covering two acres) to 18 acres and 11 buildings with a floor space of 600,000 square feet. On March 14, 1931, Dominion Motors Ltd. of Leaside came into being with Roy D. Kerby as President and, on June 1, the new company took over Durant. A sales company continued under the name of "Durant" and the commercial vehicles under the name of "Rugby." These products were distributed throughout Canada by a Durant organization consisting of some six hundred dealers.

The men at Dominion Motors started to work on a new car similar to the 1928 four-cylinder Durant. The Star was phased out and an elegant vehicle, the "Frontenac Sedan," named after Count Frontenac, a governor of New France, appeared. It had a short wheelbase, a big engine that was noticably peppy and fast, a stylish V-shaped radiator grille, sloping windshield and a deep sun visor. The Special cost $898.00 and the DeLuxe $1,018.00. The best year for production was in 1928 (22,000–23,000 cars).

At the Canadian National Exhibition, the Frontenac was called "The Absolute Sensation of Motor Car Values."[11] Over 100,000 people saw it over a 14 day period. One hundred new cars were sold to dealers across Ontario.

Kerby made a deal in 1931 to build Nash cars in Leaside. But this was not accomplished and in February, 1932, Dominion announced that it had the Canadian rights to build the Reo. For two years the "Reo Flying Clouds" were manufactured in Leaside, but Reo had its own sales and service organization.

Both the Frontenac and Durant were continued into 1932, but the economic hardships of the Depression had taken their toll. The Reo Company proved to be of little help, and Dominion Motors lost a quarter of a million dollars in 1931. As well, the sales of the Frontenac luxury car were poor. President Kerby decided to launch another line, the Frontenac 6–85, which resembled an updated Frontenac but with a cost of $300.00 more than the old 6-70, a decision that did not prove to be successful. At the end of 1932, Kerby dropped this line.

Later, in 1933, an even bigger, deluxe six cylinder car called the "Ace" became available. This luxury vehicle was built in the United States and imported on order to Leaside. The last Durant car was built in 1933. There were 50 cars manufactured that year, with a major Durant display featured at the Toronto Motor Show. The Canadian operation lasted one and a half years longer than the American plant.

The Depression and reliance on American builders for the Frontenac were the causes of its decline. By December 1933, the Leaside production stopped and Roy Kerby rejoined General Motors. The company sold what it could and wound up their operation by 1935, though an offshoot lingered on for years, selling parts at discount prices to its many "friends." "When Dominion disappeared so did the last bit of Canada's own automobile industry."[12]

6

THE WAR EFFORT:
WORLD WAR I AND WORLD WAR II

LEASIDE, LIKE most communities across Canada, contributed much to the war effort. Many young men and women gave the ultimate, their lives.

War touched the daily life of every household, from the dislocation of families to the effects of wartime rationing. To this newly incorporated Town of Leaside, the War brought both hardship and profit. With the Leaside Munitions Company (WWI) and Research Enterprises (WWII) booming during wartime, Leaside's economy was enhanced. At peak production, these companies together employed thousands of people. The war effort, however, placed additional spotlights on Leaside.

THE LEASIDE AERODROME

Towards the end of 1916, plans were approved by the Canadian Government for the construction of aerodromes and war equipment. The Canadian Government leased about 220 acres north of Canada Wire and Cable Company, just north of Wicksteed Avenue.

Construction began on May 21, 1917. The land was carefully drained by laying 45 miles of field tiles. The airfield would extend from Wicksteed to Broadway and from Sutherland to the Don Valley. Once hangars and workshops were built, the Leaside Aerodrome became a reality, providing a base for Number 83 Canadian Training Squadron of the 43rd Wing Royal Flying Corps.

The enlisted men lived in the top storey of the munitions factory. In reality, the Leaside Munitions Company provided their barracks. Down below the men, the shell cases for the war effort were being manufactured.

Flying instructors at the Leaside Aerodrome, 1918. The man on the left is believed to be Brian Peck, pilot of the First Air Mail Delivery to Leaside. *City of Toronto Archives, William James Collection.*

Wooden plane factory at the Leaside Aerodrome. Date: 1918. *City of Toronto Archives, William James Collection..*

Once the runways and the total of nine hangars, housing three squadrons, were complete, the instruction and repair buildings, a mess hall and a temporary hospital were built. This full-scale military hospital, there to serve the requirements of an extensive training program designed to prepare pilots for war, was located at Sutherland and Eglinton.

"Hordes of civilian workmen operating dozens of graders, ditch diggers and steam-rollers, quickly put the finishing touches to the Aerodrome as scores of carpenters completed the hangars and buildings."[1]

Other large structures sprang up to support this massive undertaking. Included were the wing headquarters building, the officers and cadets mess and quarters, and a garage capable of housing twenty large motor vehicles. A railroad spur was run into what is now the corner of Rumsey and McRae to bring men and supplies to the camp's centre.

"The airfield was old-fashioned, without many runways, and it was grassy. They used to take off heading for the Don Valley, so that if they weren't able to get off the ground in time at least they could climb out of the valley. That would give them some more time to get the airplane up in the air."[2]

By the end of the war, there were approximately 600 servicemen stationed at Leaside Air Base. "By the end of the war, there was accommodation for 89 officers, 230 cadets, 83 warrant officers and sergeants, and about 600 rank and file, with the latter being housed in yet another completed CWC building."[3]

Once peace was declared and World War I was over, the need for the Aerodrome was equally over. The Air Field, however, flickered back to brief life. In the early 1920s, Albert Munday and Earl Hand organized the Toronto Flying Club and made Leaside the first private club aerodrome in Canada. "For some years after the first war, the flying field was privately operated and it is within the memory of many of us seeing planes landing and taking off on weekends as well as the thrilling aeronautical displays which were put on from time to time."[4]

Ultimately, real estate pressures forced the airfield out of existence. The temporary buildings vanished and rail spurs hauled in road paving materials. Soon houses began to appear west of Laird stretching over to Sutherland and industries moved in to the "industrial area."

"As industry took over, the Leaside Aerodrome was gradually phased out over time, with the last remaining hangar being removed as recently as 1971."[5] The remaining Quonset huts still found in the industrial area in the seventies were never used as hangars.

A hangar built for World War I. Later, the structure was used as a warehouse for Canada Wire and Cable. In 1971, the last hangar in Leaside was demolished. Photograph taken July 2, 1955. *Toronto Reference Library, J.V. Salmon Collection.*

Leigh Capreol, Toronto Flying Club Instructor, at the Leaside Air Field. Date: 1924. *City of Toronto Archives.*

A US Army Ford single propeller plane attracts much attention at the Leaside Air Field in 1928. *City of Toronto Archives, William James Collection.*

American Curtiss Hawks, lined up at the Leaside Aerodrome 1929-30, with Canada Wire and Cable in background. *City of Toronto Archives, William James Collection.*

Today, with the many changes, nothing remains of the airfields built on the level terrain around Laird or of the wartime Aerodrome.

CANADA'S FIRST AIRMAIL DELIVERY

In early 1917, during the First World War, it became obvious that warfare by air had become a necessity. To attract more aviators, the Royal Flying Corps, with assistance from the Canadian government, leased an airfield in Leaside. This land, located just north of Canada Wire and Cable, became the Leaside Aerodrome.

During that year, the number of young men choosing to sign up for training began to dwindle. To promote the Royal Flying Corps, Captain Brian Peck and Corporal E. W. Mathers flew to Montreal to perform an aerial demonstration designed to arouse the interest of potential flyers. "Peck wangled the flight by convincing the authorities at Leaside Airport that he could become a valuable part of their recruiting program.

It was the closing months of the war and the number of recruits had fallen to almost zero. Peck offered to perform aerobatics over the centre of Montreal and end his performance by dropping thousands of recruiting leaflets. The commanding officer accepted the idea and on the morning of June 20th, with a Corporal Mathers as passenger, Peck flew out of Leaside in a two-seater biplane, a Curtiss JN4."[6]

Brian Peck had flown his own aircraft at Calgary and became one of the "Early Birds of America," the name given to the first people to fly a distance. In the early war years, he served overseas, but, in the summer of 1918, was posted to Leaside to instruct pilots of the 89th Squadron. Originally from Montreal, he had not been home for months and was strongly motivated to return.

"It was a sturdy, reliable craft with a single 90 h.p. engine that was used exclusively to train airmen in Canada. The plane was known affectionately as "Jenny" by the thousands of pilots who flew in her and learned to trust her. The flight to Montreal that day was uneventful. Peck's plane landed safely at the Bois Franc Polo Grounds outside Montreal and he immediately left the airfield to see his family."[7]

The next day, plans for the airshow over Montreal had to be postponed because of a heavy rainstorm.

Two men, George Lighthall and Edmund Greenwood, executives of the Aerial League of the British Empire, thought of the idea to make the return flight from Montreal to Toronto the first airmail delivery in Canada. The next step was to obtain approval from the postmaster-general in Ottawa. One hundred and twenty letters addressed to Toronto were randomly selected, each to have a specially designed postal stamp. Each was stamped "Inaugural Service via aerial mail—Montreal 23.6.18." However, on June 23rd heavy rain prevented the flight!

The next day, June 24, Peck raced his aircraft across the polo fields, but the small plane was barely able to leave the ground. The reason for this remained a secret for half a century. The story was finally revealed by another Canadian pioneer pilot, Frank H. Ellis, who had his history of aviation published, under the title of *Canada's Flying Heritage,* in 1954.

"...Mathers, in the passenger seat, was perched atop as many cases of "Mull Scotch" as could be stored, holding the bag of airmail on his lap. At that time, the Province of Ontario had introduced Prohibition, causing people to resort to smuggling liquor in from the United States or Quebec."[8]

Peck had arranged the illegal cargo in secret before leaving Leaside! One of his friends at the Leaside airport was to be married and had asked Peck to bring back "something suitable" for the wedding celebrations.

One of the early Airmail Express deliveries to the Leaside Aerodrome. The pilot on the right may be Leigh Capreol. Note the name T. Eaton Co. on one of the packages. *City of Toronto Archives, William James Collection*

The plane was not suited for such cargo and Peck had to fly at 40 feet above ground! He flew under telegraph wires and consumed more fuel than expected. He refuelled in Kingston on ordinary gas and, as the plane sputtered almost constantly, he needed to stop again at Deseronto by the Bay of Quinte. Here, he drained the tanks and used aviation fuel this time!

The flight began in Montreal at 10:30 a.m. and finished in Leaside at 4:55 p.m. that afternoon. Upon arrival, Peck took a car and delivered the mailbag personally to Toronto Postmaster William Lemon—the delivery a surprise to both the Postmaster and the Mayor of Toronto, Thomas Church. Each letter which was carried now is worth several thousand dollars. One of the letters was purchased for King George V and is in the royal collection.

This flight made the Leaside Airport one of Canada's historic landmarks. On September 6, 1958, in celebration of the 40th Anniversary, the Ontario government placed one of its gold and blue plaques in front of the house at 970 Eglinton Avenue East, marking the site where the plane had touched down. Unfortunately, Brian Peck[9] died in the spring of 1958 and did not live to see the plaque dedication.

A few years ago, the plaque disappeared and John Ridout, President of the East York Historical Society, said that a request for a new plaque required full research before another could be provided; that work was completed. The second plaque has been placed on an island where Broadway Avenue and Brentcliffe converge in North Leaside. This marked the northern boundary of the airfield and was thought to be a less vulnerable location.

CANADA'S FIRST AIR MAIL
1918

In June, 1918 the Montreal branch of The Aerial League of the British Empire persuaded postal authorities to sanction an air mail delivery to Toronto. A JN4 Curtiss aircraft from the Royal Air Force detachment at Leaside aerodrome was selected for the attempt. Piloted by Captain B.A.Peck with Corporal C.W. Mathers as passenger, it took off at 10:30 a.m. June 24th from Montreal's Bois Franc Polo Grounds. After refueling at Kingston, Peck landed here with his cargo of 120 letters at 4:55 p.m., thus completing Canada's first air mail flight.

Erected by the Ontario Archaeological and Historic Sites Board.

Plaque dedicated to Canada's First Air Mail flight, first erected in 1958. Presently, the plaque is standing at Brentcliffe Road and Broadway Avenue in North Leaside. *Leaside Camera Club, courtesy Herb Horwood.*

The plaque reads:
Canada became the first country to transport, where practical, domestic first class mail by air.

THE LEASIDE SQUADRON

The Leaside Squadron was formed on May 1, 1943. Under the Royal Canadian Air Force (RCAF), they were a six-group bomber command stationed in Yorkshire, England. Their role was to fly heavy bombers on strategic operations; their aircraft included Wellingtons, Lancasters and the plane known as the "Halifax." On May 23, 1943, fifteen Wellingtons

Four Halifax bombers in the 432 Squadron returning home from a European mission, escorted by a Spitfire, as painted by John Leonard. *Collection of Bessborough Public School.*

were dispatched to bomb Dortmund, Germany. This was the Squadron's first operation.

This RCAF 432 Squadron was adopted by Leaside and was officially known as the Town of Leaside Squadron. Residents of Leaside stocked their comfort station in East Moor, Yorkshire with pyjamas, chocolate bars and Lux toilet soap. Residents of the Leaside community knit sweaters and socks for Squadron members and corresponded with them regularly. As well, the unit actively recruited from Leaside.

A fund-raising drive was begun in February 1944. A consignment of cigarettes, sent along with sweaters for all squadron members, was acquired through the $1,280.00 raised.

On April 25, 1945 nineteen "Halifax" aircraft were dispatched to bomb gun positions on the Island of Wangerooge; this would be their last mission. The Squadron was disbanded at East Moor, Yorkshire, on May 15, 1945.

There is a painting by artist, John Leonard, which is of four Halifax bombers in 432 Squadron colours returning home from a European mission, escorted by a Spitfire. This painting conveys the feelings that the young crew members (many of them really teenagers) must have

The Leaside 432 RCAF Squadron overseas in 1944. This framed photograph is also on display in Bessborough School. *Collection of Bessborough Public School.*

experienced in their flimsy aircraft. It was presented to Bessborough Public School on November 8, 1986 and hangs in the office hallway today.

One former pilot returned a sweater that was knit in Leaside and sent to him overseas. He wore it as a good luck talisman on his missions. This sweater, as well, is found in Bessborough School, also mounted for display on the wall of the office hallway.

LEASIDE CORVETTE

Originally laid down as *HMS Walmer Castle*, the ship was transferred to the Royal Canadian Navy and commissioned on August 21, 1944 at Middlesbrough. Following workups at Tobermory in September, *Leaside* arrived at Londonderry early in October to join EG C-8, then forming.

Leaside June 1945.

The *Leaside* sailed on October 22nd to meet ON.261, her first convoy, and served the rest of the war as an ocean escort.

On May 11, 1945, the *Leaside* made her last departure from Londonderry to join ONS.50. She left St. John's in June for Esquimalt, where she was paid off for disposal on November 16. Sold in 1946 to the Union Steamship Company of Vancouver, she was converted to a coastal passenger vessel and renamed *Coquitlam*. In 1950, the ship was renamed *Glacier Queen* and stripped, in 1970, in anticipation of becoming a floating restaurant.

The hulk sank in Cook Inlet, Alaska, on November 8, 1978, but was raised, towed to sea and scuttled in January, 1979. The ship bell from the *Leaside* can be found today in the library at Leaside High School.

During World War II, the Leaside Board of Education ruled that the Junior Red Cross would be the only fundraising organization permitted to function in the schools.

The first project of the schools in Leaside was to purchase a heavy-duty army truck. This was followed by the outfitting of the navy corvette, *Leaside,* with a piano, record player and records. The veterans at Sunnybrook Hospital were given a piano, and an iron lung and a TV set were donated to the polio ward for patients.

Each year, the Northlea Junior Red Cross Members entertained the Divadale Hospital veterans with their songs and gifts.

7

INDUSTRIAL AND BUSINESS AREAS EXPAND

ONCE THE Town was incorporated, the newly-formed Town Council, then without financial resources, acted quickly to encourage a solid industrial base to help defray costs. The industries came. The support for industrial development in Leaside is aptly described in the words of R.H. McGregor, Leaside's member of Parliament in the Dominion Government: "...to my mind there is no place so well situated to meet the needs of industry as your municipality. You possess an abundant supply of labour of all kinds in your own and the surrounding municipalities, the best of shipping facilities and ample room for expansion. My business takes me over many parts of the Province each year and I have yet to see a place so well situated as Leaside."[1]

LINCOLN ELECTRIC COMPANY OF CANADA LTD.

In mid-1914, a partnership of four with a capital investment of $1,500.00, formed a company to sell Lincoln electric motors in Canada. The four partners were: Mr. Melville Bertram, Mr. Robert Bertram, Mr. R. E. Smythies and a Mr. Milton. In 1925, the Bellwoods property (which ran north and south between Queen and Dundas, east of Shaw and west of Bathurst) was purchased for approximately $20,000.00. In 1928, the company was appointed the sole distributor in Canada for the Lincoln Electric Company, now located in Leaside. By 1930, it was incorporated federally and began the manufacturing of motors.

From 1930 to 1940, motors formed the greater part of their manufacturing, with Stator cores and rotors being purchased from the parent company in Cleveland, Ohio. Winding stators (part of electric motors) and rotors (armatures), making shafts and machining end yokes comprised the factory operations in Leaside.

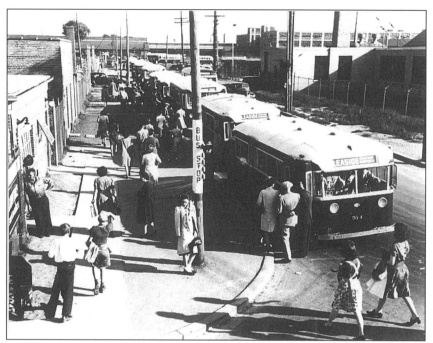

The buses are lined up to take employees home from Leaside's busy Industrial Park. *Collection of Stuart Halliday.*

An additional 2.5 acres of land were purchased in 1937 and four years later, in 1941, operations moved to the current Leaside Industrial Park site, the present location of the Company, approximately 400 to 500 feet east of the site of the old Canada Wire and Cable. Their new location boasted of being the first welded steel building in Canada.[2] The facilities have grown from the original 30,000 sq.ft. building constructed in 1940, to the current 220,000 sq.ft. head office and manufacturing facility. Completed in 1952, this industrial site is set on 5.67 acres of land located between 163 and 179 Wicksteed Avenue. In addition, the company owns 1.14 acres of land on the north side of Wicksteed Avenue, currently used for employee parking, and leases a 50,000 sq.ft. building three blocks to the south on Esandar Drive which serves as their eastern Canada Distribution Centre.

The enlarged manufacturing area not only provides for expansion of electrode manufacturing, but also releases other space for manufacturing: d-c welding generators, both motor and gas engine driven; transformers; combination ac-dc welders and an extensive line of motors. Low-hydrogen and straight iron-powder electrodes—comparatively recent developments in welding—are now being produced.

Since 1918, Lincoln of Canada has been a pioneer in instruction courses for prospective welders, with welding schools organized right within the plant. A four-week basic arc welding course, a very special course, is offered on a regularly scheduled basis.

With more than 200 employees, the Lincoln Electric Company is well-known in academic and business communities for its profit sharing program for its employees and its incentive management programs.

Lincoln is Canada's only manufacturer of arc welding equipment and is the largest manufacturer of arc welding consumables. The company also markets integral horsepower industrial electric motors, manufactured by the Cleveland plant. In 1993, it received ISO 9002 registration, the first welding consumable manufacturer in North America to do so.[3] Today, its products are marketed not only in Canada, but also in the USA, Europe, Middle East and Southeast Asia. Lincoln Electric has been an active member of the Leaside Business Park and is currently expanding its ordering and shipping operations.

Sangamo Company Limited

This company, originally located at Laird Drive and Eglinton Avenue where Canadian Tire is currently found, began producing electric meters in 1904. Displayed above their buildings, clearly marking their presence to the public, was a large rotating oval sign. Their electric meters, designed to measure watt hours of hydro consumption, were exported to 16 countries, including Mexico, Portugal, Africa, Central America and Japan. Sangamo products were designed by Canadians, manufactured in Canada, made from Canadian materials and used by Canadians every day of the year in every province. The company had plants in Leaside and Three Rivers, Quebec, with sales offices in Toronto, Montreal, Winnipeg and Edmonton. The Leaside plant covered 180,000 square feet and had employed 825 people.[4]

In 1970, Prestolite acquired the Sangamo Motor Division which was located in Sarnia, Ontario. Sangalarm, a device developed by Sangamo Company Ltd. of Toronto, monitored the use of electricity and warned when the electrical load was passing a predetermined peak. The company believed the alarm would assist in more efficient energy use. It permitted users to distribute the electrical load by shifting power use to times when requirements were not so high. Some time later, Sangamo moved to Guelph, Ontario.

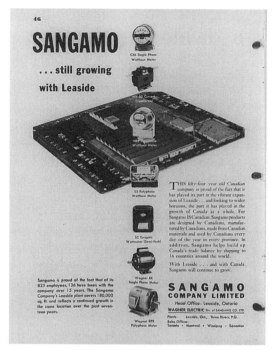

A Sangamo advertisement, 1958. *Taken from* The Leaside Story *by Charles Clay.*

CANADA VARNISH LIMITED

In 1924, R. E. Edwards founded the Canada Varnish Limited, a factory occupying 4.5 acres of land in Leaside on Canvarco Road. The highly skilled and trained employees worked with very specialized equipment to manufacture a diversified line of paints, enamels, varnishes and

An early photograph of Canada Varnish Limited. S. Walter Stuart Library, Elmore Gray Collection.

lacquers for all uses, for both amateur and professional, and for either home and industry. The varnishes were used on the gumwood of many of the Leaside homes.[5]

TREMCO LIMITED

Tremco's origins were with a young Cleveland businessman, William C. Treuhaft, who believed that a successful company is based on well-trained salesmen who understand their customers' requirements. In working as a sales trainer, Treuhaft perfected methods and concepts to the point where he believed he could start a very successful company that would prosper in the building maintenance and construction areas. Therefore, in 1928, the company was launched—TREMCO (TRE for Treuhaft, M for manufacturing, and CO for company). Simultaneously, the company's sales horizons were expanded into Canada.

In the mid-1930s, Tremco enlarged its Canadian interests by establishing a small plant in Leaside in 1931 and consolidating the manufacturing operations previously performed by other companies. In 1950, they moved up the street on Wicksteed Avenue.

Within two years, Tremco's growth and emergence into the international marketplace required the construction of a new facility at 220 Wicksteed Avenue, with subsequent expansions and the addition of a facility at 215 Wicksteed Avenue. Today, Tremco's operations in Canada include: its head office, main distribution and manufacturing operations in three facilities in the Leaside Business Park; a manufacturing and distribution facility in Boucherville, Quebec; and an extended distribution network located in Dartmouth, Ottawa, Winnipeg, Edmonton, Calgary and New Westminster, BC Tremco Inc. has its international headquarters in Cleveland, Ohio, with more than 20 global locations including the United Kingdom, Europe, Asia, Australia and Mexico.

William Treuhaft expected much from his employees and, in return, provided them with a rewarding environment in which they could excel. Possessing a love for the environment, Treuhaft, in 1942, purchased Salisbury Island, about 60 kilometres north of Toronto. This was to be used as a recreation getaway for Tremco employees. The island, approximately seven acres in size with two cottages, continues to be a popular vacation spot enjoyed by Tremco people and their families.

Tremco Ltd. is now structured and operated under the following Divisions: Sealant/Weatherproofing; Roofing and Building Maintenance; and Retail Products. Tremco leads the market with a full range of products responsive to the changing technology appropriate to today's needs.

At 220 Wicksteed they have 8.4 acres, with a total of 207,000 square feet. The 215 Wicksteed warehouse and office, set on six acres was purchased in 1979. In 1984, they added the Roofing building and, again in 1985, a new addition was built.[6]

The business continues to expand and contribute to the industrial well-being of Leaside.

W. E. DILLON COMPANY LIMITED

W. E. Dillon Co. Ltd., originally established in Toronto by Mr. Dillon in 1890, commenced operations at the corner of Wicksteed and Copeland in 1942. The firm started as a branch plant to make ammunition boxes and other wartime supplies. The complete plant moved to Leaside in 1945, and buildings were expanded to cover their two-acre property and accommodate their production needs. The company's post-war manufacturing included: hollow metal doors; fire doors; elevator doors and cabs; electrical control cabinets; toilet compartments and perforated metal grilles; Kalamein doors and custom sheet metal work.[7]

REGAL GREETINGS AND GIFTS INCORPORATED

The Regal story starts with one man, the founder, William S. McCartney. Originally from a farm, he came to the city in the 1920s looking for work. He started by apprenticing as a carpenter, but as there was very little building going on, he obtained a job selling envelopes. The experience led to his developing a great desire to manufacture greeting cards. Fortunately for McCartney, the woman he was dating at the time provided him with $500.00 to set up a business. He later married her and from that time on never worried about the business failing.

It was Edith McCartney who suggested the name "Regal." They began by importing cards from the United States and Britain, but, by 1929, he was printing his own cards in Canada.

The business moved from a basement on Pape Avenue to a store on Greenwood Avenue and from there to a building on Pearl Street in downtown Toronto. The turning point was the purchase of a building at University Avenue and Simcoe Street which Regal occupied from 1946 to 1953.

Not only did Regal bring the first giant four-colour presses to Canada, but it was the first greeting card company in the world to manufacture its own envelopes. As well, the company was the first to produce its own gift wraps.

The first Regal catalogue was produced in the late 1930s. McCartney supported local artists by using their art design for his cards. The company had an interesting relationship with the sales representatives. Each year the reps would write to McCartney, telling him what their earned money had allowed them to do.

In 1974, Regal was sold to Canadian Corporate Management Company Ltd. This acquisition began an era of great expansion and, by 1986, Regal became part of Federal Industries Ltd.

The head office, manufacturing plant and store outlet is at 939 Eglinton Avenue. Customer mail orders come in to Leaside—where they are sorted and sent electronically for fulfillment. A supporter of the local community, Regal has sponsored such groups as the Leaside Garden Society, Leaside Hockey Association and the South Leaside Monday Group.

From an initial investment of $500.00 in 1928, Regal has grown into a business exceeding annual sales of one hundred million.[8] Recently, Regal moved to Mississauga but still has a presence in Leaside.

APCO INDUSTRIES COMPANY LIMITED

APCO's business is marketing to the coatings, ink, adhesive, rubber and specialty chemicals industries in industrial southern Ontario and Quebec.

In 1935, C.I. Grierson borrowed $3,000.00 from his mother, obtained credit with key suppliers and, with two good friends, launched the business. Grierson's good friends, Frank Abernathy and Adam Capling, held shares in the company and the $3,000.00 loan was finally paid in 1944. Adam Capling handled the technical duties, C. I. Grierson the marketing and Frank Abernathy looked after the office. The offices are in a century farm-style house which was acquired in 1935.

One of the company's strengths is being able to capitalize on new and emerging markets. As the company expanded, there was a need for more land to accommodate their growth. The additional four acres obtained in 1965 contained manufacturing facilities laboratories, a tank farm and a warehouse. The business is split between distribution and manufacturing.

During the 40s they struggled to gain acceptance. For them, the 50s were a turning point that saw chemical solvents being added to the line. The 60s represented a period of change. APCO Petroleum Products split into APCO Sales and APCO Industries. In 1981, they became APCO Industries Company Ltd.

It is a family business. C.I. Grierson's son, Jim, became the President in 1965. Approximately 20 years later his son, David, took the reins. As well, many of the 50 employees are the children of original workers.

APCO Industries is celebrating its 65th year at 10 Industrial Street in Leaside, in business as a distributer of petrochemicals and as a manufacturer of a wide range of products used in the metal working and heat treating industries.[9]

E. S. & A. ROBINSON (CANADA) LIMITED

In 1844, the founder of the Robinson group of companies, Elisha Smith Robinson, at the age of 27, set up a modest business in wrapping-paper and paper bags. His business was in Bristol, England and his first customers were grocers. Elisha took his youngest brother, Alfred, into the business in 1848. From this original combination comes the name— E. S. & A. Robinson.

One of the largest overseas operations of the Robinson group is in Canada. In 1932, the first Robinson factory was opened in Toronto. By 1960, there were over 1,000 employees with factory space of 393,000 square feet.

This company designed and produced a wide range of flexible packaging materials using paper, transparent film, plastics and aluminum foil, in single wall, duplex or laminated construction. The products are supplied to customers in either bag, pouch or reel form. Multi-colour printing embraces labels, calendars and advertising. Folding boxes and vacuum packaging for the food industry were also manufactured. Over the years, E. S. & A. Robinson were generous supporters of many Leaside hockey and baseball teams.

The E. S. & A. Robinson Canada Ltd. plant on Laird Drive. *Courtesy Paul Beatt of Winpak Ltd.*

The Sellotape Canada Ltd. company was formed in 1954 to market and distribute pressure-sensitive tape. This was the Canadian competitor to producers of "Scotch-tape."

In 1969, the name of the company was changed to DRG Packaging. However, twenty years later, a venture capital group out of New York bought the company and the company was known as PNG Packaging. Finally, in 1992, Winpak Limited purchased the assets of the company and the name changed to Winpak Technologies Inc.

At their peak, the company employed 1,510 individuals in their facilities at both 73 and 85 Laird Drive and much of what we see in use today was developed here in Leaside. Some of the products are: labels on beer and soft drink bottles; cookie bags with tin-ties; In-Theatre popcorn bags; the window envelopes; "Sello-tape" and plastic packages for bacon and hot dogs.[10]

CORNING GLASS WORKS OF CANADA LIMITED

While Corning Glass Works' head office is in Corning, New York, the Canadian Company branch was incorporated in 1945. Property was purchased from Research Enterprises in 1946, east of Brentcliffe and north of Vanderhoof. Production of glassware in Leaside began in June of that year.

That year, Corning melted the glass and made pyrex products through a process involving a big glass tank. Gradually, green glass blanks of preformed glass were brought in from the United States. By 1959, Corningware was introduced and a sales force established. One of their very popular products, the pyrex glass decorated with the blue cornflower design, received wide distribution. Television picture tubes were also being manufactured at that time.

In 1978, the name changed to Corning Canada Incorporated. Shortly afterwards, an expansionary move was made to Bracebridge, Ontario, but the Leaside plant continued and all of the packaging was done in Leaside.

In Canada, the greatest growth period for the company was from 1960 to 1990. However, Corning left Leaside in 1991-1992 and moved to West Beaver Creek. Many functions (including packaging) were moved to the United States.[11]

VALVOLINE OIL COMPANY

Valvoline Oil, established in Lexington, Kentucky, in 1866, began in Leaside shortly after the town was incorporated in 1913. Its facility was at 31 Industrial Street, having moved there from Laird Drive.

The Corning plant at Brentcliffe and Eglinton, 1967. *Leaside Camera Club, courtesy Herb Horwood.*

The firm blended and packaged high quality lubricants and rust preventatives for distribution throughout all of Canada. During both World Wars, the company donated the Valvoline Victory Award Flags. These flags went to the three competitors representing the country which accumulated the greatest number of points at the International Band show.

In the late 1970s, they moved to Royal Windsor and Winston Churchill in Mississauga. They are still located there. Valvoline produces car products such as Pyroil and Eagle One. With 86 employees in Canada today, the company supports the Molson Indy.[12]

REO MOTOR COMPANY OF CANADA LIMITED

At the end of the war (WWII), Canadian truck and bus operators needed new vehicles by the thousands, to replace worn out equipment long, long overdue for scrapyards. Of course, this was also the case the world over—a demand that would take years to satisfy. In 1946, this was an opportunity for the Reo Motor Company of Canada Ltd. to launch an extensive assembly and plant operation at Leaside's Vanderhoof Avenue. The company would produce some of the needed vehicles. [13]

The location selected was a large and modern plant which had been part of the wartime Research Enterprises complex at Laird and Eglinton.

With the war over, the property was offered for peacetime development through the War Assets Corporation, as, in fact, were other wartime plants which were attractive to automotive companies. Studebaker acquired one such plant in Hamilton for Canadian production, and several other plants were disposed of in much the same way.

Reo had been active in Leaside since 1931, initially with Dominion Motors and then later in buildings acquired from Dominion when that firm closed during 1933 and 1934. Reo stayed on in its ex-Dominion premises on Commercial Road until just after the war, when it moved a little northwards to its new and spacious stand on Vanderhoof. While shutting down on Commercial Road, Reo opened a new sales and service depot in downtown Toronto, seen at the time as more convenient for the city's truck owners.

The operation on Vanderhoof Avenue was on a substantial scale and far exceeded anything Reo had achieved with Dominion Motors while on Commercial. Some 250 workers were employed at peak production times, in addition to personnel in the company's general offices, sales and export departments. These offices were also located right in the plant.

Ideal for assembly lines, the property offered 60,000 sq. ft. of production area, space that was ample for three lines: one for trucks; another for buses and coaches; and a third for the Canadian assembly of Kaiser and Frazer cars. The latter had just come on the market and was a new name in the automotive industry. Both cars sold reasonably well initially when their sponsors managed to get them into a market clamouring for new cars, before many of their rivals had reconverted from military production to automobiles. For a time, at least, most of the taxicabs in Toronto were Frazers, many presumably from the Leaside plant.

Reo had no interest in the marketing of these cars, the assembly program was simply a contract the company had with the Canadian Kaiser-Frazer organization for the supply of completed vehicles to be sold and distributed by the latter. The plan was one that Reo had entered into with Dominion Motors back in 1931. Dominion Motors would assemble Reo cars and trucks under contract for sale by Reo, however the Depression did not allow this to happen.

Reos were quality vehicles and they sold well and widely in Canada. The firm excelled, especially with a unit which it called the Reo Safety School Bus, which was a genuine bus, not a converted truck. The vehicle was suitable for charter service as well as for transporting school children. It cost more than the competitive models, but it sold well and the

Leaside plant turned them out by the hundreds. Reo produced the body as well as the chassis. Usually, a customer bought his chassis from one manufacturer and sought a body from another. Reo had specialized in buses for decades and the firm always commanded a large share of the Canadian market.

Export orders were important, too. A large order for highway-type rear-engined buses was filled for Chile, in addition to business generated in Australia, New Zealand and South Africa. Output would have ranged around 2,000 vehicles annually. This was an impressive output of heavy trucks and buses. The production of Kaiser and Frazer cars, however, was a matter of fits and starts and it is doubtful if more than a few hundred passed through the plant.

Canadian-made tires, batteries, paint, radiators, mufflers and upholstery went into Reos to hold down the price (tariffs on imported parts and components were high). This helped increase the Canadian content, a feature important for some government and provincial sales. Accordingly, Reo was anxious to increase the Canadian content in as many ways as possible. They worked with A. V. Roe (Canada) Ltd. at Malton, to see if the aircraft company could produce some of the stampings Reo needed. A. V. Roe had excellent facilities for the processing of stampings and pressed steel panels, but nothing developed beyond a few trial pressings for Reo buses.

Reo stayed on Vanderhoof Avenue for six or seven years, but eventually the plant was closed following the decision to import complete vehicles from Reo's big Lansing plant. The general offices were retained for a year or two after that, but eventually they were moved to new quarters. The building was torn down four or five years ago and all that remains is the concrete floor with a few conveyor racks still evident. [14]

While Reo as a maker of automobiles disappeared from Leaside and elsewhere many years ago, the name was memorialized by Canada Post in a series of automotive stamps a year or so ago.

DIESEL EQUIPMENT LIMITED (DEL)

DEL opened for business in 1945 as Diesel Equipment Limited. Jack Martin, along with several partners, formed the business plan while overseas with the Canadian Army during WWII. Upon their return to Canada, the men established their company and built a shop at 139 Laird Drive, on the site of a coal storage yard bought from Standard Fuels.

Diesel Equipment started out doing general repairs on any and all vehicles. Early clients included Leaside businesses of the time: Sangamo;

Frigidaire; Canada Wire and Cable; MacNamara Construction; Lincoln Electric of Canada; Philips; Ontario Department of Transportation; Town of Leaside; Ontario Equipment; and E. S. & A. Robinson. DEL's British American (BA) gas pumps are long gone.

While DEL still does diesel fuel injection repairs, the company has evolved to a manufacturer of truck bodies and equipment, the largest in Canada. The original company has become three: DEL Equipment, Canadian Liftgates and Unicell Body, run by Jack's sons, Paul, David and Roger Martin respectively. It is not uncommon to find DEL equipment parked on their roof, moved there by means of a ramp.

While he was building Diesel Equipment's shop, Jack and Mary Martin built a house at 1 Annesley Avenue, their home for over 50 years. Their five children attended Northlea Public School and Leaside High.

DEL still calls Leaside "home" for its branches from coast to coast in Canada, with DEL operations in the United States, the United Kingdom, and South Africa.

In the 1970s, a DEL company built hundreds of high quality sailboats in Leaside. Two of these boats sailed around the world. One voyage is the subject of the book *Maiden Voyage* by Tania Abel.[15]

DOROTHEA KNITTING MILLS

Dorothea Knitting Mills is located on the former site of Research Enterprises (REL), a company which owned property from Brentcliffe Road, north of Research Road, south of Eglinton Avenue East, spanning to the valley. REL assembled radar units which would be fitted into radar trucks for the war effort.

The knitting company moved into one-third of the top floor in 1946, eventually buying up the entire top floor and then the entire building. The company also owns the property at 51 Beth Nealson Drive. They still maintain their partnership with Parkhurst Clothing Company, a similar clothing company.

Dorothea Knitting Mills moved from downtown Toronto into Leaside, where they made scarfs, berets and gloves for Canadian and Russian soldiers. They were formally recognized for their contribution to the war effort by the Federal Government in 1967, as noted on the commemorative plaque that hangs in the second floor lobby.

Initially, the company started knitting wool for ladies' hats, as well as sweaters, scarfs and gloves. Their first overseas shipments during wartime were woollen goods which crossed through the Japanese U-boat infested waters of the Pacific during the Second World War. Nowadays, instead of wool, the company relies mostly on cotton for their products.

The company was named after owner Louis Borsook's wife, Dr. Dorothea Borsook, one of Toronto's first women doctors. Much of her work was at Women's College Hospital.

The current owner, Beryl Borsook, is the son of the founder, Louis. In 1939, he began as a part-time staff member at the age of ten. After completing university at Harvard and MIT in 1952, Beryl Borsook assumed his first full-time position in the family business.[16]

HONEYWELL LIMITED

When a relatively minor firm, Small Electric Motors Company, in Leaside closed at the end of World War II, Honeywell purchased the plant at 107 Vanderhoof. It was here that Honeywell entered the manufacturing field on a significant scale. The first product, the 56 aquastat, a water temperature gauge, was completed in 1956. At that time, the Minneapolis-founded company changed its name to Honeywell Controls Ltd.

The facility later moved to Scarborough. They produce systems and services for energy management and environmental controls for heating, ventilating and air conditioning systems in Canada's schools, as well as for commercial buildings, industrial processing centres and for ships, trains and planes.[17]

GEORGE CROTHERS LIMITED

Leaside was "home" and headquarters for several of the largest construction companies in Canada. Serving the needs of these companies were the many and varied suppliers of machines, equipment and specialty services also located in the Industrial Area. All or most are gone now, but for a time it was an area of intense activity and high local employment.

Crothers Drive (now Redway Road) claimed a tractor "parking lot" at one end and a completely landlocked "boatyard" at the other. Crothers Drive owed its name to George Crothers Ltd. The firm started in a small way before the war, specializing in the overhaul and the sale of used construction machinery, typically crawler tractors, cranes and allied equipment. Growth was very rapid indeed with the outbreak of war and the addition of new shops and services which expanded the firm's mushrooming facilities.

The first office and yard area of George Crothers Ltd. *S. Walter Stewart Library, Elmore Gray Collection.*

The yards were filled with equipment drawn from major wartime construction projects, mostly in eastern Canada, and were sent to Leaside for overhaul and renewal. Replacement parts were in scarce supply as were skilled mechanics. The machines were serviced and revived and sent back out on projects. Many of these machines lasted a lot longer than their manufacturers ever intended, thanks to the continuing and unremitting efforts of Leaside's depots and machine shops. New machines were reserved for the military during the war and only the most essential of civilian customers. The picture did not improve much in the early postwar years with strikes and persistent shortages, but at least Leaside's agents and distributors had a few new machines to sell now and then.[18]

HOWARD FURNACE COMPANY LIMITED

The Crothers organization had a neighbour at the end of the street, the Howard Furnace Company Ltd. This outfit was a large manufacturer of hot air furnaces with its main plant and head office on Yonge Street, a block or so above Davenport Road.

Howard's stand in Leaside was the firm's "boatyard," which was a very large complex of temporary buildings and welding facilities for the production of landing barges and pontoon bridge equipment. The site was one of intense activity with the fabrication of these units, powered by Detroit Diesel engines. They were 20 to 30 feet in length and, at the time of 1943 and 1944, were presumably designed to aid with the invasion in the D-Day operations.

They were not easy to build as the plate, while not armour, had a thickness of about one-quarter of an inch to perhaps an inch, which meant heavy shearing and much flame cutting. There was a sequence in building these barges, culminating with complete assembly to see that everything fitted. After such inspection, the units were dismantled for shipping as sub-assemblies by railway flatcar to what was described at the time as "a Coastal port," probably to the UK and then on to the European continent as troop and equipment craft.

A special railway siding was provided to facilitate transport and to aid next door neighbour Crothers, in the movement of machines and heavy equipment into and out of the yard. The Howard operation was marked by large cranes, imperative in the transfer and the handling of heavy barge components.

With the end of the war, Howard got back to the production of furnaces in its Yonge Street plant.[19] The site on Crothers Drive eventually disappeared as the temporary buildings were moved elsewhere, one by one. The railway siding also vanished.

SHERIDAN EQUIPMENT

Of course, there were other equipment suppliers besides Crothers. Sheridan Equipment had sizeable premises on Laird Drive just above the railway underpass. Sheridan operated a very large shop which claimed to have one of the heaviest cranes in Leaside, needed to ease the handling of heavy tractor and machine parts. A large lot beside the company's frontage on Laird always intrigued onlookers with its amazing array of 30-ton crawler tractors, rock crushers and other machines that Sheridan's always had to offer.[20]

The building, with its high bays out back, is still there, but today it serves new and different clients in its role as the Leaside Business Centre.

WAJAX EQUIPMENT, KNOX AND ONTARIO COMPANY LIMITED

A major centre for the construction industry, Leaside attracted other agents and machinery outlets. Wajax Equipment had premises on Wicksteed for years, as did the Knox Equipment Company Ltd. located just across the street.

In 1976, the Milling Division of Wajax moved its offices and plant from Leaside to Markham, Ontario, to occupy a 30,000 sq. ft. facility.

These new premises house the offices, fabricating and warehouse departments and complete engineering and design services. Knox simply closed its doors and shut down completely.

Just around the corner on Copeland, the Ontario Equipment Company Ltd. sold, repaired and leased construction machinery from a much modified hangar left over from World War I, when this area was a military airfield. Ultimately, the company closed down.

C. A. PITTS CONSTRUCTION AND MCNAMARA
CONSTRUCTION COMPANY LTD.

Two leading contractors faced each other across Commercial Road: C. A. Pitts on one side and McNamara's on the other. The latter was a paving contractor and the firm participated in the construction of dozens of wartime airfields in connection with the Commonwealth Air Training Scheme. This was a British-inspired program established during World War II for the training of airmen across the Dominion.

The company's large storage yard, during the latter part of the war, was filled with a fleet of very hard-used Ford and Chevy dump trucks sent back to Leaside from projects out in the field. They had seen long and demanding service and the firm had obviously despaired of keeping front fenders and running boards free of dents and other evidence of hard times. Instead, these appendages were simply removed or, at the most, were replaced by rough-and-ready shop-made fenders which did nothing to improve appearances, not that this was even remotely a consideration. The firm had a large repair depot which is still in use by tenants who occupy the site and property now.[21]

C. A. Pitts across the street was primarily an excavating outfit, but a very large scale operation. At the time, 1943 and 1944, the firm was busy draining a large lake in Northern Ontario and creating another one to gain access to iron ore deposits at the bottom of the drained lake. "Steep Rock," the project's name, was an undertaking of heroic proportions and, like Hercules, Pitts was involved in the redirection of a river flowing into one of these northern lakes.

Leaside was "home" and headquarters for Pitts. Their operations radiated out from a large and well-equipped machine shop which, like its neighbour across the way, Ontario Equipment, had been a World War I hangar which had been rejigged many times since 1918. Small boats, barges and similar craft were sometimes stored in the company's yard, testimony to Pitts' interest in dredging and harbour work. The firm left Leaside for a new location outside of Toronto.[22]

The company yard of C.A. Pitts, an indication of the range of their operations, 1967.
Leaside Camera Club, courtesy Herb Horwood.

Ultimately, Leaside became less and less attractive to contractors and their equipment suppliers because of increasing traffic and the often difficult access to their yards and lots. Then, too, the problem was compounded by tractors, shovels and similar machines growing in size and weight by leaps and bounds. If one wanted to be in the business, Leaside was no longer the attraction that it had been, lacking the "wide open spaces" that had been the inducement to contractors and suppliers in earlier years.

RESEARCH ENTERPRISES LTD.

Research Road in Leaside is named for a short-lived but amazingly productive high technology war industry company named Research Enterprises Limited (REL). Located two blocks south of Eglinton between Brentcliffe and the proposed Leslie Street extension, the street is now home to contractors, a theatrical equipment supplier and a stage set painter, two innovative recycling companies, a plumbing supplier, and a wood flooring manufacturer, among others. Not much remains of the original plant, just a few red brick buildings facing Eglinton, in the block including the Business Depot, and those on the south side of Research Road near Brentcliffe. The final few structures to the east, including the tall smoke stack, were demolished in the fall of 1999, to make way for the Kosmor development.

Research Enterprises Limited (REL) at Leaside, 1944. This gives a rather complete view (looking northeast) of the manufacturing facilities towards the end of the war. At the top of the picture is the ravine that was later to become the Eglinton Avenue East extension. The street in the middle is Vanderhoof and the one to the south, Research Road. Truck bodies ready to be filled with "radar" equipment are parked upper right. *Credited to the Photographic Survey Corporation Limited. Collection of Bruce Whitehead.*

Occupying 55 acres southeast of Eglinton and Laird, REL at its peak employed over 7,500 people in buildings covering 750,000 sq. ft of engineering and manufacturing plants. It produced an incredible $220 million worth of high technology radio machinery and precision optical instruments in its six short years. To gauge that value, it is interesting to note that at the time, a semi-detatched home at the east end of Parkhurst Boulevard could be purchased for $5,000.00.

Incorporated on July 16, 1940, and closed in September, 1946, Research Enterprises was the largest single employer ever to operate in Leaside. At the time, Canada was essentially still part of the British Empire and was sufficiently far enough away from the threat of invasion to be of strategic value as a supplier of war materials. The United States had not then entered the war and was technically not permitted to be involved. This opportunity gave Canadian engineers, managers, scientists, and technicians, a chance to prove to be among the world's best in rapidly establishing a high technology facility and at maintaining very high production volumes throughout the war. Leaside had excellent rail and road access, vacant flat land (home of a former airport) and was located near a pool of highly skilled people. In addition, there was room for moderate cost housing to accommodate the great many workers, many of whom walked to work. It was at this time that the houses on Parkhurst Boulevard and to the north were begun.

Also noteworthy were the equal staffing numbers of men and women, with females comprising the majority of the inspection staff, and the in-house training program, with as many as 1000 staff members simultaneously receiving instruction on their own time. Because of a shortage of manpower during the war, the facility operated two 60 hour a week shifts, eventually reduced to about 45 hours each. Despite this, there was a 20% increase in productivity.

There were two major sections within the single company: Instrument Division (optical), and the Radio Division (manufacturing radar machinery). The name "Research" was actually not quite accurate since the operation involved primarily engineering and manufacturing. The research function was essentially undertaken by the National Research Council in Ottawa in cooperation with similar departments in other countries.

"Radar" was a development of the 1930s. In February 1935, Sir Robert Watson Watt, head of the National Physics Lab in the United Kingdom, demonstrated "Radio Direction Finding," i.e. the reflection of radio waves originating in ground based antenna, from an approaching aircraft. The first application was a network of 25 "early warning stations" situated along the southeast coast of England. These prototypes quickly proved the usefulness of the concept and encouraged the British government to pursue wider use.

Bringing together the necessary funds, technical talents, ideas, and materials for this secret new invention is a fascinating story. The following is but a brief introduction to the subject. The concept of radio direction finding involved the timing of an echo. A very high frequency radio burst was emitted from a narrow angle transmitter and a fraction of a second later an echo at the same frequency would be received at the base station. Knowing the speed of radio waves in air, the travel time could be calculated, i.e. the time from the transmitter, to the approaching aircraft, and back again.

Advanced models were later developed for use on airplanes and ships, as well as the IFF (Identification, Friend or Foe) system. In use, a ground-based radar sweep would activate an automatic aeroplane or ship transmitter which would then send a coded message to the radar station identifying the vehicle as friendly. Normal radar screens showed only a blip for each encounter, leaving the ground crew to guess as to the identity.

In 1946, with the threat of war gone, the War Department sold off many of the Crown Corporations involved in the war effort. The glass works building of REL was sold to Corning Glass, and other buildings to the Canadian Radio Manufacturing Corp. (previously known as Rogers Majestic Ltd.), which in turn was taken over by Philips Electronics. Both Corning and Philips had left the area by the late 1980s. Canadian Arsenals Limited, another Crown Corporation, was given the task of disposing of the REL production equipment and inventory.

Many of the skilled staff returned to their pre-war employment or moved on to careers in electronics. There was some thought of maintaining the REL Crown Corporation intact after the war, but this was voted down by government, likely due to a policy of not competing with private enterprise in peacetime. Had the skills been maintained under one extended roof, who knows how the future may have turned out. Perhaps Leaside would have been home to another IBM, Sony or Microsoft.[23]

PHILIPS ELECTRONICS LIMITED

In 1881, Gerard Philips, a graduate mechanical engineer, established a company in Eindhoven, the Netherlands to manufacture incandesent lamps and other electrical products. His brother, Anton, became his partner to help bolster sales.

The company initially concentrated on making carbon-filament lamps and became one of the largest producers in Europe. In 1914, a research laboratory was established to develop new lighting technologies.

Philips began x-ray radiation and radio reception in 1918. They then became involved in experiments in television in 1925. In 1927, radios were a major Philips product and, by 1932, they had sold one million radios around the world.

Their first electric shaver was launched in 1939. Its research led to the development of the Plumbicon TV camera tube and improved phosphors for better picture quality. In 1963, Philips introduced the compact audio cassette and, by the 1970s, inventions such as the Compact Disc were developed.

A Philips VHF transmitter was installed in the CN Tower in 1974 to strengthen and extend the range of television signals in the Toronto area.

Philips House was built on Vanderhoof Avenue in 1966, adjacent to the company's factories, warehouses and other office buildings. Inside were the executive offices and office space for three marketing divisions in Canada. This three-storey block, constructed on a former Leaside garbage dump, had a spectacular view over parkland and was a striking landmark on Eglinton Avenue East. An illuminated Philips sign on the roof dominated the skyline.

"The White House," as it was called, was opened by Paul Hellyer, then a Liberal cabinet minister, and William Davis, then Premier of Ontario. It was the hub of the Company's Canadian activities. In the summer of 1976, the equipment and people moved to 601 Milner Avenue in Scarborough.

In February 1994, this building, along with others along Vanderhoof Avenue, was demolished.

WATER AND POWER

The influx of industry to Leaside brought with it an increasing demand for the essential services of water and power. As well, the residential area was expanding rapidly, adding to the demand.

LEASIDE WATERWORKS

The first piped water for Leaside residents came from wells located in the Don Valley, north of Broadway Avenue, and was stored in a tower on the high land located at the intersection of Broadway and Bayview Avenue. "Water was pumped by diesel engine from artesian wells in line with the road allowance beside the present Northlea United Church. It was forced up the hill along the northerly limits of the lots on the north side of Broadway Avenue to the tower. From there it flowed downward in a south-easterly direction through pipes to the older sections of the town. It proved unsatisfactory as the muddy Don River clogged boilers and left great deposits of silt in bathtubs. The tower was removed and sold some time after the First World War."[24] During the war, this supply was abandoned and a supply of city water was made available at Eglinton Avenue, which was connected to the original main from the water tank.

The Town of Leaside also owned its own sewage treatment plant located adjacent to the present sewage treatment plant. It is located in the valley below Redway Road and the Leaside Bridge. Leaside allowed the City of Toronto to build a trunk sewer 60 feet deep through Leaside.

In 1930 Leaside abandoned its own disposal plant and outflow sewer to the Don River in favour of entering into a new arrangement with the new City of Toronto plant as it was thought it would provide better service.

GREAT GATINEAU POWER STATION

The Town of Leaside was selected by the Ontario Hydro Electric Power Commission as the site for the largest power substation in the world in the 1920s. This location was chosen because of Leaside's strategic location, believed to be a key position for province-wide distribution of power. As well, Leaside had exceptional railway facilities to accommodate heavy equipment.

Gatineau Power Station 1931. *Taken from* The Story of Leaside *by John Scott.*

The five million dollar Plant was the Toronto receiving end of the great Gatineau line. Each of the twelve transformers in the Plant weighed 368,000 pounds. These were the largest single-phase, water-cooled units in physical size ever constructed. Each day approximately 1.5 million gallons of water were required for cooling purposes (which is approximately enough water to supply a town with a population of 15,000).

The power generated from the Gatineau River in Quebec was transmitted to Leaside at 220,000 volts over a distance of 230 miles. This became the longest 220,000-volt line in Canada.[25]

8

MERCHANTS OF BAYVIEW, MCRAE, MILLWOOD AND SUNNYBROOK

A T THE CLOSE of World War I, the first store in Leaside opened in 1922, at the southwest corner of McRae and Sutherland. This grocery store, known as Perrem & Knight, operated for 25 years until 1947 when it became the Leaside Postal Station. The store sold and delivered groceries, meat and a few staples like thread and aspirin. The store was not self-serve, but rather it had a long counter and the goods were brought to the customer. Mrs. Perrem was a friend to her customers and to the community-at-large. It was here that the first telephone in Leaside was installed. Whenever there was an emergency, Mrs. Perrem rose from her bed to drive sick people to the hospital. One time she was an emergency midwife and fainted from the excitement of it!

In the late 20s, stores started to open up on the east side of Bayview from Millwood to Parkhurst on Eglinton Avenue east of Sutherland and on Millwood Road between Rumsey and Airdrie.

Frank Surovec, who purchased the barber shop at 864 Millwood Road in March of 1952 and eventually bought the building, was able to get some of the history of "Millwood on the Park" as it became known. A man by the name of DeMarco owned the whole block, with the exception of 850 (a variety store) and 856 (formerly the Millwood Color Copy), which was owned by an American company, Champion. At the time, Champion was the largest supplier of embalming fluid in Canada.

The shop at 850 Millwood, it seems, was always a variety store. However, in the 50s it did not do well because next door was Andy Anderson's Drug Store which carried many of the same products. When the drug store finally closed, that space was taken over by the Endangered Animal Sanctuary. When Bill Vallieres was finally forced out in about 1993, Struther's Paints occupied the store. Now Bicycle Specialties is there.

Perrem and Knight, the first store in Leaside opened in 1922 on the southwest corner of McRae and Sutherland. This photograph was taken May 21, 1955. *Toronto Reference Library, J.V. Salmon Collection.*

At 854 (now China Food), Dominion operated their first store.[1] Prior to Dominion it had been a butcher shop. Mr. Neilson had the corner store, candy and variety. A Chinese gentleman bought 852 and 854 Millwood from DeMarco and still owns that corner. As mentioned earlier, Champion owned 856 and had expanded next door to 858 before they moved their operations in 1988.

Three partners owned Leaside Electric at 858 Millwood Road. Of the three, one was involved in construction and one was an electrician. All together, they did a great business. In the front of the store they sold electrical appliances and in the back they had up to eight men working at repairing radios, toasters and other small appliances. When they moved out, the location became a Fish & Chip store that was very popular with Leasiders.

In 1988, these two stores, 856 and 858 Millwood, were bought by Michael Hibbard. Dann Dunn, an interior designer of stores and offices, renovated them and operated there until he moved downtown in 1991. Millwood Color Copy moved into 856 until 1997 (now Turning Pointe, a dance academy) and Room by Room (a paint and interior design store) occupied 858 until December of 1996. This store is now vacant.

Situated at 860 Millwood was a very popular butcher shop and small grocery shop called Hudson's Groceria. It was owned by a couple from North Toronto. When they retired, it was kept going by several people, including a couple from Montreal. Next, two men, one a manager from

Looking north from Bayview and Eglinton in 1910. The house on the hill at right is the Robert Cook House; across the road now is Brennan's Pontiac. *From the Archives of the Todmorden Mills Museum.*

Loblaws and the other from Dominion Stores, tried their hand at running this store, but no one could match the expertise of the original owners. Apparently, there was a mysterious fire there one night. Eventually, the building was bought by a business called Ekhohm's. They moved in with Millwood Upholstery and are still going strong.

A dry cleaners occupied 862 Millwood and the garages at the rear were used for car repairs and cleaning engines. There was a big cauldron in which the mechanics would boil the grease off the engine parts. This company was known as Simplex and, when the dry cleaners' lease expired, they moved into the store front and began selling parts and accessories for cars. The company was sold and eventually went out of business. For a while a print shop occupied this same store front and did the printing and mixing of inks in the back room, a room which was all tiled in white ceramic tile.

Number 864 Millwood used to be a variety store with wooden floors and pinball machines. However, in the late forties, it was a combination hairdresser and barber shop. Both occupied the same store space. When Frank Surovec bought the barber shop business in 1952, he partitioned off the space for Irene-Ann's Hairdresser, keeping it separate from his barber shop although they both used the front door on Millwood. After Frank had a stroke in the mid-eighties, he rented the barber shop portion to Sandy's Cycle. In 1988, Irene-Ann decided to retire and Frank sold the building.

Eglinton Avenue East, looking east from Bayview Avenue, September 1951. The dip in the road is being "filled in" to accommodate the new Sunnybrook Shopping Centre. The road and sidewalk are still intact under the fill. The new Leaside High School is on the right. *Toronto Reference Library, J.V. Salmon Collection.*

Across the street on the southeast corner of Millwood and Rumsey was a gas station run by a father and son. For a while it became Kentucky Fried Chicken and then reverted back to being a garage to service cars.

In 1930, the Leaside Service Station was situated at the corner of McRae and Millwood. Ideal Dairy, owned and operated by Mr. & Mrs. Brown, was located at Laird and Markham. From here, milk was delivered by horse-drawn carts.

Sunnybrook Shopping Centre, now called Sunnybrook Plaza, originally was a marsh where people dug loam for their gardens. Behind it was a wooded hill. In the early 50s, this site was cleared and levelled to make way for a new business complex.

On May 14, 1952, Sunnybrook Shopping Centre was officially opened. On behalf of the Centre, Mayor Howard Burrell of Leaside presented Sunnybrook Hospital with a 20-inch television set. Superintendent of the Hospital, Dr. Karl F. Hollis, accepted the gift on behalf of the patients.

Featuring a frontage of 560 feet, approximately two city blocks in length, the Centre offered the shopper everything from fine watches to a shave and a haircut. It opened with 17 businesses, including: a bank, a drugstore, gift shops, clothing and shoe shops, a supermarket, a five-and-ten, a furniture store, a dry cleaner, a department store and a bakery. Eventually, there was a beauty parlour, a florist, an appliance store, restaurant, shoe clinic and a sporting-goods shop. The longest running tenant, Monaco Paints, has been there for 36 years.

The Sunnybrook Shopping Centre in April 1952, just prior to its formal opening in May. Looking northeast from Bayview Avenue. *Toronto Reference Library, J.V. Salmon Collection.*

The very latest in fixtures and materials were used in the construction of the complex. The supermarket even featured conveyor belt counters that automatically took the customers groceries to the checking clerk.

Sunnybrook was Ontario's first planned community shopping centre. To celebrate the opening, roses and cigars were passed out to customers.[2] Today, the Centre still offers a range of shopping opportunities.

BAYVIEW MOTORS

During the "dirty 30s," the Lepard brothers opened the Bayview Garage. In 1938, the garage, which still stands facing the lane between Donegall Drive and Bayview at Fleming Crescent, flourished. The two brothers, Howard and Lloyd, began learning auto mechanics began with their father. They moved the garage to McRae Drive in 1948. The business lasted over fifty years before being closed.

STANLEY CLEANERS

This business was begun in 1929 by R. D. Stanley, a relative of the Stanley Cup provider.[3] The shop was located at 922 Millwood, which, at that time, was the end of the road.

The cleaners consisted of a store and pressing room in the front, a cleaning room behind and a boiler room which used coal to produce steam for the pressers and dryers. The cleaning room was in a separate building where the petroleum was used. From 1929 to 1940, the business experienced great growth. In the early days the cleaning deliveries were made by horse and buggy. Later, trucks were used, leading to the employment of nine drivers. At one time the business required forty to fifty employees.

The plant and head office of Stanley Cleaners circa 1935. *Courtesy Stanley Cleaners.*

A section of the Ladies Finishing Department of Stanley Cleaners at 922 Millwood Road. *Courtesy Stanley Cleaners.*

The second owners were Mr. Stanley's son and brother. In 1948, Norm Whitney purchased the business and, in 1977, the present owners, Mario Cuzzolino and Forunato Fusco, bought the business. The building is the original one with the original floors. Over the years the building has been painted and the equipment updated.

BELL JEWELLERS

Originally from Scotland, Mr. Bell opened Bell Credit Jewellers Ltd. on Bayview Avenue in December 1936. It was located beside the popcorn concession booth outside the Bayview Moving Picture Theatre. After twenty-two years of operation, Bell sold his shop to Mr. Files who moved the store to its present location. Formerly that space had been occupied by Aikenhead's Hardware. While Files did not work in the store, he owned it until 1963.

Next, Israel Erlich both purchased it and worked there. In November 1979, he was shot and killed by two teenagers from the Mt. Pleasant area. The eighteen-year-old was sentenced to ten years in prison and the four-teen-year-old was sent to a reformatory for three years. They had attempted to steal jewellery to buy drugs. Although they initially escaped, they were caught in North Dakota and turned over to the RCMP in Canada.

In January 1980, Photi Philos purchased the business. Today he works in his store offering excellent merchandise and service at affordable prices. He and his staff design jewellery and are watchmakers as well. In addition to a wide range of goods, they specialize in Japanese watches, Italian jewellery and Greek crosses.[4]

Bell Jewellers has been a long-standing success story on Bayview.

RUMBLE CHEVROLET LIMITED

Everyone remembers the advertising jingle "Ramble into Rumble—you'll see!".

Robert Rumble purchased the property on the west side of Bayview in 1950. It was the homesite of the last farm in Leaside: namely the "old McGinn place." The farmhouse, barns, apiary and cherry orchard were removed.

Rumble Chevrolet later became Rumble Pontiac Buick, In their peak period, there were between 95 to 125 employees. Rumble also owned and leased property at Roehampton and Bayview. Eventually, they expanded and purchased a used car lot and administrative building which had been owned by two brothers named Hurlburt.

One Leaside resident, Irene Quibell, was secretary to Mr. Rumble from 1951 to 1985. She then worked for Rumble Holdings at the Inn on the Park until 1998. Mr. Verdun Smith, another Leaside resident, was the comptroller and secretary/treasurer from 1950 to the 1980s.

Robert Rumble sponsored hockey and baseball teams in Leaside and also provided cars for the Canada Day Parade. By working with Leaside

Rotary and the Leaside Lions, the dealership sponsored educational driving lessons for the handicapped at the Hugh MacMillan Centre.[5]

Mr. Rumble sold the business to Gerald Wood in 1985. Although only
owning this agency for a short time, he renovated and tore down the
original buildings. In 1990, Brennan's purchased the business and continued the driver education classes.

BADALI'S FRUIT MARKET

Badali's business in Toronto began in 1927 at the corner of Logan and
Queen Streets. It was Gus Badali, having emigrated to Canada from
Sicily in 1920, who started his business. He sold fruits and vegetables
from his horse-drawn wagon all over Toronto.

In 1938, his son, Leo, saw an opportunity. He moved to a store front
on Bayview, and with the help of his wife Lena, brother Sam and his wife
Victoria, opened a fruit and vegetable market.

When the family originally moved to Bayview, they lived above the
store which is now Alex's Cheese Shop. In 1940, the family purchased
the 1587 Bayview Avenue location where Sam and Victoria lived above
the store.[6]

The brothers, Sal (left) and Dom Badali, in front of their Fruit Market with their Aunt
Victoria (with glasses) and their mother, Lena. Theirs is one of the oldest continuously operated family stores on Bayview. *Courtesy the Badali family*.

The first Imperial Bank of Canada on McRae Drive, just west of Laird. *Courtesy CIBC, Laird Drive.*

IMPERIAL BANK OF CANADA

In October 1918, the Imperial Bank of Canada opened its first branch, a small white building, in Leaside. The original location on McRae Drive one block west of Laird Drive was open only until December of that year.

The Imperial reopened a branch at Laird and McRae in the former Town of Leaside Bank, really the first bank in Leaside. This opening in March 1928, is recognized as the initiation date of the branch.

The name of the bank was changed to the Canadian Imperial Bank of Commerce in June 1961, brought about by a merger with the Canadian Bank of Commerce. The bank absorbed the business of 188 Laird Drive on August 31, 1962 and, in 1965, was redesignated at Laird and McRae.

MERCHANT DEVELOPMENT AS TAKEN FROM COUNCIL MINUTES

A perusal of the Council Minutes from this period of early commercial development in Leaside provide some interesting insights into the concerns and priorities of the times.

November 30, 1927	A petition received to make Millwood Road a business street.
May 30, 1928	A petition has been received to create a business section along Bayview. It will run between Millwood and Soudan.

639 Bayview Avenue at Fleming Crescent in 1931. Cars were scarce; stones were more plentiful. *Collection of Paul Clough.*

June 27, 1928	Another petition to council asks for the business section to extend from Moore Ave. to Eglinton.
May 29, 1929	Steps are being taken to create a lane behind the Bayview business section.
November 17, 1930	The lane behind the Bayview business section is to be extended from Fleming to Soudan. (Parkhurst)
October 3, 1936	The Dominion Store at the corner of Millwood and Bayview is given permission to build an addition.
November 18, 1936	Permission is given to build a gas station at Millwood and Rumsey.
February 1, 1937	Request is received to build a Moving Picture Theatre. Annual Fees for this establishment: seating under 600—$500.00, seating between 600 and 1,000—$1,000.00.
March 1, 1937	Hanson Theatre Corp. begins theatre construction on Bayview Avenue (now Bruno's).
July 5, 1937	Barber Shops are to close by 8:30 p.m. on weekdays and 11:30 p.m. on Saturday nights and holidays.

Vito Pantaleo (left) and Bill Van Vugt (now deceased). Bill and Vito's Service Station is still in business after 50 years, on the corner of McRae and Sutherland. *Courtesy Bill and Vito's.*

April 8, 1938	A medical certificate must be received from each employee working in restaurants, grocery stores, butcher shops (anyone who handles food for human consumption).
October 27,1938	Request to build a store at McRae and Bayview.
April 3, 1939	Permission is given to build a small animal hospital on Millwood Road.
July 25, 1939	Dairy operating out of 223 McRae Drive.
August 8, 1939	Service Station on southeast corner of Millwood and McRae.
May 19, 1941	Loblaws Store (where the old Bruno's was) on Bayview had wanted to install a beverage room (Brewers Retail). Hundreds of complaints from ratepayers caused Council to stop all future Brewers stores, warehouses, retail stores and government liquor stores from locating in Leaside.

The Jeffery Meat Market originally established in 1948 at 689 (now 1689) Bayview, was a popular neighbourhood business for thirty-one years until its closure in 1979. *Courtesy Bea Jeffery.*

June 12, 1950	Brewer's Warehouse asks to erect a liquor store on Eglinton between Sutherland and Laird Avenue. Council objects because of the existing heavy traffic [a liquor store was eventually built].
March 19, 1951	A used car lot for the corner of Sutherland and McRae is denied by council.
November 2, 1953	Lots of tax appeals are being made and Leonards Hobby Shop will be leaving 603 Bayview in March.
September 19, 1955	Parking meters are to be installed on Bayview and will charge 10 cents for one hour.[7]

9

A Place to Worship

As the town of Leaside grew there developed a strong desire for worship in a congregational setting. This was a time when Sunday attendance was strong and, as each denomination built a church in Leaside, it flourished. St. Cuthbert's was the first church to become established in the area.

St. Cuthbert's Anglican Church

In 1890, William Lea designated a half-acre of land to erect a small frame building, known as the "Leaside Mission, on the "Government Road" (as Bayview was then called). It opened October 1, 1890 and seated 90 people. Money to build this church was donated by John Lea and his wife, as well as by Mr. Collins who, at that time, was renting a house from John Lea. The cost of construction was $705.00. A debt of $200.00 was carried on the building until 1894 when it was paid in full.

It is interesting to note that not until 1938 was the land vested in the names of the Rector and Wardens, as is the custom. Previous to that, it was held in the names of three men who were appointed trustees by William Lea and delegated to see that the property was actually used for church purposes; if not, the land was to revert to the original Lea heirs. The name Leaside Mission was in use until 1908 when it changed to its present name, St. Cuthbert's. Its small congregation of 40 struggled through 18 years, ministered to by a variety of students and clergy.

Prior to the mission house, Canon T. W. Patterson from the mother church, Christ Church Deer Park, located on Yonge Street, had held "cottage meetings." These were services held in the homes of Anglicans who wished to have a church service close by. In order to attend the evening service, Canon Patterson would walk from Yonge Street along

The first St. Cuthbert's Anglican Church, built in 1890. Fire destroyed the church on October 28, 1937. *S. Walter Stewart Library, Elmore Gray Collection.*

Merton, carrying a coal-oil lantern as there were no street lights. Patterson named the mission after the British Saint Cuthbert, the 7th century shepherd who became a bishop. Students would be sent from Trinity College for three o'clock Sunday School and for the evening service at seven. These students would then be invited to different homes for dinner.

Until the time of the name change, there had not been a permanent minister. Finally, in January 1909, a young graduate of Trinity College, named P. Morland Lamb, was appointed curate of Christ Church Deer Park and was given charge of St. Cuthbert's, Leaside. Deer Park also gave $200.00 to assist with costs. That year, he was ordained in the Church and, in 1910, he took charge formally. Because of Lamb's hard work and his great faith in God much was accomplished. In 1910, Reverend Lamb married Miss Estella Mary Lea, the daughter of Charles Lea and great-granddaughter of John Lea. She had been the organist for the Sunday School since 1903. Prior to the marriage, we are told that she had one very bad habit—constantly being late for the service! It is said that Reverend Lamb cured her of this habit by starting the service one Sunday without her.

In 1912, Estella Lea relinquished her church duty in order to begin a family and ultimately had three children: Max, Thais and Cuthbert. The family moved into the rectory which still stands just south of the church green.

A garden party held on the lawn of St. Cuthbert's Church, circa 1920. *Toronto Reference Library, J.V. Salmon Collection.*

When Leaside was incorporated in May 1913, St. Cuthbert's Mission was the only public building and so the first town council meeting was held there. Once it became possible to build a new church, the frame mission building was moved to the back of the lot. A shallow excavation was dug and the soil from it spread around to raise the level of the site. A brick church with a basement was built.

When the new church was opened on May 3, 1914, the congregation numbered 350. The former mission building became a parish hall and remained in use until it burned to the ground in 1937.

In 1922, Mrs. Charles Lea (Charlotte Playter) had laid the cornerstone of the Church. Almost thirty years later, in 1951, her daughter, Estella Lamb, laid the cornerstone for the new Parish Hall. Three years later, when Canon Lamb retired and moved to Brighton, Ontario, the hall was named "Lamb Hall" in his honour. In 1960, two stained-glass windows were dedicated to the Canon and his wife.[1]

LEASIDE UNITED CHURCH

Not until 1928 was the need for a United Church in Leaside considered urgent. With the opening of the Leaside Viaduct in 1927, development of the community was rapid. Reverend James Miller canvassed the area and called residents affiliated with the United Church to a meeting at the home of Mr. and Mrs. G. D. Bird on December 6, 1928. He informed those present that the land, which had been purchased at the corner of Millwood and McRae as early as 1925, was available and that a portable building over on Manor Road was also available for use.

A "victory tea" reception held at St. Cuthbert's to welcome troops returning from
World War I. In the centre are the three Shuttleworth Sisters. *Toronto Reference
Library, J.V. Salmon Collection.*

Agreement was reached that night and those present became the first
Board of Managers: Gil D. Bird, Chairman; Cecil J. Woodard, Secretary;
Edwin Smith, Treasurer; R. Hancock, Envelope Secretary; John Girard
and John Dawson, Property Committee. The congregation was represented by J. Sherbett.

The Manor Road building was moved to its new location and the
Canada Varnish Company provided the paint to freshen-up the new
"church." The Women's Association made curtains for the windows.
One hundred chairs were purchased for $75.00, along with a stove and
pipe for $23.90. The first minister was Rev. Dr. Alexander Mac-Gillivray
who was paid $7.00 per Sunday. Mrs. Dawson conducted the Sunday
school. A back room served as kitchen and minister's study, as well as
being the Sunday School room where Mrs. Gil D. Bird was one of the
teachers; she taught there for twelve years.

Soon there were socials and concerts, sleigh rides and bowling nights,
and Mrs. William Page found the means to buy hymn books. Meanwhile, the Building Committee was charged with the responsibility of
investigating what it would take to erect a larger, permanent church, but
three years would pass before the new church could open.

In 1939, the auditorium of Leaside School (now Bessborough) became
available for services and seventy new members joined, swelling the size
of the congregation even more. The first sod for the new church was
turned on October 5 and the foundation stone was laid on November 2,
1940. The architects for this new structure were J. Francis Brown and Son.

The interior of the first Leaside United Church in 1928. *Collection of Robert Butcher.*

The exterior walls of the church were to be "of finest Credit Valley stone,"[2] creating a very imposing building. In 1941, the church was completed and opened its doors for its first service, conducted by the minister Reverend Harry Mellow. The church membership continued to expand and, by 1949, when Reverend Charles C. Murray became the minister, the Sunday School attendance was 704 in total!

Soon, there was a need for a Christian Education Wing as the number of people attending Sunday School grew rapidly to 1,200. The school was operating four "shifts." Correspondingly, the congregation grew from 900 in 1949 to 1,600 in 1951.

A Casavant organ was installed in 1950 and a beautiful memorial window was designed by Mr. Murray, of the old Leaside Murray family. This window, unveiled in 1955, commemorates those whose lives were sacrificed in the war. The window can still be seen today.[3]

SALVATION ARMY CITADEL

On Wednesday, October 29th, 1930, the twenty-fifth Salvation Centre opened at 541 Bayview Avenue, directly across the road from Belsize Avenue (north of Millwood). Commissioner James Hay officiated at this joyous occasion.

The Salvation Army Citadel built at 541 Bayview Avenue (now 1541), as shown in 1931. *Collection of the George Scott Railton Heritage Centre.*

Previously, Captain Margaret Campbell and Lieutenant Merle Silver worshipped in a large marquee. "Wind and weather and other causes did not deal gently with the canvas temple and thereafter the faithful handful found conditions to be more hospitable in the open air."[4]

Brother Ham of the Dovercourt Citadel was the contractor to build the handsome red-brick edifice on Bayview. This location was decided upon because 150 houses in a year had been erected within six minutes walk from the citadel.

Lads on bicycles, a brigade of marching women, cadets and laden motor cars all converged on the Citadel for the opening night. A couple of Salvation Army families living in the district joined in the festivities.

After Captain Campbell and Lieutenant Silver, a succession of dedicated people were appointed. There were three opportunities for worship on Sunday:

    11:00 a.m.   Holiness Meeting
    3:00 p.m.   Sunday School
    7:00 p.m.   Revival Meeting

Alas, visible results were negligible, even with impromptu concerts being held on the steps of the hall to attract attention.

The Citadel closed June 26, 1940, partly due to the Depression. A Loblaws groceteria later occupied the premises, then Bruno's Fine Foods and presently a designer discount clothing store and an art gallery.

Leaside Presbyterian Church during construction, August 1951. *Toronto Reference Library, J.V. Salmon Collection.*

LEASIDE PRESBYTERIAN CHURCH

In the spring of 1942, the students of Knox College, Toronto, conducted a survey of homes in the Leaside area. The official organization of a congregation began as a result of a meeting of interested people on October 28, 1942. Services of worship under the auspices of the Presbyterian Church of Canada were first held in the Bayview Theatre. Later, the congregation met in Bessborough Public School. Rev. W. T. McCrea was appointed the interim moderator and Glebe Presbyterian Church, located on the west side of Bayview, oversaw the new congregation.

By December 1942, the name of Leaside Presbyterian Church was chosen. Officers and committees were appointed to organize the church and Rev. G. W. MacKay conducted worship. Mrs. MacKay and Mrs. John Fernie directed the Sunday School. In March 1943, Mr. J. C. Hay, a student of Knox College, was asked to be the minister. Ordained in April 1945, Reverend Hay served his congregation for ten years.

Four lots were purchased from the York Land Company on the northwest corner of the intersection of Hanna Road and Eglinton Avenue in January 1944. Later the same year, a lot from the Fleming Estate that would allow for 193 ft. frontage on Eglinton, was acquired.

Because of wartime regulations, special permission from the government was required in order to erect a church with a basement. James Wilson, a church member, was contracted as the architect. The building, costing $19,000.00 and accommodating 225 people, was formally opened by Rev. A. O. Stewart, the Moderator of the Presbyterian Church of Canada, on April 1, 1945. The first two elected elders, F. A.

Willett and J. T. Carlyle, began the Kirk Session. At this time, Eglinton was unpaved and only two homes existed east of Bayview Avenue.

In 1947, while Leaside High School was being built, it became necessary to hold classes in the basement of the church, located across the street. This accommodation was reciprocated in 1952 when the church congregation met at the high school while Leaside Presbyterian, now with a capacity of 500, was expanded. Bruce Brown and Brisley were the architects for this building which cost $160,000.00.

When Reverend J. C. Hay left in 1955, Reverend Douglas G. Seaton arrived as the new minister. In October 1961, the new Christian Education Wing was built for $120,000.00. This addition included a chapel, several classrooms, a boardroom and a parlour. Today, the Leaside Presbyterian Church continues to serve the community and shares the church building with a Taiwanese congregation.[5]

St. Anselm's Roman Catholic Church

"About 100 Catholic families were living in the mostly Protestant Town of Leaside at the time. Many had long cherished the idea of establishing their own Catholic community."[6] Father Francis Michael Caulfield, arriving in an old jalopy, pulled up on Donegall Drive in 1938. His mission was to create a new parish, build a church and a school. Initially, he settled into a rented home on Donegall Drive, and began his work.

Father Caulfield spotted a bankrupt meat market and groceteria, located then at 609 Bayview Avenue (now the location of "Nestings" at 1609 Bayview). He promptly leased it. The first Mass was celebrated here on July 31, 1938, and the site was named after St. Anselm of Canterbury, a saint born of noble parents in Piedmont in 1033 or 1034.

Father Caulfield had a dog named "Tinker" who would accompany him to church. Once when Tinker was trotting down the aisle to the altar, a parishioner tried to restrain the animal. It is said that Father Caulfield gruffly told the parishioner to leave his pet alone because "he comes to church more often than you do."

Some twelve years earlier, the York Land Company had sold a choice piece of land for $8,645.00 to the diocese. This property was located on Millwood Road between MacNaughton Road and Bessborough Drive. Father Caulfield promptly began raising the $50,000.00 for his building program. The Episcopal granted him $30,000.00 and he personally advanced $20,000.00! In the meantime, since the temporary church on Bayview Avenue was satisfactory, the funds went towards the building of a two-room school. The rectory at 1 MacNaughton Road was then built

St. Anselm's Church. *Taken from the "St. Anselm's Parish Book."*

with Father Caulfield's money.

In September 1941, the cornerstone of the new church was laid by the Guiane Construction Company. The new church, designed to seat 400 people, was completed by December 1941. Inside the altar were the relics of the martyred Saints: St. Lucidianus, St. Auxilius and St. Desideria. The wooden steeple was covered by copperized metal.

By 1951, the parish had grown to more than four times the seating capacity of the church, to the degree that it became necessary to hold Mass in the church basement as well. Father Caulfield served this growing parish for twenty-three years until his health began to fail. Father Merrit T. Griffin moved into the rectory in 1959. It was clear that St. Anselm's needed a much bigger church.

Father Caulfield died in 1961, at the age of 70. To honour his dedication to his parish, the Borough of East York declared that a tract of land at MacNaughton and Cameron be called the Francis M. Caulfield Parkette.

In July 27, 1964, the new church design was approved, with the architect being Arthur Taylor of Lenz. The old church was disassembled and, while construction occurred, Mass was held at Leaside High School. The first Mass to be celebrated in the new church was held on June 26, l966. This new church could seat 957 and had an auditorium capacity of 750 people.

When Father Griffin moved to Pickering in 1969, Father Carlo J. Cerrone was appointed to replace him, beginning October 23, 1969. He erected a large cross on the sanctuary wall. In 1978, after Father Cerrone left for Barrie, Father John O'Neill replaced him, appointed from 1978 to 1992. Monseignor Edward Boehler who followed in 1992, is still serving the community.[7]

THE CHURCH OF ST. AUGUSTINE OF CANTERBURY

In 1943, the Rev. Canon P. M. Lamb of St. Cuthbert's Church anticipated the post-war expansion of the Sunnybrook area. Consequently, he began to lay plans for the work of church extension in the northern portion of his parish.

"This was a selfless venture of faith because he knew only too well that it would result in a substantial loss of membership for his parish."[8]

Within a year he had persuaded the Incorporated Synod of the Diocese of Toronto to purchase a site two blocks north of Eglinton Avenue, on a quiet country lane known as Bayview Avenue on the outskirts of the Town of Leaside. On June 6, 1944 the site was purchased for $3,600.00.

This plot of land had had a variety of previous uses, as demonstrated: "In 1816 a wooden school house was constructed. It was used also as a community centre."[9] Much later: "Between 1913 and 1919 a water tower existed here to dispense water to the community."[10] And later still: "When the tower was removed an apple orchard provided much needed sustenance."[11]

A nucleus of worshippers began to gather at the home of Eric Palin, at the corner of Rumsey Road and Donlea Drive. He became the first churchwarden and his wife, Alice, began the Ladies' Service Guild. Mrs. Norman Pickering began the Sunday School. On April 28, 1946, services of worship, led by William Bothwell, a Trinity College student, began in the basement corridor of Northlea School. The congregation was known as "St. Cuthbert's Northlea Mission."

The church requested the name of St. Augustine of Canterbury in order to perpetuate the memory of the former church of this name, which had been located at Spruce and Parliament streets, but destroyed by fire much earlier. This request was granted.

On January 19, 1947, Reverend G. I. B. Johnson replaced William Bothwell as Priest-in-Charge and, in May 1947, the parish was officially incorporated. A rectory was purchased at 38 Donlea Drive for the sum of $12,500.00. The first Rector, Reverend H. Newman Bracken led the service on June 15, l947 in the auditorium of Northlea School. Bruce,

The Church of St. Augustine of Canterbury at
Broadway and Bayview. *S. Walter Stewart
Library, Elmore Gray Collection.*

Brown and Brisley was to provide the architects for the new church (as
the firm had for Leaside Presbyterian Church) and the sod was turned
on October 3, 1948.

On February 20, 1949, the basement unit of the new St. Augustine of
Canterbury, constructed at a cost $40,000.00, was opened by the Rt.
Reverend A. R. Beverly. Four hundred and twenty-five people crowded
in for the service and sixty-eight children squeezed into a back room
with their teacher, Mrs. Phil Oglesby. By June 1950, an urgent appeal
was made for a Nursery Wing to consist of two rooms north of the existing building. On St. Augustine's Day, May 26, 1951, this wing was officially dedicated by Reverend Canon P. M. Lamb.

A great desire to expand the church above the basement led to a financial campaign being launched in 1953. Within two years, the congregation raised $113,000.00. On St. Augustine's Day in 1956, the Rt. Rev-
erend F. H. Wilkinson, Lord Bishop of Toronto, laid the cornerstone
and, on January 22, 1957, he officially opened the new church building.

The cornerstone of the superstructure to the Nursery Wing was laid on May 26, 1960 and the Rt. Reverend G. B. Snell officially opened the completed church on November 27, 1960. "The church is constructed of stone taken from the valley of the Credit River and has a vertical gothic thrust along contemporary lines."[12] Canon Bracken served St. Augustine's for thirty-five years while his wife, Alice Bracken, supervised the nursery department for twenty-eight years.

In 1982, Reverend Canon John B. Hill became the new rector. He has served St. Augustines for 17 years and is still at the church in 1999.

NORTHLEA UNITED CHURCH

A few residents of Leaside, north of Eglinton Avenue, assembled under the sponsorship of the Toronto Home Mission Council of the United Church of Canada. Their meeting, to discuss the possibility of a new congregation, took place in December 1948, at the home of Mr. and Mrs. J. L. Halpenny on 32 Glenbrae Avenue. Less than a year later, on September 11, 1949, the first service was conducted by the Reverend Clifford Torrance of the Home Mission Council. Soon after, services began in Northlea Public School under the direction of the Reverend Dr. D. A. Myers. A Sunday School, organized in that fall of 1949, grew rapidly to include over 350 children and young people.

Spring of the following year found Northlea United Church constituted as a pastoral charge with 517 charter members on the roll. In June 1950, the Reverend Donald C. Amos of Belleville became the first minister and preached his first sermon early that fall. A home at 647 Broadway Avenue was purchased as a manse.

In April 1951, a major fundraising campaign was initiated to raise money for the building of a church. The land consisted of a lot that had been purchased in 1945 by the Toronto Home Mission Council, and an additional lot acquired in 1950. An outdoor service to "Hallow the Ground" was held on the site on September 30, 1951 and the sod was turned on Sunday, May 10, 1953. Over two hundred people were present. Rev. Donald C. Amos laid the foundation stone on September 20 of that year and the church was dedicated the following spring. The architects were Barnett and Rieder, Mr. W. E. Barnett being a member of the congregation. In January 1954, the contractor went bankrupt, but Mr. Barnett saw the work through to completion.

In 1957, a building program committee was authorized to provide more space for Christian eduation. Building began May 1959 and, by November 1, the Christian Education Wing was opened by the Rev. A.

Northlea United Church as photographed in 1967. *Leaside Camera Club, courtesy Herb Horwood.*

W. Jones, Chairman of Centre Presbytery. Two years later the adjoining property at 85 Brentcliffe was purchased for a new manse and the property at 647 Broadway was sold.

Reverend D. C. Amos resigned August 31, 1959 to go to the new Oriole-York Mills United Church, and Reverend J. M. Butler from Hespeler United Church was formally inducted on September 19, 1959. Three years later the membership had grown to 1,155 people, with a Sunday School enrolment of 600. On October 20, 1974 a new electric organ was dedicated, as part of Northlea's Silver Anniversary, a celebration that lasted over the year encompassing 1974 and 1975.

When Reverend Butler retired on June 30, 1981, Reverend Bob Thompson from Sudbury became the new minister.[13]

Many groups make their home at the church. These include the

Donwood Institute for Study Sessions, Art Trek, North Leaside Women's Group and Creating Together. Today, Northlea United Church is still firmly rooted in the Leaside community.

LEASIDE BIBLE CHAPEL

Five men, belonging to the Plymouth Brethren faith, wanted to start their own church in Leaside. The five, Elwood Reed, Sydney Hoffman, Ernest Tatham, Horace Holt and Greg Marsh proceeded to approach the local council for the necessary permits. An active member, Ernest Tatham was a pastor or full-time worker for seven years, until he moved to Florida.

Construction began, in 1950, on their building site, located on the north side of Eglinton near Laird Drive. Originally, they had chosen Rumsey and Eglinton as a location, but the local council felt this was too close to the already existing Presbyterian church. The first service was delivered to a congregation of 27 people. In 1956, the second phase was completed and the church membership grew to 250 people. The church facilities include a basement, main floor and a gallery. Today, the church currently supports ten missions around the world as well as contributing to the community. In the 1950s and 1960s seniors could attend craft evenings for 25¢ a class.[14]

10

EDUCATION FOR OUR YOUTH

A 200-ACRE parcel of land known as Lot 1 Concession 2, east of Yonge Street, ran from the present Bayview Avenue on the west to Leslie Street on the east, and from Eglinton Avenue on the south to a line drawn through the present Annesley Avenue on the north. On February 10, 1797, this land was granted by the Crown to the Hon. William Allan who held it for almost thirty years. About 1816, a wooden schoolhouse was constructed on the west side of this lot. "The first Eglinton school, a chinked, unhewn log building, twenty-eight by thirty-eight feet, was operating on the east side of Bayview Avenue in 1816."[1] By 1847, this building was listed as one of the common schools of the original Township of York. "The District Council finally bought the property, 406 square feet, from Alexander McCormick in 1847. Many heated discussions took place in the old school, often in regard to free schooling."[2] Browne's "Map of 1851" clearly shows it as the only schoolhouse in School Section No. 2 in the Township of York.

In 1850, a new brick school was built on the same location. By 1879 another two-storey schoolhouse had been erected on the west side of Yonge Street across from the post office, north of Eglinton Avenue. This lot was sold to John Burke for $500.00 in 1891 and the money was given to St. Clement's Church. Until 1921, any children in the Leaside area were required to either learn at home or travel over to Yonge Street in order to attend school.

On August 16, 1920, six school trustees were elected to the Leaside Public School Board by the residents of Leaside. The town had, by this time, collected $8,000.00 for school support. The Provincial School Inspector, Mr. Jordan, chose a temporary building for a school, one that was offered rent-free by the Canada Wire and Cable Company. This frame building, for-

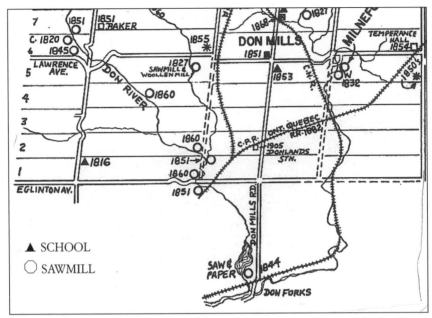

Browne's "Map of 1851." Note the location of the 1816 school, just north of Eglinton, on the east side of Bayview. *Taken from* Toronto World, *September 18, 1918. Toronto Reference Library.*

merly the cafeteria used by the Leaside Munitions Company during World War I, stood at the corner of McRae and Laird Drive. Later the building site would be shared with the Imperial Bank of Canada.[3] That year there were 24 children under the age of five years, 53 between five and fourteen years and 14 between fourteen and twenty-one years of age. Transportation to school consisted of a trek by pony-cart or a walk to and from.

The Leaside Council provided the funds to divide the donated space into two classrooms and Miss Mary C. Pepper of 151 Balsam Avenue was appointed by the Board as Leaside's first teacher on September 7, 1920. The $1,000.00 for desks and chairs, the $1,000.00 for plumbing and the $3,000.00 for repairs to the building were paid for by the Leaside Engineering Company. The remodelled building was to have an enrolment of fifty-one pupils.

J. Dawson was hired as caretaker at a salary of $1,500.00 per year. Both the *Star* and the *Telegram* announced that the school would not be open until September 15, 1920. When the York Land Company Ltd. was asked for the use of the lots adjacent to the school building for a playground, this request was granted. On September 23, 1920, Miss Gardiner was hired as an assistant teacher to teach in the second classroom.

From 1920 to 1930, the School Board was comprised of Canada Wire and Cable employees (as this company often advanced school funds to meet expenses until taxes were collected), the one exception being Canon Lamb. This was not surprising as most Leaside residents at the time worked for CWC. The Leaside Athletic Association was granted the privilege of using the schoolroom for a dance after their annual corn roast, provided they cleaned up after themselves!

On January 5, 1921, plans were submitted for a new permanent school to include four classrooms and an auditorium. The Board chose the firm of S. B. Coon and Son, Architects, to design the new building. One month later, Dr. Elliot became the first Health Officer for the school and Mr. Clime was appointed Leaside's first Attendance or Truant Officer, a position created by the School Board. That year the Leaside Board's budget was $7,500.00. In 1922, the first provincial educational grant was received, an amount of $742.50. Funds could not be raised until 1923.

LEASIDE PUBLIC SCHOOL (LATER RENAMED BESSBOROUGH PUBLIC SCHOOL)

In July 1923, a site consisting of 23 lots (3.25 acres) was purchased from both the York Land Company and Canada Wire and Cable by Messrs. Witchall and Son for $17,979.37. The property was bounded by Edith Avenue (now Bessborough), Clowes (now Sharron), Hanna and Field Avenue. The new school, with doors facing Hanna Road, consisted of four classrooms and an auditorium. The building was completed in December 1923 at a cost of $43,870.00. On January 11, 1924, the official opening of Leaside Public School took place, with Miss Pepper becoming the Principal and being presented with the keys.

A fence was built around the school to keep the cows out. To provide some winter recreational activities for the neighbourhood, the Town Council had erected a skating rink within the school grounds. Two years later, Dr. Morton, a Leaside resident, was appointed school dentist. He visited the school and provided checkups and dental work to the pupils. As numbers grew, safety became an issue and, in December 1927, the Town Constable was requested to patrol the crossing at McRae Drive before 9:00 a.m., at noon hour and at 4:00 p.m.

Contrary to popular rumours, the school (today known as Bessborough School) did not house the jail (the first jail was located on the east side of Laird Drive and is still standing today); but its caretakers were the Volunteer Fire Department. As well, both the Municipal Offices and

Leaside Public School on Hanna Road in 1924. *Taken from* The Story of Leaside *by John Scott.*

Some of the first students of Leaside Public School (later Bessborough), posed for a photograph. *Courtesy the Reed family.*

Pat (Reed) Osborne's Grade 8 Home Economics class at Bessborough School, 1953. Mrs. Warren is the teacher. *Courtesy Pat Osborne.*

the Police Department were located in the basement. The original town office was in the basement of Bessborough School in a room about 10 feet by 15 feet. After the establishment of this office, the first two elections, in 1929 and 1930, were held in a corridor in the basement of the school. It would not be until 1949 that a town hall was built at Randolph and McRae to accommodate all the municipal offices and meeting rooms. Today the building is home to the Junior Academy Private School.

In August 1928, Leonard G. Hill, the first male teacher in Leaside, joined the staff of three female teachers. By 1929, a tennis court was approved for the school grounds, continuing the process of making the schools the recreation centres for the community. Four rooms were added to the school by 1930, bringing the structure to the street edge of Bessborough, and yet another four-room addition was made in 1936. By this time, the pupil-teacher ratios were in the range of 36 to 45 pupils to one teacher for regular class sizes, and up to 55 to one in the junior room. Increasing enrolment brought the addition of two more rooms along the Hanna side of the building in 1937 and kindergarten classes were established. The following year, Home Economics and Manual Training classes began under the supervision of Miss Robinson and Mr. Keene. Children from other Leaside schools still come to Bessborough for instruction in these subjects. In 1939, Canon Lamb of St. Cuthberts Anglican Church retired from the School Board after sixteen years of service.

Class of Room 21, Bessborough Public School, circa 1951. Front row (left to right): Ian Fraser, Allan Brereton, Bill Hough, Rudy Kellerman, David Hillsdon, Doug Evans. Second row: Barbara Campbell, Virginia Ellam, Eleanor Sheare, Else Kerbekian, Susan Roden, Eleanor Pariss, Sheila Edmondson, Marlene Hodgson, Heather MacRobie. Third row: Frank Palmer, Carol Hillsdon, Margaret Johnston, Daphne Welch, Betty Scand, Jerry McIntyre. Top row: John Purkis, Larry Rosen, Huey Yee, David Walker, Paul Harrington, David Powell, Malcolm Mathers. *Courtesy Carol Hillsdon.*

On December 9, 1932, Governor General Bessborough agreed to the changing of Edith Avenue to Bessborough Drive. The Leaside community made this request after he had visited the Town. Leaside Public School became Bessborough Public School a few years later, as it was no longer the only public school in Leaside once Rolph Road School opened in 1938. To this day you can still read "Leaside Public School" in the stone over the entrance at Bessborough Drive and Hanna.

As the population of both the town and the school continue to grow, tensions related to "proximity" begin to surface. By 1939, residents were complaining that the school's teeter-totters were too noisy and should be placed in Millwood Park. The Council, however, refused to comply with the request.

However, by 1941, it is noted that payment is to be arranged for the supervision of children playing in the school yards during July and August. That same year, the School Board asked that white lines be painted on the street, marking a safe place for children to cross; thus the first crosswalk in Leaside came into being.

In 1945, when Mr. Keene became the Principal, the school population had increased considerably. Over the years this growth led, in 1949, to two rooms being added on the Bessborough side. A new gym was constructed in 1976.

Today, Bessborough Public School, with its many additions since its opening in 1924, continues to be a proud part of the heritage of Leaside.

ROLPH ROAD PUBLIC SCHOOL

With the rapid growth of Leaside's population, the need for a second public school soon became obvious. Land, between Hanna Road and Rolph Road just south of Sutherland Drive, was purchased on November 12, 1938.

John Rolph was born in Thornbury, England in 1792. After studying medicine and law, he immigrated to Canada. In 1821, he settled in St. Thomas, Ontario, where he practised law. After being elected to the Legislative Assembly, he moved to Toronto and became very active politically. In 1831, he was teaching medicine from his house (now the site of New City Hall). A radical and a Reformer, John Rolph was a supporter of William Lyon Mackenzie. In 1851, Rolph founded the Toronto School of Medicine. Rolph Road School is named for this pioneer in medical education.[4]

Plans moved ahead quickly. The school was built at a cost of $111,000.00 and the official opening was held in October 1939, 69 years

Rolph Road Public School as photographed in the spring of 1967. *Leaside Camera Club, courtesy Herb Horwood.*

after the death of Dr. John Rolph. The site of the school had once been farm fields complete with cows, ably described by Mrs. E. J. Moldan of 63 Airdrie Road in 1974. "We moved here 36 years ago and we looked out the back window and there was a cow. It just happened we were out of milk, but I didn't know how to milk a cow so it didn't help me any."[5] Originally, the town plan indicated that Randolph Road should run through to Rolph Road, right across the present schoolyard. But Mr. Percy Turner, Secretary-Treasurer of the Leaside Board of Education, arranged for the change in the plan to preserve the large play area for the school site.[6]

Mr. Willis Wright, who had taught at Bessborough since 1931, became the first principal of the Kindergarten to Grade 8 school. In 1940, the first grade nine class opened on the second floor. Up to this time, high school students had attended Toronto schools. In fact, in 1930-31 twenty-one Leaside students were attending Toronto Seconday Schools. A grade ten class was established in 1941 and eight additional rooms were added to the school at this time to meet the evergrowing demand for pupil space. Grades 11, 12 and 13 met in Leaside United Church, Leaside Presbyterian and St. Cuthbert's Anglican.

In 1945, Leonard Hill, who has been at Bessborough, became the new Principal and Willis Wright was transferred to open up the new Northlea School.

In this same year, Leaside High School was organized at Rolph Road. For three years, there were two complete schools in the Rolph building until the new high school was opened on Hanna Road in 1948. From 1945 to 1963, while Mr. Hill was Principal, the pupils excelled in music and public speaking at the Kiwanis Festival.

By the late 1950s, the Thorncliffe Park area was being developed, but as yet there was no school. The children of Thorncliffe attended classes at Rolph Road until a new school could be built.

In 1963, William R. Ruhnke was appointed Principal of Rolph Road and the school altered to include Kindergarten to Grade 6, with the Grades 7 and 8 pupils attending Bessborough. With the amalgamation of East York and Leaside in 1967, a new principal was appointed, Mr. R. J. Brown. In 1968, two rooms on the second floor were renovated to become the library.

When Mr. Brown was transferred to Thorncliffe Park School in 1970, Robert A. Cook became Principal. During his three years, the natural climber and hill were constructed in the schoolyard.

First day of school at St. Anselm's, 1939. *From the St. Anselm's School Archives.*

St. Anselm's Separate School

In 1938, Father Caulfield came to St. Anselm's Roman Catholic Parish in Leaside. Largely due to his efforts, interest and enthusiasm, and his belief that the school should be his first priority, St. Anselm's Separate School was started that same year. Both the school and church are named for St. Anselm of Canterbury, an eminent theologian of the 11th Century. This renowned saint was viewed as an excellent role model for the students as he personifies great courage and outstanding scholarship. The school, formally opened in 1939, began with two rooms, two teachers (Miss Mary Breen, Principal, and Miss Susan Carroll, teacher) and seventy-nine pupils. The pupils sat at wooden desks in the new yellow-brick building facing Millwood Road.[7]

Father Caulfield had planned to form a Leaside Separate School Board, but before his plans were carried out, the area was placed under the jurisdiction of the Toronto and Suburban Separate School Board. In 1940, Sister St. Madeleine became the Principal and the Loretto Sisters became the teachers, for the next thirty-two years, as Father Caulfield had wished. "The Loretto Sisters came from tough stock. They disciplined with the strap and expected hard work and great respect."[8] This Board subsequently became the Metropolitan Separate School Board and E. J. Brisbois of Leaside was elected as the local representative.

Father Caulfield visited the school twice a week to instruct the children in their faith throughout his time at the parish.

In 1943, two more classrooms were added and, again in 1948, two more rooms were completed. The last seven classrooms were constructed in 1951, but it would not be until 1966 that the library and gymnasium were completed.

The year 1963 was special: the town of Leaside celebrated its 50th anniversary. The pupils of Grade 5, Room 6 of St. Anselm's School sang this verse (to the tune of "Mother"):

L – is for the luxury of Leaside
E – means we're the envy of them all
A – is for the ambitions we all strive for
S – is for our service at your call
I – is for the industries we have here
D – is for the duties we perform
E – is education for us all
      Put them altogether they spell Leaside,
      The greatest little town in all the world.

In 1997, a major renovation took place, adding four classrooms, a library, a new foyer, plus two administrative offices with a staffroom. This renovation required the Toronto Catholic District School Board's approval of funds to demolish the 1938 and 1943 wings and the construction of a two-storey addition. During construction, all of the students were transported to 1107 Avenue Road to take classes at Marshall McLuhan High School. With the completion of renovations, students and staff moved back to St. Anselm's in May 1998.

NORTHLEA SCHOOL

In June 1941, negotiations were started for the purchase of a land site for a school in the Sunnybrook area. The post-war population explosion was underway and Bessborough School was bulging with pupils. On October 7, 1942, a motion was carried unanimously that the Board approve the purchase from the York Land Company Ltd., of lots (#359 to #370 and #537 to #548, Plan 1908, Leaside) together with the land portion of Mitchell Avenue (now Divadale Drive) between Rumsey Road and Sutherland Drive. The price was $21,600.00. This amount was to be paid in three installments, but such an arrangement did not meet with the approval of the York Land Company. Consequently, a new agreement was prepared offering $19,000.00 cash, an offer that was accepted. On April 7, 1943, Mr. B. R. Coon was appointed architect for the proposed

Northlea Public School on Rumsey Road, 1967. *Leaside Camera Club, courtesy Herb Horwood.*

new school on the newly acquired site. Mr. Coon was requested to submit plans for a sixteen room school, designed to be built in sections. On July 9, 1943, the Town of Leaside was asked to raise, by the sale of Public School debentures, the sum of $70,000.00 net for the construction.

Mr. Leonard Hill, Principal of Bessborough School and the Secretary of the Board was asked to buy school furniture. An order was placed with the Frank G. McKay Company for: 40 large desk chairs @ $11.50 each; 80 medium desk chairs @ $11.25 each; and 40 small desk chairs @ $11.00 each. The Kindergarten furniture was bought from the Globe Furniture Company. The order was for 20 kindergarten tables with open shelves and 76 chairs @ $2.00 each. The entire order was to be painted "school brown."

On September 8, 1943, the town was asked to build a sidewalk from Eglinton Avenue to the school property and, in the following February, 150 students and five teachers moved into the first section which contained five classrooms and a boiler room. Mr. Hill assumed the responsibility of supervising principal, in addition to his being Principal at Bessborough.

Almost immediately, as the baby boom continued to increase the enrolment, it became necessary to arrange for the building of six more classrooms. This addition was completed in the spring of 1945.

On September 1, 1945, Willis Wright was appointed Principal of Northlea, with F. J. Maw as Vice-Principal. In 1946, the Northlea Home and School Association was formed. By 1950, another eight room extension was approved and within four years, two portables were added. Mr. Wright would remain as Principal until 1970. By this time the enrolment was up to 410 students and the projection was for 800 pupils. The Board was forced to build an additional eleven rooms plus an auditorium.

Since then, Northlea Public School has undergone even further renovations, adding additional classrooms and another gymnasium, as it continues to serve the community of North Leaside.

LEASIDE HIGH SCHOOL

The burgeoning Town of Leaside needed a high school – badly. In the early 40s, students in Grades Nine to Eleven studied in make-shift classrooms in a few of the local churches (St. Cuthberts, Leaside United and Leaside Presbyterian) and in 5 classrooms on the top floor of Rolph Road School. There were 230 students in Grades 9, 10 and 11 with a staff of nine full-time and two part-time teachers.

A municipal referendum was held and the decision to build a high school passed, but only by very few votes. Some citizens felt there would never be sufficient high school students. Senior students of the time had no choice but to travel west or south to either North Toronto, Jarvis, Eastern High School of Commerce or Northern Vocational. The Leaside School Board was paying the costs.

Before the High School was built, the Board purchased a temporary building from the Air Force for $600.00. This structure was transported from the Lake Huron Air Base and re-erected by the north entrance of Rolph Road School, to house four classrooms. The "high school" was called "Joe's House" after Joe Fennell, the Maintenance Superintendent at that time.

The war was on and the expense of a new school would be high, but Town Council still intended to approve the building of a permanent high school for Leaside. It was on September 3, 1945—only months after victory in Europe and only weeks after victory in Asia had been achieved— that Leaside High School was officially inaugurated in a brief ceremony held in the Rolph Road School auditorium.

A lovely home with an inground swimming pool stood on the hill where the new high school was to be built. It had been built by Thomas Elgie on 200 acres of land on the south side of Eglinton Avenue East. This land had been owned by the Elgie family since 1860 and sold in the 1920s.

Access to the property was by means of a driveway from Eglinton to the east side of the building. The exceptional house also had a tennis

This house, built by Thomas Elgie, once stood on the present site of
Leaside High School. Wendell Lawson, artist, created this pen and
ink drawing. He used the house as a home as well as a studio and
art school during the 20s and 30s. *Courtesy Raymond Perringer.*

court and a croquet lawn. Wendell Lawson (1892-1952), an architect and
artist, and his sister lived there. He used the house as a home, studio and
art school in the 1920s and 1930s. After they moved out, it had been empty for some time. Children of Leaside thought the house to be haunted!

W. J. Stephan had purchased the house from the Lawsons and had
only recently completed renovations when the Board of Education
decided to purchase it. Mr. Stephan was quite indignant about selling,
but eventually an arrangement was made. For a while, the building was
used for art classes before being demolished in 1949.

It took three years of construction work on what was fairly swampy
tree-covered land, before the school was ready to open to its first students, 650 of them in all. Workers faced many obstacles. They tackled
wild cattails, had to bypass a small stream and even deal with a minor
case of quicksand, all of which slowed construction.

In September 1948, in a mood of pride and anticipation, the Leaside
Lions' Marching Band led the students from Rolph Road School where
they had been attending classes in "Joe's House," the World War II issue
four-room prefabricated hut, to the new high school on Eglinton. Later
that school year, at the official opening, Professor Sidney Smith, President of the University of Toronto, was the key-note speaker. With Norman McLeod as the first Principal and many of the teachers and stu-

Leaside High School, January 1, 1955. *Toronto Reference Library, J.V. Salmon Collection.*

dents being of Celtic descent, the school motto aptly was a Gaelic one: "Seas Gu Dileas." It means "Stand Faithfully."

Four years after the school opened, eight rooms were added at the Eglinton end, the population having increased more rapidly than expected. In 1954, the small gym was added and four more classrooms were built three years later. The music room was built in 1961 and a vocational wing was completed by 1963. With the addition of the new library in 1967, the building was completed.

The flagpole dedicated by the Board of Education in 1948, has a plaque on it in memory of the first school captain, Don Johnson, who drowned. He had been an extremely popular student, and his death was a great loss to the school.

During the 50s, Leaside High students had a daily prayer session, led by their own Chaplain, a practice somewhat unique to a Toronto-area public high school. The Drama and Latin Departments were thriving, reflecting positively on the highly-creative and academic-oriented student body. As well, Leaside High excelled in sports, often coming on top in Senior Hockey, boys' basketball and track and field.

The dress code for the first decade or so was quite formal. Boys were expected to wear dress trousers and button-up shirts, while girls wore a school uniform consisting of a navy tunic, white blouse and long black stockings. As times changed and the styles became more informal, a Miss Gladys Heintz, head of Girls' Physical Education felt compelled to write home to parents that "many students have been wearing extremely short tunics, a style which has created some unfavourable comment, not only within the school, but also from outside sources."[9]

Even though the times changed, Leaside's reputation as a strong academic school remained. On a snowy October day in 1969, the Duke of Edinburgh came to Leaside High School to speak to the student body. He had a quick tour of the school and presented twenty female students with the award named in his honour. When Prince Philip was offered a cup of punch made by the Grade 12 Home Economics students, it is said that he asked "Is there any rum in it?"[10] Upon finding out in fact that there was not, he settled for a cup of coffee. In his closing remarks in front of an auditorium packed full of students, staff and Principal Mitch Kerr, the Prince enthused that "this is the best example of student power that I have come across here!"[11] Many would say the tribute still holds true about Leaside High students.

11

The Leaside Library:
A Community Resource

IN JULY 1943, Leaside's first public library opened in a leased store at 645 Bayview Avenue called the Carol Davey Shop. At the time, Leaside, with a population of nine thousand residents, had three Public Schools, one Separate School and plans for a High School. A house-to-house canvass by volunteers resulted in enough members paying a one dollar per year membership fee to form an Association Library. Much effort went into acquiring books. The first book to be part of the new library, presented by Mayor Talbot, was entitled *Land Below the Wind* by Agnes Newton Keith.[1] Books were donated to the library by the Leaside Lion's Club and by the Rotary Club or were purchased. The necessary shelves and furniture were made by Board members and by library members, at the Vocational classroom at Bessborough School under the supervision of Mr. Bert Keene, now the manual training instructor. The library was staffed by volunteer workers, two of whom were ex-librarians.

From its opening until the end of that year, the library enrolled 569 members, acquired 1,056 books and boasted a circulation of 2,584. Thus began an ever-increasing attention to the place of a library in Leaside, a process which has continued until the present time. By that time, a qualified librarian had been employed and a children's librarian would soon be included.

This community-based project was so successful that, by 1944, the Association Library was incorporated as the Leaside Library and supported financially by the municipality. Early that year, plans were conceived for a possible Memorial Community Centre and Library in a two-wing building. However, this idea was abandoned, but the need for greater library space became increasingly more apparent. By 1949, there were 7,084 library members, representing about fifty percent of the population, 10,623 books and a circulation of 64,631.

The first location of a library for Leaside at 645 Bayview Avenue (now 1645). Formerly a dress shop, it housed about 2500 books. Once opened, it attracted 100 new members a month and lent out approximately 3000 books per month. *Collection of the Leaside Public Library.*

Finally, it was decided that the library should be built as a separate structure on a crescent-shaped piece of land on the northern part of Trace Manes Park, where Rumsey Road and McRae Drive converge. The first sod was turned in April 1949 and the building was officially opened on March 8, 1950. Within seven years, the library population had increased from 9,000 to 16,568. The Leaside Library Board was formed with the first members being: Mrs. G. Tait; Mr. G.A. Mason; Mr. R.S. Godbold; Mr. C.F. Holland; Mr. E. Killingsworth; Miss T.C.M. Lamb; Mr. D.E. Cooper and Mr. L.G. Wrinch.

In 1950, a working relationship between the Leaside Library and the Toronto Art Gallery was developed. An art exhibit was held featuring the artwork collection of the four elementary Leaside schools. Two films featuring the work of A.Y. Jackson and Tom Thomson were shown. The Director of the Art Gallery, Martin Baldwin, was the guest speaker. A Gallery Group began at the library and painting classes were offered to twenty members.

A class visit to the Leaside Public Library in the late 1940s. *Collection of the Leaside Public Library.*

Four exhibits were arranged: The Group of Seven, Snow Scenes by Canadian artists, Abstracts by Canadian artists and a show featuring two Leaside artists.

The building was full to capacity. Plans were drawn up for an addition of a children's wing and a main entrance. The enhanced facilities were opened on November 15, 1958.

The library continued working closely with the schools by arranging class visits to the library and by supplying lists and exhibits of books to the schools. That same year, a children's branch of the library opened at Northlea Public School and for years to follow, the Saturday morning story hour was held at both the Leaside Library and at Northlea School because of the great number of children living in North Leaside.

In 1981, the library was renovated with lighting, insulation and new dampers for heating and cooling. In 1997, some windows were replaced at a cost of $20,000.00. The addition of assistant librarians, Mrs. W. M. Corbett and Mrs. Phyllis Moffat, allowed for extended hours. The library, then, was open every afternoon and on Tuesday, Wednesday and Friday evenings.[2]

Leaside Public Library, built on McRae in 1950, with an addition of a children's wing completed in 1958. *S. Walter Stewart Library, Elmore Gray Collection.*

Chief Librarians:

1943	Mrs. Charles Manson
1944	Mrs. Alice Griffiths, assisted by Mrs. H. H. Chapman
1945-1946	Ms. Elizabeth Loosley
1947-1962	Mrs. Eleanor MacAlpine
1962-1966	Mrs. Jean Parriss

A plan was initiated, in 1999, to replace the existing library. There was a need to make the library more accessible and to update the well-used facilities. Because of the high level of the water table, it became evident that an elevator to the lower level auditorium could not be installed, except at great expense. Already, water seepage had been a problem and, given the fact that ongoing repairs would be necessary, it was decided that a new one-storey building would be the solution.

A new library would not only operate more economically, but would provide an accessible meeting room and greater space for research and study. As well, there would be space for an archival room and a place to house the special collections, so important to Leaside. It is hoped that construction will begin Spring 2000.

12

THORNCLIFFE PARK: FROM THE
RACETRACK TO RESIDENTIAL

MUCH OF both the charm and the insularity of Leaside comes from the fact that it is an exceptionally well-defined area. On the west, Bayview Avenue provides a clean-cut boundary with North Toronto. On the north, Sherwood Creek, with the Canadian National Institute for the Blind (CNIB) and other health-related institutions, effectively delineates the end of the residential area along Glenvale Boulevard. With the Don Valley on the east and south, Leaside forms a cape projecting out into a sea of space, with its neighbours on a distant shore. It would be unthinkable to contemplate Leaside without considering the ambiance of the Don River and Valley. Although Thorncliffe would not become part of Leaside until 1954, it seems that William Lea's pioneer neighbours to the east merit inclusion in any history of Leaside.

The name, Thorncliffe, goes back 111 years to 1888 when Thomas B. Taylor sold his 600 acre farm at the Forks of the Don to his brother-in-law, Robert Davies, for $50,000.00. Taylor had named his white clapboard southern style mansion, "Thorn Cliff," but Davies, it is presumed, like Anne of Green Gables, decided that, to be more fashionable and elegant, the name should be one word with an "e." Thus "Thorncliffe Farm" was born.

The Taylor and Davies families were friends and business associates. The Taylors, at one time, owned almost 4,000 acres in the Don Valley, complete with saw, grist and paper mills, a brick factory and a brewery. Davies owned a thriving brewery, a meat-packing plant and later took over the brickworks. Thorncliffe Farms became a model farm, one of the best equipped stock farms in Canada at the time. Many visitors came to marvel at its fine buildings, and the outstanding stock of thoroughbred, standardbred and Clydesdale horses, as well as prize cattle, swine

The crowds at popular Thorncliffe Racetrack, 1920. *S. Walter Stewart Library, Elmore Gray Collection.*

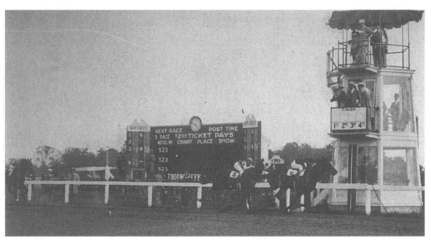

Thorncliffe Park, the popular mile track at Leaside. *Taken from* The Story of Leaside *by John Scott.*

and sheep. An ample apple orchard added to the picturesque setting where four valleys joined in scenic splendour. Taylor's paper mill, the "Upper Mill," was at Thorncliffe just west of the Forks.[1] In *Remembering the Don,* Charles Sauriol reported that the mill, built in 1846-7, for many years supplied the papers of Toronto, such as George Brown's *The Globe,* with newsprint. The millpond, about 30 acres in extent, was still

"Two Dollar Straight." Betting on the horses at Thorncliffe Racetrack, 1937. *Courtesy Dr. Robert Bertram.*

in existence until the 1920s or early 30s, when the dam was blown up because of the drownings at the site. The thick stone walls remained standing until 1942 when the huge pine roof rafters were removed by a sawmill operator. Sauriol, in the book, regretted that the mill had not been preserved as an historical site.

Early in the 1920s, Mathilda Bryan and James O'Hara from Baltimore, purchased Thorncliffe Farms from the Davies and built Thorncliffe Racetrack. It was quite fitting that the farm become a racetrack because the Davies family had been prominent in thoroughbred racing and breeding for over 50 years, first under Robert, and later his son, George, as Thorncliffe Stable. The track was under the control of Thorncliffe Park Racing and Breeding Association.

On May 31, 1920 Thorncliffe Racetrack ran its first race. This new track, Thorncliffe Park, was well-received as it joined with the old Woodbine, Dufferin and Long Branch tracks in providing Toronto racing fans with the exciting "Sport of Kings." The one mile track had seating accommodation for 4,000 people and stalls for 610 horses. Among the feature races were the Clarendon, the Prince of Wales and the My Dear Stakes, and some of Canada's exceptional thoroughbreds were cheered on at Thorncliffe. The racing greats that ran there were also winners of the King's or Queen's Plate at old Woodbine and included such names as: Willie Morrissey's "Bunty Lawless," George McCullagh's "Archworth" and Harry Gidding's "Ten to Ace." Oldtimers will remember other exceptional horses: "Queen's Own," "Casa Camara," "Magpie," "Mugwump," "Big Fish," "Easter Hatter" and "Just Mary."

Chilton Selke recalls being at Thorncliffe with his parents when "Just Mary" was the cause of a riot. She dumped her jockey before the race and ran off around the track. She was in no shape to race against the rest of the field, hence when she was allowed to compete, she finished away back. The angry spectators who had bet on her surged onto the track and prevented the next race from taking place. Chilton is not certain as to how the matter was resolved.

There was another form of gambling besides betting on horses that occurred in Thorncliffe. Some residents may recall Garity's Club, the

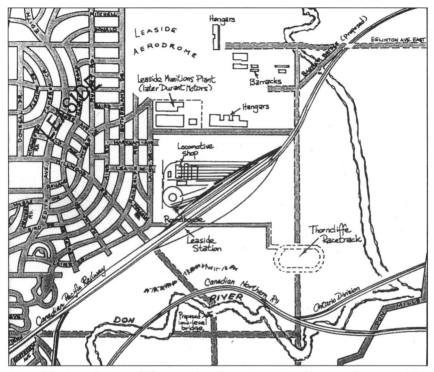

Map of the Leaside-Thorncliffe area, taken from *Toronto World, 1918.* The map clearly shows the Thorncliffe Racetrack, the Leaside Aerodrome and the Leaside Munitions Plant. *Toronto Reference Library.*

concrete block structure with the wooden planking inside the glass windows to prevent curious people from looking in. It was located near Banigan Drive which runs parallel with Overlea off Thorncliffe Park Drive and was raided many times in the late 20s and early 30s by police chief Sandy Bruce. The building was listed as a storage warehouse, but it actually blew up. Rumour has it that this was no accident but the work of a rival group!

An interesting sidelight to the Thorncliffe story involves the traffic congestion that occurred when a few thousand fans converged on the track, on a daily basis, for the two week meeting twice a year. With the residential and industrial growth of Leaside already causing traffic problems, the councils of Leaside and East York finally decided, after much talk that had been going on since 1911, to build the Leaside Viaduct, joining Donlands and Millwood.

The new bridge opened on October 29, 1927, providing metropolitan Toronto with a much needed east-west thoroughfare, since the Eglinton extension over the west branch of the Don would not be built for another 30 years.

Nothing left of the Thorncliffe Racetrack following demolition in July 1954. *Toronto Reference Library, J.V. Salmon Collection.*

Thorncliffe Racetrack operated from May 1920 until June 1952. On May 8, 1939, the TTC agreed to reduce bus fares to Thorncliffe Racetrack from 25 cents to 15 cents. Many Leasiders would hurry home early from work to attend the racetrack in the late afternoon. On most race days, you could hear the horses and the roar of the crowd, an enticement to young boys who would watch the races through the fence from the industrial area.

In 1952, the Ontario Jockey Club purchased Thorncliffe Park from its Baltimore owners for a reputed one million dollars. The Jockey Club, spearheaded by E. P. Taylor, had been buying up racetracks and dozens of inactive racing charters with the intention of building a new, state-of-the-art track at Malton. Before long, the Jockey Club sold the property to a group of residential and industrial developers, Thorncliffe Park Limited.[2]

In 1954, the Ontario Municipal Board annexed the 387 acre property east of the industrial area of Leaside to the Town of Leaside. As a result, the Leaside Planning Board was established.

The most difficult problem with the property was providing reasonable automobile access to and from the area. The only access from Millwood was Overlea Boulevard. The solution was to build the Charles Hiscott Bridge (named after a former mayor of Leaside 1956-1962) across the Don Valley linking Thorncliffe with Don Mills Road.

Construction of residential Thorncliffe began in the late 1950s. First to be constructed was the shopping plaza and 21 six-storey apartment buildings. Next came nine 17 to 23-storey buildings, all of which were completed by the late 1960s. Five of those buildings were constructed around a privately owned recreation centre, while the other four buildings had a privately owned indoor pool, sauna and outdoor pool. The last apartments, erected in 1971, were the two tall 43-storey Leaside Towers which were built on land originally intended as a public recreational site.

For many years, the large monument at Millwood and Overlea proudly proclaimed the area as Thorncliffe Park. In 1993, East York Council announced in the September *East Yorker*, "Be among the first to know that the Official Plans of both Metropolitan Toronto and East York are naming the Thorncliffe area "East York Centre..." The "Thorncliffe Park" name on the monument was changed to "East York Centre," and "Thorncliffe Market Place," reputedly the first covered shopping mall in Canada, was renamed "East York Town Centre." A unique piece of history has all but disappeared. Only the memories of a few people and today's street names of Milepost Place and Grandstand Place are all that remain to mark the 32 year history of the once thriving Thorncliffe Racetrack. The cement from the "winner's circle" is still in place today, on the property of Coca Cola located along Overlea Boulevard.

Thorncliffe contains a shopping centre, a library in the Jenner Jean-Marie Community Centre (named after Councillor Jean-Marie, 1988-1994), an elementary school, a middle school and a high school, a mosque and several churches. Today, the plaza is known as the East York Town Centre and the area continues to expand its residential sites with the recent addition of 80 townhouses built by Goldlist.

It is not precisely known how many residents Thorncliffe has, but it is in excess of 20,000. Within this neighbour area there are about seventy-two different languages spoken. This cultural diversity is reflected in an array of foods and services available to the community.

THE THORNCLIFFE SKI JUMP

With so much emphasis placed on competitive downhill skiing today, it is difficult to believe that ski jumpers from around the world once competed in the Leaside area. Canadian competitors from the Toronto Ski Club (TSC) experienced considerable success in regional, national, North American and even International ski jumping events during the thirties and forties.

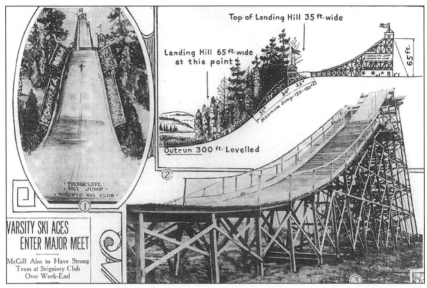

The Thorncliffe Ski Jump described in (1) the slide which "develops enough speed to fling competitors far into space;" (2) the side view diagram; (3) a photograph of the construction. Toronto Daily Star, *January 25, 1934. Toronto Reference Library.*

During the late twenties there had been some "jumping" by a daring few over a small snow takeoff on the slopes of Grenadier Pond in High Park, but ski jumping became sophisticated a little later, on a steep short hill located to the north and east of "the Hump" at the TSC's Summit property (Summit Golf Club), just north of Toronto near Gormley side road in Markham Township. At that time the maximum jump was about thirty feet. Soon they began to "out-jump" the hill, so a rickety wooden takeoff and artificial in-run were added to allow jumps of up to sixty feet, or even seventy plus feet.

As ski jumping in Canada and North America increased in popularity, the ski jumpers convinced the directors of the club of the advantages of building a major ski jump. Thus, the Toronto Ski Club's 40-metre hill was born. An appropriate site was sought. Permission was granted by the Leaside Council to build the jump in the Don Valley, on an unused portion of a hydro right-of-way. The spot was located at the end of Wicksteed and slightly to the south, behind Linda Lundstrom's warehouse of today.

Fred Hall, an experienced ski jumper and a member of the TSC, designed the Thorncliffe Ski Jump in 1933, and tested the hill himself. Then, as President of the TSC, he helped organize the Ontario Championships of 1934, which were to be hosted by the Toronto Ski Club.

Creating snow for the Thorncliffe Ski Jump. Toronto Daily Star, *February 1, 1934. Toronto Reference Library.*

SCRAPE 'SNOW' OFF ICE FOR NEW SKI COURSE

Varsity Outdoor Rink Provides Surface for Thorncliffe Jump

Toronto's first "snow factory" is delivering that flaky substance to the new ski jump at Thorncliffe at the rate of seven tons an hour. By nightfall some 100 tons of snow will have been transported the six miles separating Thorncliffe from Varsity stadium skating rink.

Officials of the Toronto Ski Club, which is sponsoring the Ontario ski championships on Feb. 10 and 11, found themselves faced with the problem of conducting the jumps on a new but woefully bare tower.

Early to-day The Star found unusual activity at the outdoor Varsity rink. A queer-looking machine with eight whirling circular blades, towed by a tractor, was scraping one-quarter of an inch off the surface of the ice in a swath six feet wide. The finely-chipped ice was then brushed up into piles, loaded into trucks and driven away.

The ice, after the scraper and brush have been over it, is as smooth as a billiard table and will be ready for skaters again to-night.

"We finally decided it would be more convenient than to bring it in box cars," said Sam Cliff, president of the Toronto Ski Club, to-day. "This snow is really finely-chopped ice and will make a much faster run."

Competitors will be able to get in some practising to-morrow.

All of the Club's efforts went towards building the jump. It was finished just two weeks before the big meet, only just in time for trials and the club championships.

With this new "Olympic-size" jump, it was estimated that jumps of 150 feet were possible. As part of the preparation for the big event, a small practice jump was built beside the big one. Everything was to be ready for the outstanding jumpers coming from across Canada and the US!

The Ontario Championships were scheduled for February 10. Two days before, a thaw took away all the snow! The ski jump loomed big, bare and dry!

What to do? Creative minds found a solution. As some of the skiers skated on local rinks and frequently skated at the Varsity Rink, they were aware of the oversized "ice shaver" used to keep the skating surface smooth.

Ross Workman, the manager, was contacted. He offered to flood the surface of

ONTARIO
CHAMPIONSHIP
SKI - JUMPING
THORNCLIFFE JUMP
AT LEASIDE
SATURDAY, FEB. 10th, 2.30 p.m.
A Special Train leaves North Toronto Station at 2 p.m. Return fare 25c.

Due to the large crowds expected and the limited parking facilities spectators are urged to use the train if possible.

Please get your tickets in the city or at the station.

More Moderate Weather is Predicted for Saturday

ADMISSION 50c

Map shows roads leading to Thorncliffe jump.

A newspaper advertisement promoting the Ontario Championship "Due to the large crowds expected and the limited parking facilities, spectators are urged to use the train if possible." The Evening Telegram, *Toronto, February 9, 1934. Toronto Reference Library.*

Varsity Rink an extra inch and then work the shaver all night. The shaved ice was piled in huge ridges along the sides. One hundred tons of shaved ice were transported by truck and train to Thorncliffe! There, fifty members of the Ski Club spread it over the hill and on the outrun. By the time of the jumping event the next afternoon, conditions were viewed as perfect.

On that day, the 10th of February 1934, the sun shone brilliantly, creating an outside temperature of 20 degrees F. Thirty of the top jumpers in Canada were competing. To cheer them on, about 10,000, the largest crowd to congregate at any ski jumping meet in Canada up to that time, assembled as spectators. Unfortunately, many watched for free from the fields at the bottom, so despite the crowd, the net gate was small. Mayor William J. Stewart of Toronto cut the ribbon to launch the extraordinary event.

The star of the meet who should have won a medal for bravery was

Thorncliffe Ski Jump, Ontario Ski Jumping Championships, Feb. 3, 1934. *From* The Globe and Mail *Negative Collection, #GO-32367, City of Toronto Archives, Spadina Ave.*

COLORFUL SCENES FROM ONTARIO SKI JUMP CHAMPIONSHIP

Photographs from the first title ski jump competition ever held in the Toronto area. The skier posed in the middle is Jack Langtry, who won both the title jump and a distance event. Toronto Daily Star, *February 12, 1934. Toronto Reference Library.*

Tom McGoey, who "zoomed down the hill, misjudged the takeoff, landed on his head—fortunately he was okay. The crowd loved it."[3] From the Toronto Ski Club competitors, Celius Skavaas placed 6th, Merritt "Putty" Putnam 8th and Ross Wilson 10th.

In a freak storm in December 1934, the jump collapsed. A decision

ONTARIO CHAMPIONSHIP SKI - JUMPING
THORNCLIFFE JUMP
At Leaside
SAT., FEB. 10, 2.30 P.M.
A special train leaves North Toronto
station at 2 p.m.
ADMISSION — 50c

Taken from the official program for
the Ontario Championship at Leaside,
February 10, 1934. *The Toronto Ski
Club's* 50 Year Anniversary Book,
1974.

was made to build an even larger jump, one that would be secured into
the ground!

In January 1935, an International Ski Jumping Event took place,
drawing 50 top international competitive ski jumpers and 8,000 spectators. Another event, the Dominion Championships occurred at the
Thorncliffe Jump on February 22, 1936 with, once again, another 10,000
spectators. Many people drove in and left their cars at the top of the
jump. Others came on a special train from Union Station. The winner
of this major event was Punch Bott of the Montreal Ski Club.

Other ski-jumping events would be held but never as successfully as
the International Invitational meets. From 1939-40, a number of military jumps were organized at Thorncliffe. However, during the war
years, the tower was dismantled, thus ending major ski jumping in
Thorncliffe, in fact ending any such jumping in the Toronto area. Toronto winters had become so undependable, that the club based their ski
jumping events in Huntsville.[4]

13

THE ORIGINS OF STREET NAMES

THE STREETS and roads of Leaside were planned out and named in 1913. While there have been some changes to these names, for the most part the original ones have been retained.

The street names are largely from three different categories. Some streets, such as Hanna Road, Rumsey Road and Sutherland Drive were named after men who had some connection with the railways: other streets such as Divadale Drive and Berney Crescent commemorate early settlers and those who contributed to the growth of Leaside. People living on Randolph Road and McRae Drive had their streets named after the first mayor of Leaside, Mr. Randolph McRae, and there are other examples of streets named for well-known politicians of the day. And of course, the original Lea family gave their name to a number of streets such as: Donlea; Parklea; Southlea; Lea; Leacrest; Leadale; Richlea Circle and Overlea Boulevard in Thorncliffe.

Airdrie Road	Mr. John Aird, President of the Bank of Commerce, the Canadian Northern banker. He supported the model town idea.
Annesley Avenue	Fred Annesley, Private Secretary to Sir William Mackenzie, of Mackenzie and Mann.
Astor Avenue	Origin not known. The street was to be renamed Mayfair, but the request was denied and the name Astor remained. (Possibly the name is after the New York Astor family from the *Titanic*).
Baird Avenue	Hugh Northcote Baird (industrialist) born July 23. 1877. The street is now called Crofton Road.
Bayview Avenue	See Junction Road. At one time the street was also known as Government Road.

Broadway Avenue, between Hanna and Tanager, looking north to Sunnybrook Hospital seen in the background, 1948. *Toronto Reference Library, J. V. Salmon Collection.*

Beaufield Avenue	Not known.
Berney Crescent	Berney Realty Corporation Ltd., the original owners of the Garden Court Apartment named it. This street was to provide visitor parking for the Garden Court.
Bessborough Drive	Formerly Edith Avenue, was named after Govenor General Bessborough in 1932.
Beth Nealson Drive	Named after Mayor Beth Nealson, 1963–1966.
Brentcliffe Road	Formerly Brentwood Road. The street was named after Brent Cairns, son of A. B. Cairns, a builder who lived on Killdeer Crescent. Brentwood Road was completed by 1943.
Broadway Avenue	Extension of a street from North Toronto
Cameron Crescent	Origin unknown.
Canvarco Road	Recognized the presence of Canada Varnish Company.
Clarke Street	Col. F. F. Clarke, of the Canadian Northern Railway, worked for Mackenzie and Mann as manager in charge of laying out model town of Leaside in 1912, the first of its kind in Canada. "Basically he separated the industrial area from the residential area and by anticipating the automobile made Leaside a town that it was impossible to speed through."[1] Clarke Street was completed by 1913.
Clowes Avenue	Now Sharron Drive. In 1940, the Post Office changed its name because of confusion with another Close Avenue in Toronto.

Donegall Drive looking south from Fleming Crescent, February 19, 1956. *Toronto Reference Library, J. V. Salmon Collection.*

Commercial Road   Descriptive of the activity on the street in the Industrial Area.

Copeland Street   Possibly named after a sheet metal fabricator, a resident of Leaside.

Cory Crescent   Origin unknown.

Craig Crescent   Thomas Craig (b. 1839) was a Montreal businessman and director of the Montreal and Southern Counties Railway Company and Secretary-Treasurer of the Lake Champlain and St. Lawrence Ship Canal Company in 1912. James Craig was the Chair of the Board of Health in 1913.

Crandall Road   Origin unknown.

Crofton Road   Formerly Baird Avenue.

Davisville Avenue   Village and street named after John Davis.

Divadale Drive   Formerly known as Mitchell Avenue, the street was named for the Divadale Estate, owned by Capt. Flanagan; his daughter's name was Diva.

Don Avon Drive   Originally named Lazard Street.

Donegall Drive   Originally Leaside had Donegal with one "l". The Borough of East York changed this to Donegall. Assumed to be named for the Irish town.

Donlea Drive   Connects the Lea family with the Don River. Originally the street was known as Donald Street, after Sir Donald Mann.

Edith Avenue	Now Bessborough Drive. The name changed in 1932 in honour of the Governor-General.
Esandar Drive	E. S. & A. Robinson's Canada Ltd., located in Leaside's industrial area. The street name spells the company's initials.
Fairland Road	Origin unknown.
Field Avenue	Refers to "the field" where Bessborough Public School now stands.
Fleming Crescent	Robert John Fleming (1854-1925) was an associate of Mackenzie and Mann, the company that laid out the Town of Leaside in 1912. He served as a Toronto Alderman and Mayor for four terms. As well, he operated the Toronto Street Railway Co. In 1924 the Fleming family bought "Donlands," the 1,000 acre farm of William F. Maclean.
Glenbrae Avenue	Origin unknown.
Glenvale Boulevard	Formerly Pine Park Avenue.
Grandstand Place	Recognizes the presence of Thorncliffe Racetrack's Grandstand (1920–1952).
Hanna Road	After David Blythe Hanna, V. P. of Canadian Northern Railway. He became its President after the government takeover and ultimately the first President of Canadian National Railways. He supported the "model town" idea. The street was originally named Glenallan.
Heath Road	In 1836, the widow of Brigadier-General Heath and her son, Charles, bought land on the hill where deer still roamed, and styled it Deer Park. Their street was known as Heath.[2]
Heather Road	Origin unknown.
Industrial Street	Descriptive of the immediate industrial area.
Junction Road	Became known as Bayview sometime after 1890. The street ran north from Eglinton.
Kenrae Road	Named after two men, Ken and Rae.
Killdeer Crescent	Named after bird. Formerly the street had been Kildare. Originally this street was part of Donlea.
Krawchuk Lane	Named after Lorna Krawchuk, Councillor for East York from 1988 to 1997.
Laird Drive	After Robert Laird Borden, Prime Minister of Canada and friend of Sir William Mackenzie.

Parade on McRae Drive at the southwest corner of Randolph Road, October 7, 1955. *Toronto Reference Library, J. V. Salmon Collection.*

	Another Mr. Laird was the first bank manager at CIBC on Laird.
Lea Avenue	After the Lea family.
Leacrest Road	On the crest of the ravine, connected to the Lea family.
Leadale Avenue	After the Lea family.
MacNaughton Road	Sarah MacNaughtan, a British journalist, wrote glowing articles about William Mackenzie's achievements and "puffed" pieces to attract prospective buyers to Leaside. Originally, the street name was spelled MacNaughtan, but after a poll of the residents, was changed to MacNaughton. As part of her payment for writing, they named this street after her.
Malcolm Road	William Lindsay Malcolm, educationalist and civil engineer. Born in Guelph, Ontario, he was involved with the town plan.
Mallory Crescent	Not known.
Mann Avenue	Named for Sir Donald Mann.
Markham Avenue	Not known.
McRae Drive	After either Alexander D. McRae, a prairie land tycoon or Randolph McRae, Mayor of Leaside, 1913–1914.
Milepost Place	Recognizes Thorncliffe Racetrack (1920–1952).

Millwood Road, looking southeast from the CPR bridge, north of Crothers Drive. *Toronto Reference Library, J. V. Salmon Collection.*

Millwood Road	A North Toronto road that continues into Leaside.
Mitchell Avenue	Now called Divadale Drive.
Moore Avenue	Originally was Laird Drive.
Overlea Boulevard	Away from Leaside (or over or above). Named for Lea family.
Parkhurst Boulevard	Formerly known as Soudan. The street was named for the Parkhurst Clothing Company, a partner with Dorothea Knitting Mills.
Parklea Drive	Formerly Phippen Avenue. Named for the Lea family.
Phippen Avenue	A Mr. Phippen was with the CNR.
Pine Park Avenue	Is now Glenvale.
Randolph Road	After Randolph McRae, Mayor of Leaside 1913–1914 (the first mayor).
Redway Road	Alan Redway, Mayor of East York (1975–1981), federal politician and resident of Leaside.
Research Road	Research Enterprises was located here.
Richlea Circle	Thought to be connected to the Lea family.
Rolland Road	Named for Senator Jean Damien Rolland who died in 1912. His father founded the Rolland Paper Mills in Quebec. Jean Damien took over the

	mills and then served as a mayor, and alderman in Quebec and, in 1887, became a senator. Many Leaside streets were named for well-known people connected with Quebec because of the connection with Montreal planner, Frederick Todd.
Rolph Road	Dr. Albert H. Rolph, Medical Health Officer for Leaside in 1913. As well, Dr. John Rolph, born in 1792, was a supporter of William Lyon Mackenzie. Rolph Road School is named after him.
Roxville Avenue	Not known.
Rumsey Road	Named for a Mr. Rumsey, a manager employed by the Canadian National Railway who supported Mackenzie and Mann.
Rutherglen Road	In 1956, the street was named Rutherglen (between Southvale and Randolph) replacing Kelway Road.
Rykert Crescent	John Charles Rykert (1832–1913) had a successful legal and political career in St. Catharines. He served in the first Parliament of Ontario. His hobby was fruit farming.
Sharron Drive	Formerly known as Clowes Avenue. The origin of Sharron is not known.
Soudan Avenue	See Parkhurst, an extension from North Toronto. Today it is named Parkhurst east of Bayview.
Sutherland Drive	Hugh Sutherland, promoter of the Hudson Bay Railway which later became the Canadian Northern Railway. He was a friend and associate of Sir William Mackenzie.
Southlea Avenue	Named in recognition of the Lea family.
Southvale Drive	Originally was called Laird Drive.
St. Cuthbert's Road	Was known as Balliol until 1939, then renamed to recognize St. Cuthbert's Anglican Church.
Tanager Avenue	Named after bird, the Scarlet Tanager. The builder of the original home on the street, #15, named it. Originally the street was Alberton Avenue.
Thorncliffe Park Drive	Recognizes the Racetrack and Thorncliffe Farm.
Thursfield Crescent	Recognizes the maiden name of the wife of A. B. Cairns, the builder of the homes on Thursfield Crescent.

Southlea Avenue from Moore Avenue, circa 1940. *Courtesy Charles Perry.*

Vanderhoof Avenue	Named for a manager in the Canadian National Railway. This road was completed by 1913.
Village Station Road	Village of Leaside, train station, still standing in its original location.
Wicksteed Avenue	Henry K. Wicksteed, Chief Engineer of Surveys—worked under Colonel Clarke for Canadian Northern Railway, designer of the Mount Royal Tunnel in Montreal. Wicksteed directed construction of this tunnel in 1912.
William Morgan Drive	Named for William Morgan, politician, Reeve of Leaside (1948–50) and President of the Leaside Lions.
Winsloe Avenue	Originally Woodbridge Avenue. The reason for the name change is not known.[3]

14

COMMUNITY INVOLVEMENT: SERVICE CLUBS AND LOCAL GROUPS

M ANY SERVICE clubs, organizations and clubs have contributed to the development of our local facilities and to the variety of sports and recreation activities in Leaside. Equally, many hours of volunteer time demonstrate the community spirit of Leaside.

KIWANIS CLUB OF LEASIDE

The motto of Kiwanis International is "We Build," while the word "Kiwanis" means "self-expression." The Leaside Kiwanis, founded in 1949, with Fred Sanford the founding President, has contributed to the Town of Leaside in many significant ways. They established the Parkette in Howard Talbot Park, set up scholarships at Leaside High School, sponsored student visits to the United Nations, sponsored Peewee Hockey and the famous Kiwanis Music Festival which is held annually and found most schools participating in choral and instrumental music and recitation.

Fundraising was achieved through the sale of Christmas trees, a Gas-O-Rama, and participation in the Horse Show, held annually at the Canadian National Exhibition.

Besides supporting the community through raising money, many Kiwaniians served on boards, committees and on the Leaside Council. In 1967, Leaside Kiwanis surrendered its charter and some of their members joined East York Kiwanis.[1]

LEASIDE LIONS CLUB

In 1939, a preliminary meeting was held at the home of the former mayor (1938-1948) Howard Talbot. The outcome was the formation of a Lions

The Parade for the Leaside Lions Carnival, heading east along Eglinton Avenue, with the Leaside Majorettes and boys' marching band in the forefront (just past Marwood Motors). *Taken from* The Leaside Story *by Charles Clay.*

Club with forty members and with Howard Talbot as the first President. At first, meetings were held at Rolph Road School and later at Northlea School. At one time in the 1950s the Leaside Lions Club was the largest in Canada, having over 70 members.

In March 1939, they were given permission to hold a carnival in June, one that would run annually from 1940 to 1960 at Trace Manes Park. Kicked off each year with an inspiring and colourful parade, the Leaside Lions Annual Carnival would begin at 6:45 p.m. on a Monday evening around June 15th. The parade included a large number of bugle, pipe and instrumental bands, along with many decorative floats from local industries. Excited youngsters would decorate their bicycles, tricycles and doll carriages to compete for cash prizes. These would be judged at Marwood Motors (now McDonald's) at Bayview and Eglinton avenues at 6:30 p.m., just prior to the beginning of the parade. Clowns, marchers, horse-drawn vehicles and drum majorettes provided colour and merriment, along with the cubs, scouts, brownies and guides, always active participants in the parade.

The parade route was usually north on Laird from Vanderhoof to Eglinton, west on Eglinton to Bayview, south on Bayview to McRae and along McRae to Millwood Park (now Trace Manes Park). As part of the carnival, the many activities in Millwood Park included a Bargain Centre under a tent selling candies, toys, books, glassware and nightly specials. Bingo was very popular, along with a range of games for young and

Some of the girls of the Majorette Corps, sponsored by the Leaside Lions, posed on a "retired" fire engine outside the Fire Hall on McRae Drive. *Toronto Reference Library, J. V. Salmon Collection.*

old. There was also a large Industrial Exhibition Tent (40 x 160 ft) housing approximately twenty-eight Metropolitan Toronto Industrial Manufacturers exhibits.

In 1954, the Dr. Ballard's Mutt Show, sponsored by the Lions, was the special guest at their carnival. There were seven competitive classes including: largest dog, smallest dog, best dressed dog, longest tail, shortest tail, best tricks and finally, the dog who ate a dish of Dr. Ballard's health food in the fastest time!

The following year, Imperial Oil and Aluminum Goods Ltd. sponsored films. One could dance to the Paul Simmons Orchestra for 10 cents per person on Tuesday, Wednesday, Friday and Saturday evenings from 8:30–11:30 p.m. On Thursday night there was square dancing, for 75 cents per person, with King Ganam and the Sons of the West, at that time famous TV and radio stars. That year the Carnival raised approximately $14,000.00.

"The Carnival was first organized as a fun and sports day for the kids but it grew into a very professional week-long operation with about 25 booths."[2]

With the Club deeply involved in recreational activities for young people, Leaside became famous for its boys' marching bands and its girls' majorette corps, both sponsored by the Lions. Between 1941 and 1963, the Lions senior and junior boys' bands won a number of Canadian championships, playing and marching in cities as far away as Philadelphia. The girls' majorettes began in 1951 for girls aged nine to nineteen. The junior and senior majorettes practised at Bessborough School and appeared in the Grey Cup and Santa Claus parades as well as the Quebec City Winter Carnival and New York City. In the mid-1960s, the girls won the US open competition for majorette corps!

Individual members of the Lions might support specific events. During that period, two hundred children were provided with free swimming instruction each year by Lion Tommy Walker. Eye conservation for all Leaside pupils was carried out by Lion Art Stemp and 2,000 pupils had their eyes examined each year.

As well, the Club sponsored a variety of activities, such as hockey and baseball teams as well as the NHL Oldtimers Hockey Game. The 172nd Air Cadet Squadron was another group sponsored by the Lions. The Squadron began in 1942 and in 1945 Lion Jim Stephen became the commanding officer. "The boys received training in airmanship, meteorology, navigation, foot drill and target practice. There were also programs in sports, summer camps and flying."[3]

For many years, the Lions also performed stage shows and musicals with an all-male cast. Some of these were "Take It Easy," "Button Busters," "Topsy Turvy" and "The Wizard of Oz," written, produced, directed and performed by members. These started as two-night minstrel shows in a local school, then moved to the Bayview Theatre and finally on to the Royal Alex for a week long, five year stint.

One of the most fascinating fundraising ideas was the "Love Nest Bungalow" raffle initiated by the Lions in 1944. The grand prize was the house at 172 Donlea Drive. Later, the Town of Leaside raffled a house on Richlea Circle in North Leaside and used the proceeds of $20,000.00 to help finance the building of Memorial Gardens.

"One does not have to look very far to see the mark left by some Lions in our community. Howard Talbot Park, Trace Manes Park (built playground and the memorial arch), the Charles Hiscott Bridge on Overlea Blvd., the R. V. Burgess Park, and William Morgan Drive in Thorncliffe are all tributes to Lions who played outstanding roles in the growth and development of Leaside."[4]

In addition, the Lions sponsored baseball teams, organized boys' hockey at the Leaside Arena, helped donate books to the library on Bayview and equipped Bessborough, Rolph Road and Northlea schools with kitchen facilities. The Leaside Lions still meet biweekly at Trace Manes Clubhouse.

Another major event was the Leaside Lions Saturday Teen Club, known as the "Sateen Club." This organization began in December 1941, organized by Leaside citizens and the Leaside Lions Club as a Saturday evening dancing and recreational activity for the young people of Leaside and the surrounding area. "It started with a record player and a coke bar at Rolph Road School and grew to a membership of about 1,000 kids after it moved to Leaside High School.[5] Funds raised were donated to charitable organizations in Leaside and the City of Toronto, and the annual Christmas dance donated hundreds of gifts to the Hospital for Sick Children. Parents were included especially at the annual June summer dance held at Leaside Memorial Community Gardens.

The Sateen Club ended in the late 1950s as there were some difficulties with complaints from the community about noise and behaviour of the teens.

LEASIDE ROTARY

The Leaside Rotary Club, sponsored by the Toronto Rotary Club, was chartered in 1940. The original 15 members met weekly on the stage of Lamb Hall in St. Cuthbert's Church. The club was conceived when some local businessmen banded together to contest a local political issue and enjoyed one another's companionship so much they decided to meet on a regular basis.

The Leaside Club reached its peak membership of 85 in the seventies, and, although the numbers are less, they continued to meet weekly in

Weekly meetings of the Leaside Rotary Club (chartered in 1940) were held at Lamb Hall, St. Cuthbert's Anglican Church. *S. Walter Stewart Library, Elmore Gray Collection.*

The Leaside Pipe Band and the 65th Scout Troop, 1930. Art Bell is the Pipe Major (the tall man in the centre back row with the pipes under his arm). Many of these boys went on to serve with the Toronto Scottish Regiment and the 48th Highlanders during WWII. *Collection of the Dade family.*

The Leaside Girl Guides during Fire Prevention Week, outside the Leaside Municipal Building at McRae and Randolph, circa 1950. *Toronto Reference Library, J. V. Salmon Collection.*

Lamb Hall. For the past two years, they have met at the Masonic building (York Banquet Hall) on Millwood every Monday at noon.

Many local endeavours have been initiated or have enjoyed the financial support of Leaside Rotary. One member who operated a gift store on Bayview had also lent out fiction books in 1945. Rotary rented a store on the east side of Bayview, took over the book rental and with proper permission, their start-up financing gave birth to the "Leaside Library."

The Leaside Memorial Gardens Community Centre and Arena was a joint venture of the Lions Club and Rotary. And at a later date, they contributed to the addition of the swimming pool. Another combined effort, this time with the Leaside Council, was the Trace Manes Park community building. Rotary financed the senior wing and half of the common areas. In more recent years, the York Lea Lodges in East York and Touchstone for troubled youth have both been Rotary projects.

Todmorden Mills Museum has always had Rotary's support, especially with the rehabilitation of the oldest paper mill in Upper Canada. The building now provides premises for the Don Valley Art Club and the East Side Players.

Ongoing local projects include such endeavors as scholarships awarded to all East York secondary schools in recognition of achievement and in support of continuing university or college education. Public speaking contests for students are conducted annually.

Rotary conducts weekly Bingo for the veterans at Sunnybrook "K" wing and Saturday morning Bingo at Columbus Hall to raise money to finance their many endeavours.

Each year, Rotary supports a reforestation project in the Don Valley. With the participation of local students, thousands of trees are planted. The club conducts vocational guidance sessions at the high schools, in cooperation with local businesses and, as well, they support foreman skills meetings designed to advance workers of local industry.

On the International level, the Rotary Club finances student exchanges between countries. Visiting high school students usually billet with Rotary families. At Leaside High School, the Leaside Rotary sponsors Interact. Here, the students who are interested become active in Rotary and assist with a variety of events such as the Annual Leaside Rotary Corn Roast.[6]

LEASIDE PROPERTY OWNERS ASSOCIATION (LPOA)

The Leaside Property Owners Association began in 1947 as a result of opposition to a potential bus service along Broadway Avenue. A group of young mothers protested this initiative and began the Association. By 1967, the membership numbered approximately one-sixth of the entire Leaside population (roughly 3,000 out of the total population of 18,000).

Initially, the association dealt with minor property problems of individual citizens. These Association challenges began to form certain patterns that became at first unwritten law and later actual legislation. High-rise apartments were not favoured in the residential area, spot re-zoning was discouraged and the LPOA was always on guard against any mixing of the strictly segregated industrial and residential areas.

As the town and Association matured, the Association became more ambitious. It was largely responsible for many of the most pertinent measures in Bylaw No. 1916 which set the plan for Leaside in the future. The fight against a high-rise development proposal in the Mallory Crescent area was led by the LPOA. When their submission went to the Ontario Municipal Board, the Association was successful. The Association was also in the forefront of a battle that prevented Leaside and East York from being annexed by the City of Toronto. As a compromise, Leaside joined East York, creating a one-city and five-boroughs organization. The LPOA also opposed the "Bayview Ghost" and the Kosmor/Bramalea development at Brentcliffe and Eglinton in 1990.

There are approximately 20 directors who meet monthly and each work on committees which include traffic, municipal affairs, the industrial area, education, fundraising and membership. The Leaside Property Owners Association is one of the strongest and oldest ratepayers groups and continues to keep the community of Leaside an attractive community with neighbourhood-based co-operation.

THE BUSINESS AND PROFESSIONAL WOMEN'S CLUB:

This club, started in October 1954, was organized by Mrs. Ethel Armstrong-Collins with an original membership of thirty-two. At the inaugural meeting, the Ontario President, stated that the club should work "...to improve the status of women and to improve women to fit that status."[7]

The charter meeting was held at St. Cuthbert's Church on January 27, 1955. To raise funds, an annual Valentine Bridge was held at Leaside Memorial Gardens. The club sponsored a scholarship at Leaside High School and paid for buses to take children to the Santa Claus Parade.

Previous members included Beth Nealson, True Davidson and Lenore Crawley.

THE LEASIDE DEBATING CLUB

The Leaside Debating Club, incorporated in 1938, was formed by a group of dedicated men who moved out of the central YMCA Speaking Club to hold regular meetings at the Leaside Library. Each year there was an annual show which the public were invited to attend.

This was a democractic club open to all men, regardless of race, colour, creed or occupation. The programs stressed parliamentary procedure and public speaking, without using lecture or classroom technique. All criticism was conducted in a constructive way, to build each others confidence.[8]

THE LEASIDE-EAST YORK UNIVERSITY WOMEN'S CLUB

The organization, part of the Canadian Federation of University Women, began in 1956, with True Davidson, later the Mayor of East York, playing an active role in its initiation.[9] The first president was Mrs. Jean Auger. Beth Nealson (a former mayor of Leaside) also became a member.

The club meets once a month from September to April at Northlea United Church, 125 Brentcliffe Road. Invited speakers address these meetings on a variety of topics with an annual dinner being held in May. Membership is open to all women graduates of accredited unversities, with an associate membership also available.

One of the fundamental objectives of the club is the encouragement of young women to pursue post-secondary education, and to render financial assistance to deserving students.

Three $500.00 scholarships are presented every year to each of the East York High Schools—East York Collegiate, Leaside High School and Marc Garneau Collegiate.

As of 1999, the club has 85 members, 64% of whom live in Leaside.

LEASIDE GARDEN SOCIETY

The Leaside Garden Society was organized in 1950 with 36 members. By 1953, membership had increased to 193 members, growing to 250 members in 1999. They meet monthly at the Leaside Public Library on the second Thursday, except in July, August and December.

The Leaside Garden Society first planted gardens at the Library, a garden on Laird Drive and other gardens at traffic intersections. In 1963, for Leaside's 50th anniversary, plaques were placed on various trees. Northern Dancer roses were planted at the Library as a centennial project.

Members have participated in several flower shows, but in the early 1970s interest dwindled and it was disbanded.

In 1986, a group of gardening enthusiasts started the society again and on June 9, 1988 they were declared a Horticultural Society under the Horticultural Society Act, by the Ontario Ministry of Agriculture and Food. Today the Society is an affiliated society with the Ontario Horticultural Association.

The children from Grades 2 and 3 from three local schools assist in the spring public planting at Leaside Memorial Gardens Community Centre, the Leaside Library and Father Caulfield Parkette. Flower beds are also maintained at Lyndhurst Hospital.

The original members of the Society wanted to create an informal environment for people to meet and share information and advice on gardening problems and horticultural and environmental issues.[10]

15

The Parks of Leaside

Parks are more than just a place for children to play. They provide green space, a breather from the concrete to beautify the residential areas. But equally important, they allow for a variety of recreational and sports activities. As well, in Leaside, parks have been named after notable Leaside residents, thus helping to keep our heritage alive.

Trace Manes Park

The space for Trace Manes Park, originally known as Millwood Park, was acquired in 1932. After 1950, the name was changed to recognize Trace Manes, a popular former mayor of the town, from 1948 to 1950. The final grading of the surface took place in 1940 when a ball field was built. That same year the Leaside Lions Club opened the town's first playground at the park, a project which had been led by Mr. Keene, when Principal at Bessborough School. The Lions Club, under President S. N. Schatz, also held its first carnival there in June of 1940. The asphalt tennis courts, initiated by Matt Sayliss, followed in 1949 and 1951. An outdoor skating rink is divided for pleasure skating and hockey. At one time in the 1950s, lights and music were provided. A small field house provided changing facilities.

Today, the Leaside Library, about to be rebuilt at the north end of the same site, occupies the apex of this triangular-shaped park.

Bruce Park

Named after Sandy Bruce, a former Police Chief in Leaside, the park was acquired in 1945. As it consisted mainly of ravine property, landfill was used to level the area in 1947.

The "Archway" entrance to Trace Manes Park, named after a former mayor. The park, originally known as Millwood Park, was established in 1932.

The Centennial Project of 1967 was the building of this clubhouse at Trace Manes Park. *Leaside Camera Club, courtesy Herb Horwood.*

A 21-inch storm sewer from Bayview Avenue to Moore Avenue was constructed throughout the park and the grading followed shortly after the filling operation was completed. Located between Leadale Avenue and Moore

Bruce Park, at Moore Avenue and Bayview, was dedicated in 1947 to Sandy Bruce, a former Leaside Police Chief. *S. Walter Stewart Library, Elmore Gray Collection.*

Avenue, the park provides playground equipment for children and green space for all.

TALBOT PARK

Named for Howard Talbot, a former Mayor of Leaside, the park was completed in 1944. The property consisted of swampy lowlands bounded by high banks on the south, with a small creek flowing through the park from west to east. Eventually, the water from the creek was collected in the town sewers at Hanna Road. A sewer was installed from east to west throughout the park, with weeping tile for under-drainage. Grading of the park was started in 1948 in the location of the rugby field and was finished in 1949 and 1950 opposite Donegall Drive. The ball fields were built in 1950 and the bowling green commenced in 1951.

The creek that flowed through Talbot Park originated in North York and crossed into Leaside where the Sunnybrook Shopping Centre is located. It flowed easterly crossing Hanna Road, Rumsey Road, Parkhurst Boulevard, as well as Sutherland, McRae and Laird drives, and on along the west portion of Commercial Road before crossing onto private property. The creek was first picked up to enter the town sewage system at McRae Drive and Randolph Road.

Pauline Whitworth pulling son Leonard and daughter Pauline through the park. The photograph was taken from the end of Donegall Drive, looking northwest towards Eglinton. This area was known as Cedar Hill and was popular as a spot for tobogganing and skiing. Taken by Howard Harold Whitworth, January 1927. *The Leonard Whitworth Collection.*

While Howard Talbot was Mayor of Leaside (1938 to 1947), much of the town's growth occurred. Born in England, Henry Howard Talbot grew up in Galt, Ontario. A carpenter by trade, he moved to Weston in 1920 and started a construction business. In 1928, he bought property in Leaside and began building homes on Donegall Drive, Cameron Crescent, Bessborough Drive and Parkhurst Boulevard. He built the row of duplexes north of Parkhurst on the east side of Bayview Avenue, south of Eglinton Avenue. His largest project was the low-rise apartment complex on Bayview south of McRae Drive and north of Sutherland Drive.

As Mayor, he was determined to keep taxes at a minimum. To do so, he stressed the development of the Leaside Industrial Area. Talbot was also responsible for the federal government's decision during World War II to locate Research Enterprises in the area (buildings later occupied by Philips and Dorothea Knitting Mills). He also encouraged E. S. & A. Robinson, Sangamo and Honeywell to come to Leaside. As part of the war effort, he arranged the sponsorship of the Canadian Navy *Leaside* Corvette and the "Leaside" Bomber Squadron during World War II.[1]

Howard Talbot arranged for the purchase of Talbot Park, was the first president of the Leaside Lions, initiated the Leaside Memorial Community Gardens and planned the construction of the town hall at Randolph and McRae.

Recreational skating at Millwood Park (now Trace Manes Park) *Taken from* The Leaside Story *by Charles Clay*

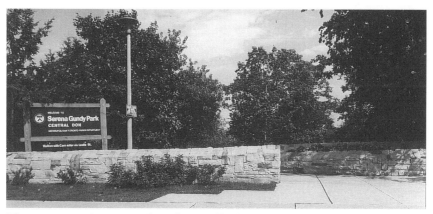

The entrance to Serena Gundy Park, just off Rykert Crescent. *S. Walter Stewart Library, Elmore Gray Collection.*

OTHER PARKS

A parkette was designated in honour of Father Caulfield from St. Anselm's Church. It is located where Cameron Crescent and MacNaughton Road converge.

The R. V. Burgess Park was named after Richard (Dick) Burgess, the Leaside Town Treasurer who held the position from 1929 to 1962, over 30 years. The park is located in Thorncliffe.

When Metro took over the former Gundy Estate it was designated as Serena Gundy Park. This extensive area can be entered from Rykert Crescent in North Leaside.

16

LEISURE TIME IN LEASIDE: SPORTS AND RECREATION

I N THE EARLY days of Leaside there was much open space and much leisure time activity was spent in the out-of-doors, from swimming in the Don River to hiking through woods, cross-country skiing and some cycling.

In 1923, the first outdoor rink was provided at the first public school site at Laird and McRae and a few years later a rink opened at Bessborough School and also at Millwood Park (now Trace Manes). As well, there was skiing in the Don Valley and, when the Toronto Ski Club built a jumping tower at Thorncliffe in 1932, much attention was focused on the Leaside area.

Leaside teams played Bantam Baseball in Pears Park in Toronto in 1941 and a Leaside hockey team played against Etobicoke in Canada's first Peewee game. Leaside's team was sponsored by Bill Morgan.

The town's first wading pool was built in Trace Manes Park in 1944 and the first asphalt tennis courts in 1948. The community softball league was organized in 1946 and quickly outgrew the facilities at Millwood Park. After a short stay under the floodlights at Talbot Park, the league disbanded in 1950.

Late in 1946, the Town Council decided to employ a Sports Director and hired Phil Stein, to begin in early 1947. By May of that year, Ron Hanegan was the Recreation Director and immediately began to organize activities. Classes in shellcraft, pottery, weaving, leathercraft and painting were offered in the fall of 1947. The Recreation Committee's first Day Camp was conducted in Serena Gundy Park in 1961.

The first Saturday morning hockey school was held in Millwood Park in 1947 and, also in that year, the Leaside Lions Band travelled to Philadelphia to the Lions International Convention where they led the parade.

Two boys on bicycles after swimming in the Don River. Todmorden Mills is in the background. *City of Toronto Archives.*

In the early 50s, the Leaside Rifle and Revolver Club was organized and the Tennis and the Badminton clubs separated to become two separate groups, after having been combined for the three previous years. Both the Badminton and Rifle clubs met at Leaside High School.

In 1952, as the Memorial Gardens neared completion, the Leaside Hockey Association was formed with Doug Franks as President. That same year the Leaside Skating Club was formed and performed their first carnival at the Gardens in the spring of 1953.

Opportunities for recreational activities continued to grow so that, by 1962, there were 5,722 participants in 27 activities.

LEASIDE LAWN BOWLING CLUB

In the late 1940s, when Talbot Park was being planned, it was suggested that a lawn bowling green be provided. Clem Hancock had belonged to the North Toronto Lawn Bowling Club and was insistent that Leaside would benefit from this green. After a number of meetings were held, Art Donahue, editor of the *Leaside Advertiser* became the first president of the new bowling club.

To help finance the building of the green, an agreement was reached with the Leaside Council. The club would return to the town all monies over and above operating costs each year; approximately two thousand

Leaside Lawn Bowling Club. Bowlers on the green near Leaside High School.
S. Walter Stewart Library, Elmore Gray Collection.

dollars per year were returned towards capital costs. With the original cost of installation with lights being $20,000.00, it was some time before the debt was paid. The clubhouse built in 1952 is still standing.

In June 1952, Joe Davis, popularly known as "Mr. Bowler," became the President and the club officially opened. A great deal of the club's ongoing success was credited to the forming of an active ladies section. In 1990, the ladies and men's sections were amalgamated and, the following year, Dorothy Ranta was the first lady President of the entire club. Over the years, the women have prepared food for tournaments and kept the clubhouse clean, as well as having been involved as players. This is a busy club. Participating in the croquet and lawn bowling are about 170 members. As well, in winter there are carpet bowling, bridge and court whist available as activities for members.[1]

THE LEASIDE TENNIS CLUB

In 1944, when Leaside's Millwood Park was only a field choked with weeds and covered with rocks, an oldtimer took out his racquet and taught a group of youngsters the fundamentals of tennis. In the spring of 1948, the Leaside Tennis Club had its official beginning, formed in partnership with the already existing Leaside Badminton Club. (They separated into two clubs in 1951).

Photograph taken at the Leaside Tennis Club in 1951. From left to right: William "Bill" Morgan, Trace Manes, Matt Sayliss, Howard Burrell, J. Allen. *Courtesy Pat Cole-Sayliss.*

Two seasons earlier, Matt Sayliss, a fortyish "go-getter" originally from Sheffield, England, had decided that he and his three friends, Al Ogue, Norm Lamport and Norm Ramsey and their children needed a place to play tennis. At that time the Sayliss family lived across from the park at 99 Rumsey Road, so he provided a net and they played on the grass in Millwood Park.

The courts were made of earth with lines marked with lime. After approaching the Town Council with his request, Matt Sayliss laid out the lines of a court on the grass and dirt where the present Courts 3, 4, 5 and 6 are located. Then, in 1948, assisted by Leaside Recreation and the Leaside Lions, two asphalt courts were put down. In 1949, two more asphalt courts were added and, in 1953, two more lower courts were installed. The estimated cost was $10,000.00. A "pay-as-you-play" policy was put into place.

The lights, those strung overhead, used for the hockey rink in winter, were transferred to the tennis courts in the summer of 1949 so that play could continue until 11:00 p.m. However, neighbours objected to the light and noise and the closing time was cut back to 10:00 p.m.

Unfortunately, after building the club, Matt Sayliss died in 1952. His son, Bob, and daughter, Pat, have been active members and directors. A trophy was established to reward the "most promising" junior member each year in the name of Matt Sayliss.

Leaside Tennis Club at Trace Manes Park. *S Walter Stewart Library, Elmore Gray Collection.*

A clubhouse was built in 1953, by a group of enthusiastic members and, in 1960, the club launched a major membership drive. By 1963, progress was made for increased clubhouse facilities.

The Council approved an addition to the field house at an estimated cost of $82,000.00, to be a 1967 centennial project. For the first time, lockers and modern dressing room facilities would be available. That year, a series of House League matches began. The next year LTC shoe tags were introduced and the Leaside Tennis Club was officially incorporated. Approval for Sunday play, to begin at 9:00 a.m., was granted in 1969, by the Borough of East York.[2]

Today, the Leaside Tennis Club is an active part of the life of Leaside with a waiting list for membership.

LEASIDE AQUATIC CLUB

In 1963, the Town Council met with 45 guests in the audience and presented the annual Recognition Certificates. One went to the divers of the Leaside Aquatic Club coached by Don Webb (winner of the World's High Diving Championship of 1963).

The outstanding divers were:

Judy Stewart—Champion—Canadian Indoor and Outdoor 1-3 metre.

Liz McGoey—Champion—Ontario Outdoor—3 metre.

Beverly Boyes—Champion—Junior Canadian Outdoor—1 metre for 11–12 years old.

Jim Lambie—Canadian Indoor—1 metre.

Bobby Eaton—Canadian Indoor—1 metre 11–12 years old.

David Brereton—Ontario Indoor—1 metre 10 years old and under.[3]
The club is not in existence today.

The Leaside Memorial Gardens Swimming Pool, 1967. *Leaside Camera Club, courtesy Herb Horwood.*

LEASIDE BASEBALL ASSOCIATION (LBA)

The Leaside Baseball Association had its beginnings in 1946 through the efforts of Leaside's Sports Director, Phil Stein, Mayor Howard Talbot and Reeve Trace Manes. Because the screening for the ball diamond had not yet been put in place at Howard Talbot Park, the initial six Peewee teams began play at Rolph Road School. Later, after Stein had scrounged the necessary screening from a local company, play started on the east diamond at Talbot Park. The land for the park had been donated to the town by the Talbot family for recreational use. A good part of the property had been a creek bed with a great quantity of stones. Over the first few years, players were asked to bring baskets to the park and take away the stones that continued to work their way up through the ground.

By 1947, the number of teams doubled and the Leaside Baseball Association was on its way to become one of Toronto's most successful minor ball organizations. The first Metro Toronto Champions were the 1947 Leaside Electric Peewees, coached by Bruce Henderson who also captured the Eastern Ontario title. In 1950, the Leaside Rotary Peewees, coached by Phil Stein, Wes Taylor and Frank Cronk won both the Metro and Ontario championships. Among the players were Ron Taylor, a future major leaguer, and Bill Kennedy who had an outstanding Junior and university hockey career.

Family baseball in Talbot Park circa 1940s. The boy at bat is Gary Reed, the catcher is his father, Dave Reed. The other children that can be identified are: Bob Keyser (hands on knees), Carol McGovern (hands on hips), Linda Mae Keyser (checked shirt). The house on the hill is at the end of Cameron Crescent. *Originally in the* Toronto Telegram, *courtesy the Reed Family.*

The west diamond had lights installed in 1952 and had been first used for local softball games, but the growing Baseball Association required more space. Additional age series were added, with Juvenile beginning in 1953 and Junior in 1955. Ron Roncetti's Metropolitan Motors teams dominated Metro in those years, winning an unequalled four consecutive championships. Unfortunately, from 1952 until 1968, the City of Toronto was not a member of Baseball Ontario, thus preventing those great clubs from additional further laurels. Professional baseball leagues signed on Ron Taylor, Jack Caffery, Don Graham, Charlie Burns, Gary Collins, and Gerry Manale from those teams.

The LBA, whenever feasible, generously hosted other Toronto associations that had inadequate park space. For many years North Toronto Midgets, coached by Roger Neilson, dominated their age series in Toronto while playing in the Leaside Midget League.

By 1968, there was no senior age baseball in Metro Toronto. It was that year that the Leaside Maple Leafs were founded, using uniforms from the now defunct Toronto Maple Leafs of the International League. The team was undefeated in league play that year and, from that auspicious start, an exceptional history of success developed. Leaside senior teams have won seven Metro and ten Ontario championships. Managers Joe Irvine, John Winter, Ric Fleury and Ron Dominico were at the helm for the team's lengthy run of success. Outstanding players have demonstrated their skills for Leaside Senior clubs. Some of them are Terry Adams, Ron Blackmore, Steve Breitner, Ron Dominico, Ross McDonnell, Alf Payne, Alf Riverso, Robbie Stevens, Bill Weedon plus many others.

The Leaside Junior League has become recognized as the top loop for its age group in Ontario. After other Toronto leagues had all folded by 1969, the Leaside league took in teams without a league. This practice has continued until today as the only Toronto area junior league with teams from across the city and from outside communities.

The inadequate lighting was upgraded over the years and completely replaced in 1989 with the present system. However, the establishment of the new system proved to be a difficult and expensive undertaking. It was found that the water table was very close to ground level, necessitating the installation of twenty-foot-deep concrete pylons to support the steel poles. The result, in the end, was an excellent lighting setup offering safer playing conditions.

Leaside teams have won 40 Toronto and 17 Ontario titles, many more than any other local organization. Among the highlights, along with the previously mentioned Rotary PeeWees and Metropolitan Motors teams, would be: 1959 Moores Drugs Midgets led by Dick Krol; Richardson Sports 1971 Juniors with Tim Ampleford, Dave Gardner and Brian Marks; 1975's Bantam All-Stars featuring Wayne Thompson, Scott McGeown and Paul Papodopoulos; the 1977 Pitts Juniors with Mike McEwen, Clint Dadswell and Marty McGeown; the 1986 PeeWee All-Stars led by Paul Evans, Brad Appel and Adam Pettle; the 1993 and 1995 Leaside Lightning Midgets with key players George Georgiadis, Mike Wesson, Mike Dryden, Doug Dimma. A special highlight occurred in 1992 when the Leaside Lightning Midgets represented Ontario in the Canadian Championships in Trois Rivieres, Quebec. The team matched, in some cases, against provincial all-star teams came away with bronze medals, a fine achievement.

Many players have been signed to professional contracts from our teams. From the extensive list, Ron Taylor and Mike Kilkenny went on to major league careers. Taylor, now Dr. Ron, is a member of the Canadian Baseball Hall of Fame (CBHOF)and also the father of two boys now playing in the LBA. In 1986, the west diamond was named Taylor-Roncetti Field to honour Taylor and his former coach, Ron Roncetti.

Roncetti, after an outstanding coaching career, scouted for several major league teams for nearly 40 years. He too, is a member of the Canadian Baseball Hall of Fame.

Talbot Park's east diamond is named Bush-Hibbert Field in recognition of two exceptional volunteers, Carmen Bush and Leith Hibbert. Bush, another member of the CBHOF, was "Mr. Baseball" in Toronto for 60 years, acting as the godfather and conscience of amateur ball. Carmen served as Junior Chairman and Registrar for the LBA for more than 20 years. Hibbert was a tireless worker for kids' baseball in Leaside, serving on the Leaside Baseball Association executive for many years, including as President in 1960 and 1961.

Leaside people have contributed to senior levels of amateur baseball as well. Jim Adams and Leith Hibbert were vice-presidents of the governing Toronto Baseball Association (TBA); Roy Fleming and Howard Birnie served as Presidents of the TBA and Howard has been a member of the Baseball Ontario Board for 20 years, including two years as President.

No history of baseball in Leaside would be complete without mention of the Leaside Midget Tournament, for many years the most outstanding minor ball event in the area. After hosting a successful Junior tournament in 1959, the LBA initiated the Midget tourney in 1960 under the capable direction of Neil Morris. Later, Charlie Wilkins was director of the tournament for many years, followed by Colin Macdougall. Unfortunately, changes in the operation of other competitions within Baseball Ontario made it unavoidable that the tourney be dropped after a run of more than 30 years. There were numerous highlights through the years, starting with the upset win by the Leaside Haughtons in the first year. Huge crowds lined the hills of the park to watch the province's best 16 and 17-year-old players show their talents.

When Baseball Ontario decided to move to tournament style playoffs in 1978, the Leaside Baseball Association was quick to volunteer to host a championship and the Junior "A" title event was played in Leaside on the Labour Day weekend for 10 years. Then, in 1988, Leaside became the hosts for the Midget "AAA" playdown, an event which has continued to be hosted by the LBA through 1999.

No mention of baseball in Leaside could omit the Leaside Atom Baseball Association (LABA) at Trace Manes Park. This league for 9, 10 and 11-year-olds debuted in 1952 and has continued to give area youngsters their start in baseball. Norm Ahier served as president of the LABA for many years and his great work has been carried on by son Norm Jr., better known to all as Charlie.

Throughout the years, it has been the contributions of dedicated volunteers that have enabled the LBA to be successful. From the first President, Phil Stein, to the current group, it has always been the efforts of the administrators, coaches, sponsors, umpires and others that have placed Leaside Baseball at the forefront of the sport in Ontario. The assistance of the municipality has always been critical to the success of the LBA. The former Town of Leaside, the Borough of East York and the City of Toronto all have been important contributors to the operation of amateur baseball in Leaside.

Talbot Park has become known in local baseball circles as "The Shrine." For some it is a somewhat sarcastic description, but for most it expresses the special spot that the park occupies in the memories of participants. The unique character of Talbot Park has made it a very special place for those involved in minor baseball.[4]

LEASIDE SKATING CLUB

Barbara Ann Scott's Olympic and World figure skating victories in 1948 raised the profile of figure skating in all corners of Canada. No doubt this increased interest in figure skating was behind the decision in Leaside in 1952 to form a neighbourhood skating club. University Skating Club and Silver Blades Skating Club, both in Toronto, sponsored Leaside Skating Club's application for membership in the Canadian Figure Skating Association (CFSA). Dr. Sidney Soanes, a local adult skater, represented the club at a CFSA meeting on October 25, 1952 at which time its application was accepted. Leaside Skating Club officially became club number 472.

In that first season 400 skaters, from 3-year-olds to adults, joined the club; Dr. Soanes designed a club crest, which is still used today; and Marjorie Cook was chosen president of the nine-member, volunteer board of directors. Almost 50 years later, with the exception of professional coaches and administrator Kathy Mackenzie who was hired in 1991, the club continues to be fuelled by volunteer effort.

On April 15, 1953, Leaside Skating Club held the first of many carnivals. In the "Skating Revue" Easter eggs, bunnies and chicks impressed their parents with their on-ice antics; Muri Burbidge, a professional skater, performed a Ballet Comique to 'Dance des Heures'; and T. Eaton Co. Ltd. provided decorations and stage settings. The local Studebaker dealer, Starks, on Mount Pleasant, congratulated the club on its first carnival, in a full-page ad in the program.

Many Leaside skaters have been content to star in the annual carnival; others have sought a larger stage. Tracey Wainman, Canadian Ladies Champion in 1981 and 1986, began her skating career at Leaside. Vern Taylor who successfully landed the first-ever triple Axel jump, skated at Leaside as a little guy. Sarah Kawahara is another success story. She competed up to the senior national level under the tutelage of Leaside coach, Osborne Colson, the 1936 and 1937 Canadian Men's Champion. Today she is a world-renowned skating choreographer.

The formation of the first Leaside Skating Club precision team in 1975 offered club members another skating option. In precision skating (now called synchronized skating), 12 to 24 individuals perform complicated on-ice manoeuvers as a team. The hosting of the COS (Central Ontario Section) Sectional Precision Skating Championships in March 1990 at Leaside Gardens is typical of the club's involvement in precision skating. Three Leaside teams, Moonbeams, Footwork Formation and Laserlites were among the 26 teams competing at that event. Leaside's two current synchronized skating teams, Ice Wonders and Synergy continue the team-skating tradition.

Great coaching has been an important component of the club's and its skaters' success. Bruce Hyland and his future wife, Marg Roberts, along with Bess Henry got the club off to a great start in 1952. Andra Kelly, wife of hockey great, Red Kelly, and a former member of United States World and Olympic figure-skating teams, coached at Leaside in the late 1970s. A yearly award begun after his untimely death in 1987, recognizes the esteem in which skaters, young and old, held long-time Leaside coach, Chuck Kiel. Sandy Johnston, a current coach, is going for a record. She has coached at Leaside since 1970 when she returned home after a year with the Ice Follies. Tom Kalweit and Teri-Lynn Black-Calleri (Teri-Lynn and her partner Mirko Savic were Junior Canadian Ice Dance Champions in 1982), as amateurs, performed with their respective dance partners at Leaside carnivals, and then both eventually joined the coaching staff.

Leaside Skating Club connections are well represented in the Canadian Figure Skating Hall of Fame. Dr. Soanes was inducted into the hall in 1992 as an official, Bruce and Marg Hyland in 1994 as coaches, and Osborne Colson in 1995 as a coach.[5]

LEASIDE CURLING CLUB

The Leaside Curling Club, established in 1963, is rumoured to have been founded and built with money from the sale of the Thorncliffe Racetrack.

This club is run by its members while the city owns the facility, and is operated on a cost recovery basis. The rink can accommodate 32 teams playing at one time because there are 8 sheets of ice.

The current registration is 590 members. An open house event is held every fall with February being "learn to curl" month. Three to four times a year the men host a breakfast. There are 8-10 bonspiels each year.[6]

Some of our members have achieved curling awards: Jim Staples won at the provincial level in the late 1960s, Neil Lazar (skip) won the Canada Life Bonspiel, with Ted Paradis (skip) winning in 1997.

LEASIDE MEMORIAL GARDENS

Leaside Memorial Community Gardens was opened in 1951 on an irregular eight hectares of land at the intersections of Millwood, Southvale and Laird Drive. While space for the building was donated by the historic Lea family of Leaside, it was the Lions Club who were the main driving force in the constructing of the Gardens. The recreation facility was named in honour of the World War II veterans, a recognition that many people felt was long overdue. The outdoor plaque reads "In memory of the men of the Town of Leaside who gave their lives for their country in the Second World War—seventeen Leasiders."

The historical nature of this site is recognized by another outside plaque, erected by the East York Historical Society, which reads: "An octagonal brick farm house built in 1851-1854 by William Lea (1814–1893) a York County Councillor, a Magistrate, amateur poet and nature lover. In 1873, it housed the newly established post-office Leaside junction and in 1884, the name Leaside was given to the Canadian Pacific Railway Station built nearby. In 1912, the York Land Company which had considerable property in the area surveyed a town site, appropriately called Leaside. Incorporated in 1913, the Town of Leaside became part of the Borough of East York in 1967."

The first Chairman of the Leaside Gardens Board of Management was Mr. Trace Manes, elected to the board in 1952. The original board consisted of Councillor Charles Hiscott, R. H. Frith, K. Smith, W. Smart, William Morgan and V. Silk. After amalgamation with East York, the board members, residents of the local community of Leaside, were appointed by the former Borough of East York Council. Currently, the board also includes two members of the East York Community Council. The board independently manages the operation of the complex with support and co-operation from the City of Toronto.

Throughout the years, board members have dedicated enormous amounts of time and professional expertise to the affairs of the complex.

The exterior of Leaside Memorial Community Gardens, 1951. *S. Walter Stewart Library, Elmore Gray Collection.*

Leaside Memorial Community Gardens is considered to be a model for other facilities with community involvement at the local level. The previous Board Chair, Peter Oyler, served this community for the past 20 years; Peter Simmie is the current chair.

The goals of maintaining a clean, safe and fiscally responsible recreational environment have been kept to the highest of standards, while simultaneously being responsive to the needs and concerns of the Leaside community. The demand for ice time by the major user groups such as the Leaside Hockey Association (some 750 boys), the Leaside Skating Club, Learn to Skate (some 360 young people), the Leaside Girls Hockey League (180 players), plus many other groups, such as private rentals, public skating, shinny hockey etc., far exceeds the supply or availability of ice time. Despite this pressure, ninety-five percent of the ice allocation goes to local community groups.

An important and integral part of Leaside Memorial Community Gardens is the elegant banquet hall, the William Lea Room, with its glistening original maple wood floor. This room has been a "meeting place" or focal point for three generations of grandparents, parents and children attending a variety of functions from wedding receptions, dances, rock shows, sport card shows, sport celebrities autograph sessions, antique furniture sales, rug sales, auctions, to club meetings and so on. As well as providing a special community social facility, this hall generates necessary revenue for the complex.

The first swimming pool, 1958. *S. Walter Stewart Library, Elmore Gray Collection.*

Attached, but somewhat out of view, is the Leaside Swimming Pool built and opened in 1958. At the time, it was considered to be a modern, open facility which won a design award for the window wall which was rebuilt in 1993. The Leaside Memorial Community Gardens maintains and operates this facility, however the City provides a variety of swimming programs. The pool is well supported by the local community. What better way to keep fit than in the swimming lanes at the Leaside Pool, or participating in the 'learn to swim' classes!

Over the past number of years, major upgrading projects, such as a new floor in the arena, a new roof in 1979 and new walls for the pool, have taken place. The old, worn out seating was replaced in the 1997-98 season with comfortable modern seats at a cost of about $85,000. Much of the money is being raised by selling the seats to groups and individual in the community for $100 per seat, each one with a small plaque inscribed with the donor's name.

Leaside has been, and still is, a small town in the big city. Everyone who grew up here, went to the same arena, even if it was at 7:00 a.m., tying up the youngster's skates and sipping coffee on a cold winter morning at the rink. This was the gathering place where public friendships were made. In the 1960s and 70s, young people would gather and hang out on Saturday nights to watch the East Metro Hockey League with Leaside teams from PeeWee level up to the Midget level.

The Leaside arena where so many National Hockey League players began their hockey careers. *Leaside Memorial Gardens Management Board, courtesy Peter McMurtry.*

Leaside Memorial Community Gardens has been a source of part-time employment for many local young people, such as the snack bar attendants, rink guards, etc. Back in 1960, a young lady by the name of Maureen Kempston worked in the snack bar on her road to success. Maureen Kempston went on to become the President of General Motors of Canada!

A number of illustrious National Hockey League (NHL) hockey players such as Peter Mahovlich Jr., Paul Gardner, Dave Gardner, Tom Edur and Terry Caffery began their hockey careers at Leaside Memorial Gardens. At a recent special event, the NHL Oldtimers against the Leaside All Stars, banners and sweaters of retired NHL players were raised to the rafters.

The inaugural game that opened the Leaside Memorial Gardens in 1951 was between the Toronto Maple Leafs and the old Pittsburgh Hornets of the American Hockey League. Some of the notable participants were George Armstrong, former captain of the Toronto Maple Leafs and resident of Leaside, Harry Watson and Cal Gardner also Leasiders and the immortal Tim Horton.

Another very unique personality or institution at the rink was the late Peter Mahovlich Sr., the skate sharpener and Zamboni driver who was devoted to the kids and who had a special place in their hearts. He was known as the "fastest ice-flooder" ever at the rink. Peter Mahovolich's plaque reads as follows: "worked this arena and served our community for over twenty-four years—a friend and helper to the boys and girls (of all ages) active in this arena. Every ice rink should be blessed with such a warm spirit." Born in Yugoslavia, July 14, 1906, he died in East York on June 13, 1981.

All arenas have inimitable characters like George Turell, the self-appointed traffic and people director in the parking lot who maintains good order and discipline. A familiar presence is still an off-ice player in the arena's culture.

And finally, one could not discuss famous people of Leaside without talking about Dr. Tom Pashby who is known worldwide for his work on sports injuries, in particular those that surround the eyes, neck and back. Dr. Pashby is the heart and soul of the Leaside community and promotes Leaside in his world travels.

Leaside Memorial Community Gardens has not only been a part of the lives of famous celebrities, but also of the many local residents who have devoted so much of their time, energy and expertise to coaching, instructing, refereeing, club administration, timekeeping and those many jobs that keep a community venture going. Those life skills and leadership roles, learned and developed at the arena, have made significant contributions to their own lives in the outside world as well as to their local community.[7]

It is well known, that arenas in every town are part of "Canadiana," the focal points of community life. And so it was in the "Town of Leaside." Long live the nearly half century tradition, a facility built by the community, operated by the community and for our community.

17

SAFETY AND SECURITY:
POLICE AND FIRE PROTECTION

FOR EVERY community the well-being of its citizens is a priority. Leaside was no exception. As the town grew, so did the need to have a stable police presence and fire protection.

DAVID T. LINDBURG—MAY 21, 1913 TO MARCH 7, 1917

It was May 21, 1913 and Leaside had become a town. In the vestry of the English Church, Mayor Randolph McRae and four councillors held their first meeting. Setting up a police force was given top priority as one hundred homes were under contract to be built. David T. Lindburg was appointed Chief Constable, but with a town population of about 43, his main duties would be for the enforcement of "the regulation of firearms and the molestation of birds." The building of the first few streets would find him being assigned extra duties of "preventing cattle and horses from running at large" and submitting a weekly building and road report which Council titled "the state of affairs within the town."

During the war years, the daily influx of thousands of workers at the munitions factory, the research station and the CNR yards transformed the scene. Added to this were the airmen training at the Leaside Aerodrome. Leaside's first chief, seemingly, continually failed to report to Council. On March 7, 1917, the Mayor would bring his career to an abrupt end.

ERNIE BELL—MARCH 7, 1917 TO OCTOBER 2, 1918

Council now decided to operate without the benefit of a formal force. For the next year and a half, Mr. Bell, the town's superintendent, would take over as temporary chief. During his time, the maintenance of good bus and rail service to Leaside's industries was given top priority.

W. Ross Davis—October 2, 1918 to August 21, 1922

By October 2, 1918, WWI was nearly over, but it was believed that the Leaside industries would remain strong. Mr. Davis would now assume the dual role of Fuel Controller and Chief of Police. It was anticipated that the construction of about seventy-five Canada Wire homes would create the first housing boom. And with more workers arriving almost daily at the new Durant Motor Plant, the economic future looked promising. Mr. Davis was "to issue restaurant and jitney service licenses [private bus services] to worthy people." However, with the advent of the automobile and more individuals acquiring their vehicles, cars and speeding had become a real problem on Leaside streets. The absence of a police patrol, it was believed, contributed to the concern.

Sandy Bruce—August 21, 1922 to June 1, 1946

Council found it necessary to hire an experienced law enforcement officer in 1922. For Sandy Bruce, this appointment would be service in his fourth police department. Immediately, he was put on motorcycle patrol to apprehend speeders. Those who were caught were brought before Mayor Horsfall who acted as chief magistrate. If a criminal offence did occur, Chief Bruce would receive the assistance of a lawyer when prosecuting cases before the county magistrate.

By 1929, the town population had increased to 605 people and 15 industries were now located there. A Bayview business section had started developing and the completed Leaside Bridge contributed to more traffic than ever before. The era of a "one man" force had come to an end.

A small police office was set up in the basement of the Leaside Public School (now Bessborough Public School). Here, a second officer, Mr. Gordon Naggs, would receive calls at night. During the day, the school caretaker would switch on a red signal light which had been installed on the school flagpole. This would notify a passing patrol that a call had been received.

Everything changed with the Depression. For a time, the town and police department would wait until growth resumed once more.

By the late 1930s, the town and its industries would be on the move once more. The year 1938 would see the purchase of the first Plymouth Police Cruiser, with two vehicles in service by the end of WWII. About the same time, a radio hook-up was established through the Toronto Police dispatchers. The early radios were not reliable and many calls went to the garage where the fire engines were kept, at McRae Drive and Millwood Road. When that happened, the station attendant would turn on the pump lights if a message had been received.

Over the next few years, North Leaside and the industrial area would grow at an incredible rate. The times and town that Sandy had patrolled alone for twenty-three years had profoundly changed. The size of the force had been brought quickly to ten men, but now strong leadership would be needed to run the department. On January 15, 1946 Council asked Chief Bruce to "resign in order to facilitate the organization of the police force."

JOHN MCGRAIL—JUNE 1, 1946 - JULY 14, 1949

Leaside's next chief was John McGrail, a man with seventeen years experience in law enforcement and service in two wars. An increasing crime rate would see Bert Fyfe become the town's first detective in 1948. On McRae Drive, a new police station containing an outside holding cell was built in conjunction with the fire hall. But, by 1949, Council would see that their dream of a force united had become a force seriously divided. The men complained of a lack of leadership and discipline. Low morale and misconduct among the men were evident. Half the force had quit and one officer had even struck the chief. Council would bring seven charges against Chief McGrail and force him to resign on July 14, 1949.

The town united with John McGrail, protesting against his dismissal. Over the next several months, Rev. Galloway and the North Leaside Rate Payers collected signed petitions and private citizens pressured Council to reinstate him. Throughout, Council stood firm: "The chief is guilty."

RUSSELL SPANTON—JULY 14, 1949 TO NOVEMBER 3, 1952

On the day of John McGrail's resignation, Council acted quickly to rebuild the force. The Police Committee and Police members agreed to promote one of their own. This was Russell Spanton, only a five-year member of the force. He was given the assistance of two advisors and the department size was increased to fifteen men.

To help the force work as a unit, a system of merit points was introduced. Points could be added or subtracted on the mens' service records for performance of their duties and conduct. In 1951, the force became unionized. However, requests for wages and working conditions equal

Leaside's "first jail," on Laird Drive at the southeast corner of Markham Avenue. The building has since been remodelled. Photograph taken on July 3, 1955. *Toronto Reference Library, J. V. Salmon Collection.*

to that of other police forces was denied. Satisfactory progress would be made in these areas through arbitration awards.

Despite the changes, in 1952, Council was still dissatisfied with police administration in Leaside. The Attorney General's Office was asked to report and make recommendations on all aspects of Leaside Police procedures. Their review, when implemented, would help bring about the necessary improvements.

From the perspective of some, the force and chief had perhaps been too much under Council's control for several years. And all was not yet resolved, for on June 29, 1952, Chief Spanton resigned. Council accepted his decision with regret and offered him a less demanding position as an inspector. This Russell Spanton would accept.

CLARENCE H. ANDERSON—NOVEMBER 3, 1952 TO DECEMBER 31, 1956

On November 3, 1952, Sgt. Clarence H. Anderson of the Toronto Police would take his place as Leaside's last chief. The efforts of Council had paved the way for creating an effective force. The department would grow to twenty-one men. Two cruisers and a motorcycle would patrol the streets in three shifts, twenty-four hours a day. The names of detectives Walter Naulls and Des Bryan would often appear in the local papers, cited for solving Leaside's crimes.

By 1955, plans were being made to build new police quarters, but first a new battle was to emerge for the force. Leaside would officially fight against police amalgamation with the Toronto force. A fight they were soon to lose.

At a special meeting held on December 17, 1956, Mayor Hiscott would address the force for the last time. He congratulated them on the performance of their duties. Each member was then presented with a set of cufflinks and a tie pin by the mayor and council members.

It was time to meet their new boss, Deputy Chief H. Smith, of the new Leaside and East York Division of the Metropolitan Police Department. The Leaside Police Force had come to an end.

The department over its fifty-four year history had its share of hold-ups, break-ins, murders, suicides, car thefts and even shoot-outs. This is a story on the lighter side.

It was about one in the morning on a hot summers night, when a car with its headlights out rolled into Sunnybrook Plaza. Stopping at the Cigar Variety Store, two youths got out. One hurled a newspaper box through the storefront window and the two then entered.

On the hilltop at the end of Donegall Drive, which overlooks the plaza, sat Officers Walter Naulls and Des Bryan, observing the scene. Within thirty-five seconds they, too, would be rolling into the plaza. When the officers entered the store, one man was apprehended on the spot. The other man, however, now carrying one hundred and sixty-seven dollars in coins, went momentarily unnoticed. Clutching his coin-laden pants, he attempted to escape by crossing Eglinton Avenue into the blackness of the ball diamond with Officer Bryan in pursuit. His added weight gave him little more speed and grace than that of a waddling duck. About twenty seconds later freedom came to an end as officer Bryan brought him down with a flying tackle, sending the coins spewing from his pockets. In just over a minute from when the crime began, the two men were in custody.[1]

DEVELOPMENT OF A FIRE DEPARTMENT

In the early years of 1913 to 1924, only a few houses and industries existed in Leaside. At that time, the fire protection was provided by Canada Wire and Cable and Durant Motors who had developed their own fire-fighting force. As well, the CNR had a volunteer team and Toronto had agreed to provide assistance. When a fire occurred, the factory whistles were sounded to summon the men. A 75,000 gallon water tower supplied a number of fire hydrants throughout the area.

Fire fighter, Bruce Catchpole, standing beside first piece of protection from fire for the Leaside community. *S. Walter Stewart Library, Elmore Gray Collection.*

In 1924, Leaside took its first step to create its own fire protection. A used fire hose was purchased from Canada Wire and set up in a special hose house at the corner of McRae and Laird. The pressure to form its own brigade came about when, in 1925, a large fire at the CNR yards showed how inadequate Leaside's protection really was.

The year 1927 saw Leaside divided into fire sections, with residents supplied with the phone numbers of whom to call. When, in 1928, the first petitions to Council to create a business section along Bayview started appearing, the need for greater service became evident. It was time to put volunteers into active service.

On September 24, 1929, the Leaside Volunteer Fire Department was formed at the ratepayers meeting at the public school. Canada Wire, Durant Motors and the CNR donated a new Rugby Fire Truck for town use. Mr. D. J. Bell, three deputies and eighteen volunteers would form the first force. The Council meeting of November 3, 1930 gave each man $25.00 per year, providing they attended 75% of all fires and at least two fire practices a month. The first "alarm" was a length of railway iron which was struck by a hammer.

The Leaside Volunteer Fire Brigade in 1934. Gil Bird was Chief. *S. Walter Stewart Library, Elmore Gray Collection.*

The fire truck would spend the next few years being moved about. At first, it was kept in several similar-appearing sheds, owned by Canada Wire, at Laird and McRae. Problems arose when the volunteers did not know in which shed their truck would be. Next, the truck spent some time at Markham and Laird, but vandalism forced its removal to the chief's property at Parkhurst and Bessborough.

When Mr. Gilbert Bird was appointed as the new fire chief in 1933, the fire hall was set up in the town's park (Trace Manes). Two years later, the garage was moved again; this time to the corner of Hanna and Sharron. At this location, the school caretaker would be contacted in case of fire. He alerted the volunteers by racing across the schoolyard to sound the siren which was mounted up top the garage roof.

In 1936, there was a change of fire chief again. At the January 14th meeting, the Fire Brigade accidently voted their chief out of office for being overzealous. Council insisted that the Brigade should agree on who they wanted as chief. Since, by June there was no winner, the Council appointed Ernie Bell (son of the first chief) to the position.

Once more in 1937, the garage would move again, but this time Council soon found a more permanent solution. One of the service bays at the gas station at McRae and Millwood could be rented. Mr. Marrin, the station owner, even set up a two-man shift to take night calls. But, when in 1938, Council challenged his rental fees, Mr. Marrin ordered the removal of the fire equipment. His pricing would not be questioned again.

Recognizing Fire Prevention Week, October 7, 1955. From left to right: Joe Banigan, name not known, Fire Chief Ernie Bell, Charles Hiscott, Lloyd Dickinson. *Toronto Reference Library, J. V. Salmon Collection.*

That same year, an agreement was set up with Toronto for fire assistance for 1938, with $25.00 being donated for each fire they attended. In the January Council meeting, pay raises were given to the firemen. The pay would be $75.00 per year providing the following conditions were met:

—75% attendance to all fires

—100% attendance to all fire practices

—$2.00 to be deducted for not attending a night fire and $3.00 to be deducted for not attending a fire practice.

With the acquisition of a second fire truck in 1940, space became a serious issue, requiring Council action. By 1942, Council was planning the building of a Municipal Office, Fire Hall and Police Station at the north end of the town's park. When much opposition was voiced, the Police and Fire Committee were asked to find a proper spot. They settled on the fire hall's present location on McRae Drive.

The station was completed in 1949 and the volunteers became part of the permanent force at a salary of $2,000.00 per year. The force grew slowly through the fifties, reaching eighteen by 1958 and forty-four near the time of the 1967 amalgamation with East York.

Initially, much of the training for firemen had been a one-week course on hydrant hookups, ladder removal and eventually the use of air packs. Two hours for each five days was spent on training given by the captain. Today, training is an eight-week course with daily training seven days a week.

Generally, fires in Leaside were kitchen and basement fires, but one much more serious fire at 85 Thorncliffe would injure six firemen. One unusual fire stood out in firemens' minds. It was a cold and very windy afternoon when the fire department responded to a call at the Crothers Plant near where the Loblaws Super Store is today. Freezing rain had turned the roads to glare ice, causing the fire truck to spin out of control at the intersection of Laird and McRae. It came to rest at the entrance of the CIBC building. Arriving at the site, firemen faced wind-driven flames of some forty feet, racing through the structure. Next, they found that the hydrants were shut off as the building was undergoing demolition. Two pumpers and an engine set up a relay of hoses from a Laird hydrant to the site. Several hours later, as dusk approached, the fire was finally out. Leaking water from hose couplings had turned the area into a skating rink. Not only had their lines frozen, but they were embedded in ice. The following day the morning shift returned to the scene. The solid lines were loaded onto a flat bed truck and returned to the firehall floor to be thawed out.[2]

18

SELECTED HIGHLIGHTS OF
LEASIDE COUNCIL MEETINGS

THE FOLLOWING selected highlights as recorded by the Leaside Town Council from 1913 to 1966, are provided to give a flavour of the changing times. Mr. John Naulls of Crandall Road is to be applauded as he spent months reading every volume, page by page. These minutes, stored in the Records Room of the East York Civic Centre, provide the history of the town's development and the decisions made by the various governing representatives of Leaside. They reflect the attitudes of early Leaside and for those of you who grew up here, it will bring back many memories. For those who are relative "newcomers" it will explain how the town was developed. The selected minutes appear in chronological order and are believed to be accurate.

The Town of Leaside was incorporated on May 7, 1913 with 1,025 acres, 73 people and a motto of "Stability and Wisdom of Purpose."

The first council meeting, held in the vestry of the English Church at Leaside on May 21, 1913 at 12:00 p.m., with Randolph J. McRae as the first Mayor. The Council consisted of: Harvey Fitzsimmons; Lawrence C. Boulton; George W. Saunders and Archibald G. McRae. The Clerk Treasurer was Arthur T. Lawson. With over one hundred homes under contract to build, Council had to prepare the town site for their coming. "The 1000 acres of fertile countryside was incorporated by a special act of a petition sponsored by the Canadian York Land Corporation, a subsidiary of the Canadian Northern Railway." [1] "Because the new town hadn't had time to build any municipal offices, the Mayor and his Council met downtown in McRae's real estate office at 70 King St. East. Interestingly, Boulton and A.G. McRae were also affiliated with the mayor's real estate company, a company that was headquartered in Sir William Mackenzies' Canadian Northern Building." [2]

David T. Lindberg was appointed Chief Constable. His first concerns were for the regulation of firearms and the molestation of birds. The Town Engineer was Mr. E. A. James.

The first roads to be graded were Eglinton, Broadway between Bayview and Brentwood (now Brentcliffe), Brentwood to Eglinton and McRae to William Avenue.

A Board of Health, with the Hon. James Craig as Chair, was formed. Early on the agenda was the matter of water and sewers for the new town. Dr. Albert H. Rolph was made Medical Health Officer.

In October, the Council meeting was held at the Leaside Mission, the small wooden church later called St. Cuthbert's. Cement roads were to be created along McRae to Sutherland and Sutherland to Broadway (the boundaries of the Airfield) and one hundred houses were to be built for Canada Wire and Cable employees.

SELECTED MINUTES—1913

August 13—Bylaw authorizing the construction, building, purchasing, managing and conducting a sewage system was read. The construction of a waterworks and sewage system was given top priority, and the borrowing of $35,000.00 to be done through the Canadian Bank of Commerce.

The Town Constable will be paid $50.00 per month.

September 10—Plans for the sewer system have been approved by the Provincial Board of Health. Numerous dwellings and factories are coming next year, being 100 homes and several factories.

October 8—Approval of the Sewage Disposal Plant is received from the Provincial Board of Health.

October 13—Mr. Lawrence gave notice to introduce a By-law for the expenditure of $42,000.00 for establishing a system of Waterworks.

December 15—Advanced by Davidson and McRae for current expenses:
Streets: Advances for wages for cutting weeds—$60.25
Police: Advances for wages of chief (June-Dec.)—$350.00
Advertising: Advanced to *"Toronto World"* for advertising By-laws—$250.00

The Clerk-Treasurer to charge to Mackenzie, Mann & Company the sum of five hundred dollars ($500.00) for the grading of Eglinton Avenue and the sum deducted from their taxes.

SELECTED MINUTES - 1914

February 24—Roads continue to grow. Many south Leaside streets are being put in. Bell Telephone will bring in their lines to Leaside along Soudan.

March 20—The Clerk-Treasurer was authorized to rent an office in town for $25.00 per month to do the Town's work.

April—The supply of fresh water for Leaside will be accomplished by extending the pipes from Toronto to Leaside. A water main will be put in to service Canada Wire. Sewer pipes will also be extended to service Leaside.

Bylaw prohibiting horses and cattle running at large. Mr. James Lea will be the Pound Keeper.

April 17—Mr. Harvey Fitzsimmons is Chairman of the Waterworks Committee and asked that lots for sites be purchased from the York Land Company at the following prices:

N. Leaside—Sutherland to Leslie—$1,525.00

Kildeer Crescent—$1,275.00 each

Brentcliffe near Broadway—$1,425.00

Broadway—$1,825.00

The Tenders of Messrs. Mackenzie, Mann and Company Limited is to be accepted for the grading and pavement of roads.

April 22—Bell Telephone to be assessed at 60% of gross receipts of $130.47.

April 28—Earth was falling away under culvert under McRae Drive (as a large stream ran from Talbot Park).

Mr. L. C. Boulton would introduce a bylaw to prohibit horses and cattle from running at large.

Messrs. Wilson, Townsend and Saunders would get the contract for the construction of the collection basin, the pump well and pump house and the sewage disposal plant. Messrs. Connolly, Agnew and Co. would lay the sewer mains and build the brick sewers and manholes. Mr. J. L. Boyd would lay water mains.

Allis-Chalmers Co. would supply cast iron pipes, hydrants, valves and erect a 75,000 gallon water tank.

May 7—The tax rate for the year 1914 was 5 mills on the dollar. The school rate was 1 mill on the dollar for a total of 6 mills on the dollar.

July 20—Water and Sewer services to be extended to E. A. Wallbergs' new houses, the matter to be advertised in *Toronto World*.

September 28—The building of a block of homes is requested. Stacey
Builders Ltd., contractors for E. A. Wallberg, asked for permits for
semi-detached houses.
The building inspector to get $5.00 for each house inspected.
September 29—That Mackenzie, Mann and Co. be advanced $6,114.20
for the building of cement roads.

SELECTED MINUTES—1915

February 5—The salary of the Clerk-Treasurer for 1915 be at the rate of
$50.00 per month commencing the 1st day of January 1915.
The Mayor explained that he was taking an active part in military mat-
ters and asked Mr. Saunders to take the chair.
Mayor McRae explained that owing to private business necessitating
his absence he would be unable to continue in his office.
February 15— Robert P. Ormsby is elected Mayor of the Municipality
of Leaside for the balance of the year 1915.
June 2—Speed regulations for cars will be postponed.
By-law No. 70 would prohibit the use of firearms and No. 71 would
prevent the destruction of birds.
A levy of one mill was authorized for the Provincial War Tax.
September 15—It was moved that Councillors attending meetings of
Council during the year 1915 be paid at a rate of $10.00 per meeting.
It was moved that an honorarium of $500.00 be paid to the Mayor for
his services.

Robert Phipps Ormsby, Mayor of Leaside, 1915-1923. *S. Walter Stewart Library,
Elmore Gray Collection.*

James Lea, grandson of the founder of Leaside
and former Reeve, 1919-1930. *Taken from* The
Story of Leaside, *by John Scott.*

SELECTED MINUTES—1916

June 8—A letter was sent from James Lea asking County Council for
road gravelling on Millwood Road.

Up to $250.00 was authorized for road repairs for the year and putting
in a culvert at Eglinton and Bayview.

The Mayor informed the Council that the Chief of Police was necessary, but to pay no more than $25.00 per month as he was getting the
same amount for services to York Land Company.

October 27—The Mayor submitted a memo dated August 2nd 1916 to
the position of the Munitions Factory and their water and drainage
services:

"In connection with development of the Town I will inform you that
Mr. E. A. Wallberg discontinued the completion of his factory and
workmen's houses in August 1914 by the commencement of the War.
He has made a contract for the making of munitions…"

The Mayor and Mr. Lea were asked to form a committee to try to get
a rebate back from the County from the good road tax.

$50.00 per year will be allowed for clerical work in the Mayor's office.

The continuing of D. T. Lindburg as Chief of Police was questioned, the matter to be taken up by the 1917 Council. Part of Mr. Lindburg's salary to be for a horse purchased for $200.00 from Canadian Northern Railway.

December 29—A circular from Premier of Canada asking for registration of all men between 16 and 65 was submitted at meeting and registration cards to be placed in hands of residents and all parties at the Leaside Munitions Factory.

SELECTED MINUTES—1917

March 7—The Mayor has arranged for Toronto to supply water for Leaside from the hydrant located at the corner of Eglinton and Bayview. It will supply 1,000,000 gallons per day and a second connection will probably be required running along Soudan.

The sewer tunnel has been delayed due to a shortage of manpower. The Mayor reported that a small building containing a stove has been built around the Town's supply water pipe to the water tank to keep it from freezing.

May 21—Leaside Airfield construction begins.

August 15—Mayor reported difficulty in collecting payment for water from munitions factory. The water supply may be cut off.

Road on Bayview should be repaired between Merton and Balliol and charged to Imperial Munitions Board as they had done the damage.

December 28—Council will accept the offer of Leaside Munitions Co. to pay 50% of water bill in cash and the balance applied to their account which the town owes them for the use of their workmen on sewer and waterworks.

SELECTED MINUTES—1918

May 13—A large water main will be needed for the new proposed factory of Mr. Wallberg, but first a committee is to be formed of the Mayor, Reeve and Mr. Mitchell to determine the factory's share in the cost.

The Mayor was asked to appoint a permanent policeman, someone capable of filling the position.

The Town Superintendent is in need of a new car to replace the old Ford. An Overland car is recommended to be purchased for an additional $400.00.

The water rates are too low and must be raised to cover expenses.

June 24—The first Canadian airmail flight from Montreal to the Leaside Airport occurs.

October 2—Mayor is to ask Mr. Hungerford, Manager of Canadian Northern Railway for the Town to take the cinders from their shops to be used on town roads.

The Imperial Munitions Board will look after all repairs for watermains, sewers and roads and will buy the Overland car at $600.00.

November 22—The new hospital constructed at the corner of Sutherland and Eglinton is being built by the Imperial Munitions Board, they will take care of the sewer and water connections to meet their own requirements. If the Town wishes to use the facility, can do so for half the cost at approximately $5,400.00.

December 27—The Imperial Munitions Co. ask that part of Mr. D. J. Bell's pay should be born by the Town as he gives service to them. The Town to pay what they consider right.

December 30—The first schoolhouse is established at Laird and McRae using an abandoned cafeteria from Canada Wire and Cable. Meetings are now held at this Leaside Schoolhouse.

Selected Minutes for 1919

September 25—The Hydro Power Commission asked to construct a high power line along Soudan (now Parkhurst) to Laird then south to the CNR shops.

The Bishop-Barker Aeroplane Co. will be allowed the use of the roads of the Town at a nominal fee.

Permission was given to use the former Guard House as a grocery store and a temporary licence was given.

Mr. Lea asked what steps have been taken to have Toronto remove its Garbage Disposal Plant on Soudan Avenue.

November 11—Mr. Wilkinson will be allowed the sum of $75.00 towards the expense of diverting electric light wires and poles to his house (45 Sharron Drive).

Selected Minutes—1920

January 28—Leaside is short of money and has not paid the taxes owing for County Taxes. The source of money being relied upon will be from the York Land Co. who have not yet paid their taxes for 1919.

Council decides to sell York Land, if taxes are not paid, to get new funds.

Leaside houses should have their ashes (from coal burned in furnaces) out for pickup every three weeks (no glass or cans).

May 31—Thorncliffe Racetrack runs its first race.

Leaside residents are now complaining of the odour from the garbage disposal works on the north side of Soudan (Parkhurst).

Dog tags are to be issued; $1.00 for male, $2.00 for female. Dog owners slow to buy their licenses and will have to be tracked down.

June 28—Dr. Elliot to be the Medical Health Officer of the Town at a retainer of $200.00 per year. Further payments could be made.

SELECTED MINUTES—1921

February 2—The Mayor has sold to Mr. Dawson the house formerly used by the Air Force as a jail building at a cost of $400.00. The building must be removed.

York Land Co. may sell the hay that grows on its roads but they do not have the rights to hay on the Town's roads.

April 8—Mr. C. J. Woodard asked permission to operate a small store for ice cream, candies and soft drinks, using the rink dressing room.

A letter from the Secretary of the School Board of the Town asked for $2,700.00 on the current account and that $60,000.00 be raised in other ways to build a brick schoolhouse. The matter was deferred.

Bayview and Millwood, looking east in 1920. The "For Sale" sign is advertising "900 ft. frontage excellent building lots" for sale in Leaside by Wood Fleming and Company. *S. Walter Stewart Library, Elmore Gray Colection.*

June 13—The Superintendent is to survey the Town and produce a list of dog owners. The Treasurer will issue a notice to each one demanding payment.

September 6—Application from Rev. P. M. Lamb for a permit to continue the erection of St. Cuthbert's Church Rectory on Bayview.

Employees of the Town should be insured against accidents under Workmen's Compensation Act after our first accident of an employee being kicked by a horse.

December 29—The speed limit of automobiles was increased to 20 mph. and it is recommended that a man be engaged temporarily to check the rate of speed.

SELECTED MINUTES—1922

April 7—The County Council has agreed to spend $4,000.00 on repairs on Bayview.

The Mayor reported that the taxes in arrears are from the York Land Co. and their purchasers. He is trying to collect from them to raise money for the school.

Plans were submitted to build a bridge between Todmorden and Leaside. It was suggested that oil be spread over low-lying wet areas in Town to stop the spread of mosquitoes.

May 30—Mrs. Perrem given permission to sell soft drinks and ice cream on the lot she is purchasing on McRae Drive at Sutherland.

A sidewalk is proposed on McRae from the factory to Bayview Avenue. The cost of a four-plank wooden walk and cinder path is $2,500.00 for materials and $1,000.00 for labour.

August 8—The plans of the new Factory by Durant Motors Ltd. submitted to the Town Engineer have been approved.

A petition from residents complaining about the disposal plant was received. The Mayor was asked to advise the city of legal action if nothing is done.

The weeds on McRae Drive are to be cut back 10 to 15 feet and the thistles as far as possible.

August 21—The Council appoints Mr. Sandy Bruce as the new Chief of Police for Leaside.

SELECTED MINUTES—1923

March 14—Dr. Elliott referred to the outbreak of measles in the Town; he and the secretary were not always sent notice.

March 23—Mr. Pinner, a representative for York Land Company, submitted plans for a row of 10 houses on Sutherland.

Mr. Gausby, Secretary of York Land Company, asked that a plan be submitted for a new schoolhouse by the School Board so the setting aside of lots could be discussed.

Water is to be drained off the low land at the area of McRae and Bayview. The Town's garbage collection will be $7.00 per collection and a man and team can be rented for $9.00 per 9-hour day.

April 8 —Foul odours are being emitted from a settling tank which had several hundred cubic yards of sludge removed. After rainstorms the water enters a tile pipe and is carried through the Township via the ditch. This is a health hazard for children and industry.

April 16—A section known as the unrestricted area on the map was referred to as Laird Avenue District to be opened for business and small factories.

The Chairman of the School Board expressed very forcibly the urgent need for a new school. A site has been selected.

Since April 5th the Heaslop Company made application to erect 14 houses on Sutherland Drive but were unable to build because of the waterway throught the lots. They verbally have now chosen Kenrae and Lea.

It was decided to adopt for the Town, Daylight Saving Time in accordance with that of Toronto.

May 11—Mr. Beatty stated that the school site was estimated at $18,000. and a four-room school with auditorium at $50,000. The loan to be at 5-1/2% with an annual rate of $4,678.76.

Mr.Horsfall explained that his company, Canada Wire and Cable could be authorized to extend their present Electric Light System to the core of new houses where possible and the Town would reimburse the Company.

May 17—Mr. Horsfall is elected as Mayor.

Leaside Public School Board consists of three teachers, one caretaker and 75 students.

Houses on Markham begin building.

May 30—Water meters are to be ordered for houses without them.

Major Hearne asked if the little bridge on Eglinton could be whitened for the safety of motorists at night.

June 12—The County Council might not legally be able to maintain the bridge over the Don as it lies within the Town. Also a new bridge might be required.

H. Horsfall, President of the Canada Wire and
Cable Co., and Mayor of Leaside, 1922-1930.
Taken from The Story of Leaside, *by John Scott.*

July 4—There was traffic congestion during the period of the Thorncliffe Race Meets.
The Town is only responsible for road repairs and is not liable for accidents.
The Bridge was closed over the Don and because there was no traffic there is no need to repair it.

SELECTED MINUTES—1924

January—Leaside Public School opens on January 11th [now Bessborough].
The building of a High School is proposed.

SELECTED MINUTES—1925

January 22—The Perrem and Knight Store at McRae and Sutherland
applies to have a gas pump. Permission is granted for a $10.00 fee.
November 27—Council meeting at Leaside Public School. The dis-
charge of firearms within Leaside is now prohibited.
There is a concern of bicycle riding on sidewalks.
December 29—A bylaw should be introduced to prohibit children from
skating and sliding on the main street of the town.

A committee is investigating the need for a high level bridge to connect Leaside to Todmorden.

January 11—Bus service has started on Mt. Pleasant Road.

November 1—The Leaside Bridge is ready to proceed and costs have been determined.

The York Roads Commission wants to build a concrete bridge over the Don on Eglinton and wants Leaside to build a sidewalk on the east side for $112.00.

January 10—Mr. Stocking, representing the Hydro Electric Power Commission, stated that soon it may be possible that the Town could install its own substation.

The Viaduct to connect to Pape Avenue and Donlands in East York with Laird Drive in Leaside—the Viaduct shall consist of steel and concrete having a roadway of 44 feet in width and two sidewalks of six feet and designed to carry a double track electric railway.

January 26—A Committee composed of James Lea, Mr. Wilkinson and Major Hearne are to select a suitable site for the Town's Municipal Offices.

March 8—Several cases of Scarlet Fever and one of Diphtheria have been reported. Concerned are Dr. Elliott and the School Board.

March 30—Mrs. Godfrey asked for a permit to erect a temporary Post Office on Laird Drive which was granted.

Letters are read by the Treasurer from owners willing to contribute ten feet of their property for the widening of Laird Drive.

June 1—The mud slide repair costs are settled for the damage done during the bridge construction.

June 29—A letter to York Land Co. from Durant Motors asking that Commercial St. become a public highway.

Millwood Rd. is to be diverted according to the plan submitted by the Town engineer and will meet Laird Dr. by a windy route.

July 14—The Reeve explained that a By-law needed to be passed to close certain streets in the northeast corner of Town to enable 68 acres to be turned over to Mr. Gundy of Wood Gundy and Company.

August 3—Millwood Rd. will be 28 feet wide from Donegall to Laird Dr. with curbs, sewers and water mains.

Paving Markham Street in 1927. Both the Durant Motors factory and Canada Wire and Cable can be seen in the background. *S. Walter Stewart Library, Elmore Gray Colection.*

September 28—Letters were read from the Bank of Montreal announcing the gift of Peony plants from H.R.H. the Prince of Wales to the cities, towns and villages of Canada as a memento of his visit during the Diamond Jubilee Year of Confederation.

October 28—A letter from East York Township asks for a donation toward the opening ceremonies of the Bridge. $300.00 will be given.

November 3—The Committee is further impowered to arrange with the Toronto Transit Commission for a bus service from the Danforth to Yonge St. via the Bridge through Leaside.

November 30—A petition of nearly all the lot owners on Millwood Rd. requested that it become a business street.

In the event of fire the factory whistle will be blown. A voluntary fire brigade divided by town sections will respond.

Toronto Hydro has agreed to run their lines through Leaside to the power plant.

Selected Minutes—1928

January 23—The question of putting the Chief of Police on a regular salary was discussed.

It was moved by Mr. Woodard that Mr. Bruce be salaried at $150.00 per month commencing the 1st of February 1928 and be allowed expenses for the use of his car on town business and to use his best judgement as to his hours of being on duty.

February 29—A letter from the Aeronautic Association of Canada Ltd. requesting part of Town for a flying operation.

March 28—The question of purchasing our own team [of horses] for Town use was discussed. It was recommended the Town purchase an acre of land adjoining Commercial St. to create a Town Yard. A stable could be built to house the horses and town's materials and tools.

May 30—A letter from Mr. R. C. Harris, Commissioner of Works for Toronto asks that the name Bayview Avenue be changed to Kilgour Avenue to honour the donor of Sunnybrook Park to the City.

The majority of land owners along Bayview ask that Bayview be made into a business street from Millwood to Soudan. Council recommends that the area be increased and be from Moore to Eglinton.

June 27—A letter from the Leaside Public School Board addressed to the Works Committee asking the Town's forces to undertake the work of making a tennis court, charging the cost to the School Board. Approved.

An application from the Bell Telephone Company for permission to erect 13 poles and wires on the bridge approach from the subway to the Race Track on the south side of the road was read.

Mushroom beds are outlawed from being in Leaside home properties.

August 1—Council receives complaints about planes flying in the early hours from the airport. Starting time will be changed from 6:00 a.m. to 7:00 a.m.

October 1—Complaints are received that Council meetings and dealings are too private. These meetings should be open to the public.

SELECTED MINUTES—1929

September 9—Paving and sewers will be constructed on Edith Avenue [now Bessborough].

The tennis court at Leaside [now Bessborough] School is being enjoyed by the townspeople.

SELECTED MINUTES—1930

December 1—Leaside has elected a new Mayor, George H. Wilkinson. A petition to get partial postal delivery for the town will be sent to the Post Master General in Ottawa.

Mr. Blain can operate a laundry business on Bayview Avenue provided he does not employ Orientals.

The town purchased 600 trees.

The Leaside Town Council, 1931; G. H. Wilkinson, Mayor and Major F. G. Hearne, Reeve. Councillors are: Robert Clark; W. P. Henderson; S. J. Hobbs, J. A. Macdonald; John Scott; J. A. Woodard. *Taken from* The Story of Leaside, *by John Scott.*

SELECTED MINUTES—1931

June 1—Postal delivery to residents is ready to proceed and Council wants someone sworn in to do the job.

The Depression—Leaside decides to help the unemployed by providing relief work. Workers are paid $0.45 per hour and must have been a resident for at least six months.

November 31—Mr. John Scott is to distribute the "Story of Leaside" and is given $300.00.

A red signal light is to be placed on the school flagpole for police signal.

SELECTED MINUTES—1932

March 7—The Depression—Town employees will be getting a salary reduction of 10% for the period April 1 to December, 1932.

April 23—There is now a Relief Committee. All single men to be paid off. Married men to be employed for only three days per week.

August 5—A letter is sent to Governor General Bessborough to ask if "Edith Drive" could be named "Bessborough."

November 7—Bylaws to prevent canvassers going door to door after dark should be set up.

SELECTED MINUTES—1933

January 14—Single men can now apply for relief assistance.

February 6—Leaside requests unemployment legislation and a larger allowance for unemployed.

March 17—No more personal remarks and discussions are to take place during Council meetings.

SELECTED MINUTES—1934

February 5—A ski jump is built by the Toronto Ski Club in Thorncliffe at the east end of the airfield.

April 30—Regulations are needed for barber shops as one barber wants to cut hair and sell ice cream.

May 9—Approximately 47% of Leasiders are unemployed.
New conditions set by the Relief Committee:
Married men—4 children, 3 and 1/2 days—$12.60
            —3 children, 3 days—$10.80
            —2 children, 2 and 1/2 days—$9.00
            —1 child and under, 2 days—$7.20
Single men, 1/2 day—$1.80

SELECTED MINUTES—1936

June 1—A speed limit of 20 mph is to be posted on Millwood Road.

October 19—A new school is urgently needed. Class sizes are between 45 and 55.

SELECTED MINUTES—1937

February 1—Charles Bolus will operate a Golf Practice Course on Millwood Road. Request to build a Moving Picture Theatre.
Leaside officially opposes any annexation or amalgamation with Toronto or any other municipality.

SELECTED MINUTES—1938

July 4—The Leaside Public School Board ask for police supervision around the school grounds at night.
July 26—A medical officer is sent to investigate the burning refuse at the East York Dump south of Moore Avenue.
Milk delivery will be from 6:30 a.m. to 7:00 p.m.
November 12—Land for Rolph Road School is purchased for $25,000.00.

SELECTED MINUTES—1939

February 21—Durant Frontenac Motors will be vacating their building and request a business tax rebate.
March 22—The Leaside Lions Club is given permission to hold a carnival in the park.
May 1—A letter is sent to the Village of Swansea to state no interest in annexation.
August 25—Residents complain about noisy teeter-totters at schools and want them moved to a park. Council refuses.

SELECTED MINUTES—1940

June 3—$50,000.00 is set aside to build an 8-room addition to Rolph Road School.
August 2—Municipal laws are changed to enable overseas soldiers to vote.
September 3—A private request is made to Council to eliminate "foreigners" from Leaside.

SELECTED MINUTES—1941

April 2—Dr. Fleming tests Bessborough and Rolph Road students for tuberculosis. Thirty-five students test positive.
May 19—Ratepayers are angry about a beverage room (Brewers Retail) inside Loblaws on Bayview.
July 7—Building bylaws are introduced for air raid shelters.

September 2—The oil controller for Leaside hopes to conserve fuel by cutting back on service station hours.

Council decides to pay a wartime bonus to each town employee. It will be 5% for each $25.00 they earn.

Selected Minutes—1942

Population is 9,000. 600-700 homes built. One-half of Leaside's work force live outside Leaside.

January 12—Howard Talbot is Mayor.

June—Council asks the School Board to use the Bessborough auditorium to hold Council meetings [they had used Bessborough School basement].

First Leaside Library opens in storefront at 645 Bayview (now 1645).

November 23—Public School Board is given $14,000.00 to purchase a school site somewhere north of Eglinton Avenue.

Selected Minutes—1943

January 11—Hockey will no longer be allowed in the park [now Trace Manes] on Sundays between 1:00 p.m. and 6:00 p.m.

February 3—Residents of Leaside will have restrictions placed on the purchase of certain goods. Ration books will be issued at Bessborough Drive School.

March 1—Leaside Public Library Association is formed and asks for support ($1.00 per family).

Clothing is collected as part of Canada's "Aid to Russia."

Amalgamation threatens—they support East York's fight against it.

May 12—The 24th of May will be a legal holiday.

July 12—$70,000.00 is needed by School Board to build school north of Eglinton.

Selected Minutes—1944

January 10—There is a need for a "Public Swimming Pool" and a committee is set up.

March 30—Teachers are requested to check their pupils' dental charts to ensure that they have had dental check-ups.

May 13—The School Board secretaries will handle the Wartime Savings Stamps.

July 21—Plans are made to welcome the return of Leaside's Canadian Armed Forces.

Dr. V. E. Henry is to be appointed as a school medical officer. His pay will be $0.25 per pupil.

October 2—A number of street names were changed at this time: Donald to Donlea, Brentwood to Brentcliffe, Clowes to Sharron, Alberton to Tanager.

December 5—A Leaside Memorial Committee is to be created. They are to setup a centre in the Millwood Road Park.

December 11—Various companies are laying off employees. One thousand Research Enterprises workers live in Leaside and 600 are being laid off.

SELECTED MINUTES—1945

January 8—At Mayor Talbot's inaugural address he made it a goal to place a light at every pole on one side of every street at a cost of $8.00 per pole. Flags will be needed for VE Day.

July 5—A request from the Jehovah Witnesses to use the Leaside Park for bible education instruction is refused by Council.

September 4—The Federal Government should be approached on their intentions to dispose of the government-owned munitions plants. New companies are looking for locations in Leaside.

September 17—The Railway will be contacted to stop using their whistles at night to eliminate unnecessary noise.

October 23—$580,000.00 is set aside for a new high school.

December 5—The Leaside Memorial Library will received $100,000.00. The use of Talbot Road as a street name is rejected.

SELECTED MINUTES—1946

January 7—Council opposes the erection of a hotel in Leaside.

January 28—St. Anselm's Church can proceed with bingo games after the clerks received rulings re bingo from the Crown Attorney.

February 4—Hockey sticks are banned from use on the pleasure rink. A banquet is to be held for the returning servicemen.

March 20—Council wants the paper carriers to pick up their newspapers from one spot only.

April 29—Cat owners are to put bells on their cats for the months of May, June and July.

September 9—The annexation of part of East York east of Bayview and south of Moore will be too expensive.

November 21—The south end of the park at Moore and Bayview will be called Bruce Park (after Sandy Bruce, Police Officer).

The VE Day Parade, standing in the middle of Fleming Crescent in 1945. The children identified are: girl with head turned to left of V, Patricia Reed; to the right side, Marion Conroy in front; Ted McGovern next; 5th girl, Carol McGovern. *Collection of Pat (Reed) Osborne.*

November 27—East York and Leaside suggest forming a "Public Health Unit."

SELECTED MINUTES—1947

April 7—Another street name change: Laird Drive South becomes Southvale.

The hydro station at Parkhurst and Sutherland will be disguised by making it look like a house.

Newly formed Leaside Board of Education, uniting the public elementary and high school boards in 1945. Back row, left to right: Rev. P. Morland Lamb; J. J. Knights; D. G. Brown; Percy G. Turner; Ernie Frey. Front Row: Mrs. H. V. Shaw; Miss M. E. Livingston (Peg Holloway) (Secretary-treasurer); P. A. McClelland (Chair); Mrs. N. F. Jones. *From the* Toronto Evening Telegram *June 24, 1945. Courtesy Peg Holloway.*

May 20—Leaside's new municipal office will cost $124,775.00.

August 11—Coca Cola offers to erect a baseball scoreboard in Howard Talbot Park.

November 3—The need to form a Don Valley Watershed Authority is seen at this time.

November 22—H. Talbot will resign as Mayor and T. Manes will become Mayor by acclamation for 1948.

SELECTED MINUTES—1948

February 2—J. H. Gundy donates the sloping portion of his land to use as a park.

March 8—An application is received by Rev. Bracken to open an Anglican Church on Bayview.

April 16—Objections are being raised by Leaside ratepayers to having a bus service running through North Leaside. A business section is being planned for the area at Eglinton and Bayview.

June 7—The Don River on the Gundy property is found unsafe for bathers and this should be posted.

July 6—The library can be built in the park for under $75,000.00.
October 4—The Bayview Theatre cannot show movies at midnight prior
  to a holiday.
November 13—An additional two tennis courts are proposed to go into
  Millwood Park. Hydro shortages are occurring in Leaside.
December 13—School children are asked to write essays on "How to
  Conserve Hydro Power." Two bikes valued at $100.00 will be given
  as first prize.

SELECTED MINUTES—1949

January 26—Leaside has had two small newspapers for several years:
  The Leaside Advertiser and *The Leaside Mail*.
March 12—The Leaside Home and School and the Rolph Road School
  associations request that council stamp out the sale of crime comics
  and other obnoxious publications.
June 16—The Memorial Centre has become an issue with Leasiders.
  The people have donated their money for a recreation centre and not
  simply an addition of a school wing. Council agrees.
November 25—A list is needed of all those who enlisted in the armed
  forces while residents in Leaside. A memorial plaque will be put in
  the library honouring those who died.
December 5—Again the idea of amalgamation will be fought by the
  Mayor but maybe certain services could be unified.
December 19—$175,000.00 should be set aside for an addition to Bess-
  borough School. It will consist of seven classrooms and one kindergarten. At the present time four classes at Rolph Road School are
  occupied by Bessborough students.

SELECTED MINUTES—1950

By 1950, Mayor H. H. Talbot and Reeve Trace Manes declared that the
  population had hit the 11,000 mark. They suggested a "sold out" sign
  should be hung on the Town of Leaside sign.
January 7—Amalgamation is seen as a problem to fight against for the
  year 1950.
June 12—Each member of council will be given a magazine produced
  by the high school. Principal Norman McLeod and editor Dennis
  Wiley will present the publication called *Clan Call*.
October 3—TTC fares should be four for $0.25. This was East York's
  view.

December 17—From the Civil Defence Committee: The Committee asks Council to set aside $400.00 in the 1951 budget to purchase 5,000 copies of "Survival Under Atomic Attack."

SELECTED MINUTES—1951

January 22—Council was asked to advise "Leaside United Church" that everything has been done to try to stop the establishment of a Liquor Store on Eglinton Avenue.
Council will endorse a 15 mph speed limit in school zones.
The proposal for tree planting in North Leaside has come from the North Leaside Property Association.
April 17—Sunnybrook Nurseries will build a bowling green in Howard Talbot Park for $5,497.00.
June 18—The Don Valley Conservation Association wants support for the "Gundy Property" becoming a park.
A shuffleboard court is to be built in Millwood Park at a cost of $375.00.

SELECTED MINUTES—1952

March 3—Part of Bruce Park will be sold to Mr. Slightham for $125.00 per foot for 93 feet along Bayview Avenue. The money received will be used to fix up the Park.
May 5—The Leaside Lions Club donated a $6,000.00 Hammond organ to the Board of Management of Leaside Memorial Community Gardens.
June 23—Last race is run at Thorncliffe Track.
November 17—A ten-room addition will be needed for the high school.

SELECTED MINUTES—1953

February 16—Leaside favours lifting rent controls but it should be done at the provincial level.
June 10—A petition is received against the building of a hotel at Laird and Kenrae. Council says that it no longer has the power to prevent a hotel, cocktail lounge or similar establishment. These matters are up to the Liquor Licence Board.
August 4—There is a complaint that too many taxis are in our area from outside of Leaside. The Police Committee says that it is discrimination if they try to prevent it.

September 14—One hundred and four acres of the Don Valley within the town, from the bottom land to the top banks, should be for agricultural purposes.

SELECTED MINUTES—1954

February 1—The Leaside Board of Education is asked to make provisions for a school site on the Thorncliffe Racetrack property.

March 15—The addition of fluoride to our drinking water has been approved by the health unit.

April 5—A Leaside Planning Board is formed and seven members are appointed. Any further building in Talbot Park will be stopped.

SELECTED MINUTES—1955

March 7—Leaside will oppose the unification of police departments. A special committee will be set up to create the opposition.

May 26—Leaside is to annex the Thorncliffe property. Approximately 387 acres make up Thorncliffe.

September 19—Parking meters are to be installed on Bayview and will charge $0.10 per hour.

Our council should be increased from four to six councillors.

Leaside is now to oppose fluoride in drinking water and support Forest Hill against Metro Toronto.

October 31—Any bowling in Leaside on Sunday is denied.

December 19—Thorncliffe Park Ltd. can start to build in 1956.

SELECTED MINUTES—1956

Sometime in 1956 Councillor Vern Page started a traffic safety campaign for children. It featured "Elmer the Safety Elephant."   •

January 3—Mayor Hiscott, at his inaugural address, says that the "Thorncliffe Development" will be the largest of its kind.

January 23—No overhead wires are to be part of the Thorncliffe development.

March 19—The Sunnybrook Shopping Centre is in.

June 5—The Library is asking for more space. The adult library is central and the children's library is in Northlea School.

SELECTED MINUTES—1957

Leaside population for 1957 is 16,568.

November 11—Council gave permission for a swimming pool at a cost of $130,000.00.

SELECTED MINUTES—1958

January 20—The land at the northwest corner of Leslie and Wicksteed is approved for the manufacture and storage of potash soap.

February 24—Those on direct relief in Leaside are to work on the park cleanup programme.

Water rates for Leaside to increase from $0.28 to $0.33 per 100 gallons. This is up by $0.05.

March 3—The new bridge over the Don River in Thorncliffe will be called the "Charles H. Hiscott Bridge" after the Mayor.

March 17—A request for the building of a 47-suite apartment at 990 Eglinton Avenue East gets it first reading.

April 8—The Brochure Committee will publish 10,000 copies of *The Leaside Story*. 5,800 copies to go free to every dwelling, commercial and industrial establishment.

April 21—Four-way stop signs are to be considered for Leaside intersections. Overlea Drive at Thorncliffe needs to be paved and sewers put in.

The Eglinton Extension being built over the Don River. The photograph is taken from North Leaside, looking south. Once completed and opened in 1957, Eglinton Avenue connected Leslie and Brentcliffe. *Courtesy Bernadine Carroll.*

May 12—A meeting with the Ontario Society for Crippled Children is held regarding their forthcoming building. CNIB has objected to using their road to gain access to the Society's facility.

July 14—Canada Wire wishes to build a 100 ft. tower at 147 Laird Drive. Leaside Baseball Association has created a Town of Leaside trophy (donated by Stanley Schatz, Q.C.) to be awarded at the Leaside Bantam Championships.

July 28—The Dept. of Travel and Publicity will unveil an historic plaque to commemorate Canada's First Domestic Airmail Flight on September 2nd at 2:30 p.m.

October 6—Thorncliffe has a problem in raising money from mortgage companies for the development.

November 3—Mayor recommends that the town offers to buy the Gundy Estate for $45,000.00.

November 18—A model of the gate to Thorncliffe is shown to the Work Committee showing a plaque and wrought-iron fences.

SELECTED MINUTES—1959

February 18—Council reviews the possibility of creating a parking lot on Donegall Drive on properties 62 to 76. The lot could hold 256 cars and cost $375,000.00.

March 5—Residents of Rumsey Road are complaining about the Carnival in the Park and nine items are listed: e.g. bright lights, traffic, garbage, people trespassing, teenagers being there all night and causing problems. They want it relocated.

April 20—Pollution concerns from the industrial area are discussed.

June 1—The Police Station of Division #26 in Leaside will now relocate in East York on June 1st. We want, in writing, that Leaside will still have proper protection.

June 15—35 children now live in Thorncliffe and a playground with a sand box, swing set and benches should be set up.

Council prepares for the Queen's visit; Eglinton Avenue to have a "Welcome" sign, and could the Queen and Prince sign a guest book.

July 16—A meeting held at the King Edward Hotel discussed the closing of Pottery Road at Moore. Leaside is trying to cut down on traffic. The Bayview Extension will soon be opened—August 14th is scheduled.

A request to use the Post Office (Perrem and Knight Store) for the sale and manufacture of fibreglass boats is turned down by Council.

September 21—Council receives traffic complaints from residents on McRae Drive. Eglinton is now open and motorists use McRae to reach it. This creates a fast and heavy flow of traffic.

It is recommended that the licencing of bicycles be discontinued.

October 13—The Works Committee points out that landfill sites are a problem and they need some options for new locations.

October 26—Special meeting was held between Council, CNIB and Crippled Children. It is felt that the opening of Rumsey Road is best and more practical access to the new facility.

November 2—Mercedes Benz informed Council of their intent to locate in Leaside.

November 21—The potential dump site at Eglinton and the Don River is now planned for a park.

SELECTED MINUTES—1960

January 4—Children should be allowed to play in school play areas as long as there is no vandalism during off hours. Could evening and weekend supervision be provided?

The Traffic Committee recommends that Leaside buy six properties north of Millwood and six properties north of Fleming for off-street parking areas.

May 4—Thorncliffe is now out a lot of money but the Mayor agrees to review the case at a later date.

June 6—A request for a Thorncliffe Public School is tabled.

June 20—The ratepayers want Council to prevent the building of an apartment on Bessborough Drive. Many of them were approached by a builder to sell their property and Council has sent the builder's request to the Planning Board.

The Post Office grounds at Station R at Laird and Malcolm Road are untidy. Frank McGee, the Postmaster General, is to be informed.

July 4—There was a meeting of Council and the Leaside School Board to discuss the new proposed Thorncliffe School. The school is to have nine classes and one kindergarten at a cost of $327,750.00.

July 21—Metro has requested a name for the Bayview Extension so Council called it the "Bayview Parkway."

The Kiwanis Club wants to put a playground into Howard Talbot Park at cost of $10,500.00 minus $1,500.00 to be underwritten by the Kiwanis for the year 1960. Council will lend them $9,000.00 to be paid back over the next nine years.

SELECTED MINUTES—1961

From Finance and Personnel Committee: Four rooms are to be added
to the west side of the present high school. The cost will be
$118,000.00. A new boiler will bring costs to $150,000.00

Parks Committee: Serena Gundy Estate is developing into a Park and
toilet facilities are to be installed.

A running track is proposed for the High School and gets approval.

The Lions Club will give a Memorial Gate to Trace Manes Park.

Metropolitan Toronto Conservation Authority requests five parcels of
land to form a green belt. Leaside was hoping to use the Eglinton and
Leslie site for landfill [garbage dump].

SELECTED MINUTES—1962

February 5—*Leaside Advertiser* Editor, A. E. Donahue, suggests that
Leaside purchase equipment to shovel snow. Cost would be added to
our taxes

Zoo near Thorncliffe: Mr. T. Thompson of the Metro Parks Commission has made a request to create a Zoological Garden. The Zoo
would be north of the Hiscott Bridge and access would be from Don
Mills Road. Council asks for more information and the Town's engineer is objecting because part of the site is the town's garbage dump.

February 19—Fluoridation questions to be with the voting ballot on
election day -December 3, 1962.

March 19—Leaside Lions Carnival in Trace Manes Park—This will be their
last year in 1962. In 1963 they will run a Bingo at Leaside Memorial
Gardens.

April 2—Committee to Oppose Amalgamation will be set up with ten
members assigned.

Canada's Centennial Year is 1967. Leaside will join with Toronto in
some sort of project of permanent and lasting value.

Amalgamation—Council will be sending an official letter opposing
amalgamation to the Minister of Municipal Affairs.

May 7—Leaside Lions Minor Bantam Team are winners of the East York
Hockey League Championship.

May 22—Mr. F. Esiner advises Council that the Four Seasons Motor
Hotel is being erected at Leslie Street and Eglinton Avenue.

June 14—The Bayview Business Men's Association is still working on
creating a parking area for customers. They want the homes on Donegall bought and then the backyards could be made smaller. The new

area would be used for parking space. Council's decision is quick and the proposal is turned down because of the devaluing of property in the area.

September 17—Bayview Theatre: Rev. J. McAlister requests the Bayview Theatre for church purposes. Council takes no action.

November 5—The City of Toronto has made application for legislation effecting the amalgamation of the 13 Area Municipalities of Metropolitan Toronto.

December 3—Starting in January 1963 Beth Nealson will be our new Mayor. 51.38% voted in the election.

Selected Minutes—1963

February 18—The Metro Planning Board has submitted a report to extend Leslie Street to Wicksteed. The sale of land, south of Wicksteed, should be looked into for this purpose.

February 23—The Theatre of Bayview has been opened on Sundays and now Bowlerama in Thorncliffe Park. A letter will be sent informing them of the violation of the Lord's Day Act.

March 4—Metro Toronto advises that Laird Drive is to be widened to four lanes from Eglinton to Millwood Road in 1963 for $145,000.00. Leaside will share the cost of the project.

May 6—The Leaside Property Owners Association was given permission to hold their Annual Fireworks Display at Howard Talbot Park.

May 21—The Parks Department request an addition to the field house in Trace Manes Park.

The Leaside Lions were given permission to hold a "Bingo" at Leaside Memorial Gardens on June 19, 1963.

June 3—Mr. Richard V. Burgess has been Leaside's Clerk/Treasurer from 1929 to 1962. The park in Thorncliffe will be named in his honour.

June 17—Leaside Library advised the Library Board that they will be setting up a permanent collection of local history.

July 11—Leaside Memorial Gardens are to pay their profit to Leaside at the end of each calendar year.

The road allowance of Leslie Street through Leaside known as the "Don River Boulevard" is now parkland and should be transferred to the Municipality of Metropolitan Toronto Parks Department.

The symbol for our Golden Anniversary will appear at the Town Office and Town buildings and a Memorial Plaque placed on the wall of Leaside Memorial Gardens. Leaside industry will contribute to Anniversary costs.

August 1—Leslie Street could be extended to Wicksteed Avenue but not further. Metals and Alloys would like to buy the extension. Council decides to close it.

September 3—Council chambers are overflowing as Leaside residents confront Council. A 14-storey apartment is proposed for Bayview Avenue and Craig Crescent. Five hundred people have signed a petition against it.

September 16—A letter will be sent to the Goldenberg Royal Commission advising that Leaside will be sending a brief opposing amalgamation.

October 30—The Amalgamation Committee is preparing a brief against amalgamation and will integrate information from the other Town Boards into the report being made for Council.

Information at this time is confidential and council approves the hiring of a Research Assistant.

The brief should oppose amalgamation but also contain a constructive proposal to preserve the present form of Metropolitan government.

November 4—The CIBC opened its first bank in 1918 and the second in 1937. They have been the Town's bank for over 35 years. They gave direct assistance to the Town in the 1930s. They are close to the Municipal Offices and have 1,280 branches world-wide. Of the 5,600 employees, 500 live in Leaside.

Council will further discuss the decision to switch to the Toronto Dominion Bank.

November 18—The field house in Trace Manes can be constructed.

December 2—The Leaside Lawn Bowling Association reports their most successful year. A cheque for $2,300.00 is presented to Council.

December 16—Fire Department: 194 Randolph Road to be expropriated at a price of $16,700.00 for the site of new fire hall.

SELECTED MINUTES—1964

April 6—The Town Solicitor is to prepare a bylaw for merchants to display their goods 18 inches from the street line and 24 inches above the ground.

April 20—Bylaw 1950 will prohibit the sounding of train whistles at the Wicksteed crossing.

The Leaside Property Owners Association can stage the fireworks display at Howard Talbot Park on May 18th. Victoria Day will now be referred to as Commonwealth Day.

May—The new proposed road to connect Wicksteed to Thorncliffe should be surveyed.

June 8—Prudential Insurance of America wish to construct a 10- to 12-storey building at the Garden Court Apartments. The Leaside Property Owners Association will be advised along with a copy of zoning bylaw 1916.

June 25—The Donwood Foundation at 15 Horsham Avenue in Willowdale requests water and access to its new property via Brentcliffe Road. A 50-bed hospital is to be built with funds acquired from the Government of Canada. A non-profit organization, it was established in 1959 by private citizens to supply treatment, research and education in the field of alcohol, drug, tobacco and food problems.

June 29—Vehicles going south on the Don Valley Parkway cannot exit to Thorncliffe Park. The Thorncliffe Market Place merchants have requested an exit for north-bound traffic.

Metro Parks Department has given the name of Ernest Thompson Seton Park to the new park in the Don Valley.

August 17—Thorncliffe continues to grow with the paving of William Morgan Drive and an unnamed street north of Overlea.

Mr. Raymond of Central Park Lodge wishes to build a Nursing Home in Thorncliffe Park. Mr. Stieneger is in charge of their operation across Canada.

November 2—An exit from the Don Valley to Don Mills Road has been approved by Metro.

November 16—The Leaside Planning Board allowed Goldlist to increase apartment heights in Thorncliffe from 20 to 24 storeys.

November 26—Two new apartments are to be built in Thorncliffe by Goldlist.

SELECTED MINUTES—1965

January 4—From Mayor Beth Nealson's Address: "The years of 1965 and 1966 will be the most crucial time in the history of our municipality. It would be foolish to think that such a change will not occur. The Province very much controls the municipalities.

The institution of a metropolitan form of government for the Toronto Area is needed. Leaside does provide good service but this is not true of the Metropolitan area as a whole.

There is a need for change. Financial adjustment among the 13 municipalities is needed but this is a Provincial decision."

January 18—The Board of Education requests an addition for the Thorncliffe Public School. 215 are enrolled but 385 are anticipated with the development of high-rise apartments.

The Parks Committee recommends that no action be taken on the development of toboggan and ski runs in the park.

March 1—The Metropolitan Separate School Board wishes to expropriate 178 and 180 Bessborough Drive for a parking lot for St. Anselm's Church.

Tennis was added to the list of games permitted on Sundays.

May 17—After several complaints about dogs, the Parks Committee recommended that Council pass a law to prohibit dogs in all parks in Leaside.

June 7—The Masonic Temple and the Pentecostal Head Office Buildings ask for space in Thorncliffe.

June 21—The Safety Council recommended the licensing of motor scooters.

June 24—Canada Wire has requested the removal of three buildings in order to erect a 22,000 sq.ft. addition. This will create a two million sq.ft. facility under one roof.

Miss True Davidson, Reeve of East York, sent correspondence relating to the Goldenberg Report. A public meeting is to be set up on September 17th to inform residents of this report and its effect on Leaside. Council will officially oppose the four city plan.

September 7—The Town has bought a piece of land on Bessborough which will become part of Howard Talbot Park (small parkette).

September 9—Mr. Hollis Beckett, MPP for East York, was opposed to amalgamation and the four city plan. He also favoured the six city plan where Leaside would be a Ward in the East Toronto Borough with a representative on council.

October 4—The new city hall is opened and the City of Toronto acknowledges our telegram of congratulations.

A drop-in centre for the elderly is proposed by the Rotary Club. It could be added to the Centennial Project at Trace Manes Park and $25,000.00 will be provided.

October 25—The Committee of the Whole recommended to Council that $1,500.00 be spent on a float to be entered in the Grey Cup Parade.

November 1—Final plans for the Centennial project are shown. The Senior Citizens Drop-in Centre is included. The banners of Leaside will be green and gold and are to be ready for November 19th.

November 15—A turkey is to be bought for each town employee as a Christmas gift.

December 20—East York advises Leaside of their intention to re-zone an area of Bayview south of Moore to Mallory Crescent for a high-rise. Council objects.

SELECTED MINUTES—1966

Beth Nealson is Mayor.

January 16—Leaside and East York Boards of Education are to meet for informal discussions.

January 22—Council wants their employees in the best possible position for amalgamation. Leaside's department heads should learn East York's operations.

Leaside to meet with East York at their council chambers on January 27, 1966. The meeting will be open to the public.

January 24—The Leaside Property Owners Association advised East York that they will create an enlarged unit to help resolve problems.

February 21—Mr. Anderson and the Leaside Property Association presented a 200-resident petition against an apartment bounded by Moore and Mallory Crescent. Traffic, sunlight and privacy are cited as problems. Council asks the Planning Board to back the residents against it. East York should be advised.

May 16—Leaside and East York are to write up points to be included in the application for amalgamation to the Ontario Municipal Board. The four main points are: (1) Political Set-up, (2) Hydro, (3) Integration of Staffs, and (4) Appointed Boards and Committees.

May 30—A ward system has been proposed for the new municipality and it is growing in favour. The Board of Education will recommend it.

June 6—A name of the new Thorncliffe Park is recommended to be "Leaside Park." The name of the new road to the park is to be "Leaside Park Drive."

June 13—Amalgamation to bring more changes and the next election is in November. Voter lists are to be prepared for Leaside and East York.

July 28—The notice that the Amalgamation of East York and Leaside will be applied for at the Ontario Municipal Board is to be published in *The Globe and Mail, Telegram* and *Toronto Star.*

September 19—Received was a request to re-zone Blocks D and J to permit the erection of two 44-storey apartments to be known as the "Leaside Towers."

October 17—With amalgamation approaching, many projects are removed from the Leaside agenda.

November 14—The emblems drawn up for the Centennial Year will now read Leaside-East York and not East York-Leaside.

The Committee of the Whole requests that E. H. Bell, Leaside's Fire Chief becomes the Fire Chief for East York when their chief retires.

November 15—An all-candidates meeting for the new Borough of East York will be held at the Council Chambers at Coxwell and Mortimer Avenues on November 21, 1966.

The building of Leaside Towers is endorsed by East York, North York and Metro. The builder will be Goldlist Properties.

December 12—Application to build a hotel at 927–955 Millwood at Southvale is fought by residents. Council finds the area not suitable.

The new road connecting Wicksteed and Thorncliffe should be named Beth Nealson Drive after our Mayor. This is recommended by the Recognition Committee.

December 21—A meeting of Council was held on Wednesday, December 21, 1966 at 8:00 in the auditorium of Leaside Memorial Gardens in order to give the Mayor and Councillors an opportunity to present Recognition Certificates to those who served Leaside.

The clerk read the names of the recipients of the Recognition Certificates. The Mayor: Beth Nealson; Reeve: V. Page; Deputy Reeve: G. S. Flagler; Councillors: R. Perringer, G. Bird, K. Stainton and D. Jagger all presented awards to the various boards and committees.

The clerk asked C. Hiscott, Treasurer to present gold cufflinks and tie pins to the male members of Council and a gold brooch showing the Leaside crest to Mayor Beth Nealson.

Certificates were given to: the Mayor, six council members, four staff, six planning board members, four from Committee of Adjustment, two members from Board of Health, nine members of the Board of Education, thirty members of the Safety Council, five members of the Memorial Gardens Board of Management, eight members of the Library Board and ten members of the Recreation Committee.

The nine members of the Centennial Committee, one member of the press and six employees with more than 25 years service.

Note: All committee reports are filed in back of 1966 Book.

December 22—New Appointments are made for six departments and Leaside Members took positions on East York Council being Jagger and Page.

December 28—The Leaside Fire Department will be the dispatch centre for East York and their phone number will be used.

A notice went to all permanent employees of Leaside and East York as follows:

(1) January 1, 1967—all employees will be transferred to the new Borough in their present classification at their existing salaries or wage.

(2) Employees should report to their usual place and their same supervisor.

(3) No changes in duties and responsibility until the integration of staff of the two municipalities has been completed under Council direction.

(17) Leasiders' present office will continue to operate until March 1, 1967.

(18) Any changes of employees will be done by the department heads.

(19) Leaside Fire Department is now the dispatch centre.

(21) The Toronto Dominion Bank will continue the banking affairs for the new borough.

SELECTED MINUTES—1967

January 23—East York begins to look for more space to create a larger Borough Office.

East York would form a Centennial Committee for the visit of the Centennial Train at the Leaside Station. $10,000.00 would be needed to prepare and arrange the site.

February 20—The clerical staff was assigned from Leaside.

Leaside Municipal Building at the corner of Randolph and McRae. 1967. *Leaside Camera Club, courtesy Herb Horwood.*

The Building Inspector from Leaside was assigned to the Fire Prevention Bureau.

March 1—The Leaside staff are integrated into the East York system and one current employee from 1998 reported that hard feelings were created when employees were losing jobs due to union rules and seniority. Recreation Committee to take on Dorothy Ward of Leaside to the Department of Parks and Recreation.

19

RALLYING TO THE CAUSE: ISSUES TO BE RESOLVED

NO HISTORY of a community would be complete without recognition of those issues that arise from time to time. Such events, while rousing the spirit, and sometimes the ire, of local residents, often serve to strengthen the fabric of a community. Fortunately for Leaside, Alan Redway, in writing a column for a local newspaper, the *Leaside Advertiser*, has provided a record of the community's response to some compelling events.

THE "WHITE ELEPHANT" ON THE BAYVIEW EXTENSION

The partially completed apartment building which stood for many years on the west side of Bayview, south of Nesbitt Drive was known locally as the "White Elephant." In 1953, the Hampton Park Company had acquired 28 acres in this area before the Bayview Extension was built. In 1957, Metropolitan Toronto expropriated eleven of these acres.

The Governor's Bridge Ratepayers Association appeared before East York's Council in 1959, and had a bylaw passed to prohibit the clearing of land larger than one acre. However, the developer had outwitted them by dividing the property into several parcels, each less than one acre.

On the 2nd of October 1959, the developer then applied for two 105-suite apartment buildings. This was approved by Council without water or sewage service and, two days later, the developer began work, even working through the evening by floodlight. In an interesting turn of events, Council passed a resolution October 19 to prohibit the construction of sewers on the property and revoked the building permit on November 9th. The construction stopped, but, by that time, the developer had roofed over the walls and floors of the unfinished seven-storey building. The whole issue went into litigation. The courts had great difficulty deciding on the legality of the building since neither the Council nor the developer could agree on the facts.

Metro Parks were approached but refused to acquire the property. Another proposal led to a brief consideration of the possibility of turning the unfinished buildings into a home for senior citizens. The Hampton Park Company, however, asked for three high rise apartments to be developed on the site. In response, the Borough of East York attempted to reclaim the property based on upaid taxes. But this, too, failed to settle the issue; a tax payment arrived!

Another proposal put forward by the Province was for construction of a 1200 unit condominium building. This project would have included two tennis courts and an indoor pool and health club. Nothing came of this.

After many years, the structure, long an eyesore in the community, was torn down. At the present time, sixty single-family luxury homes are being built on the site.

THE DEVELOPMENT BATTLE OF MALLORY CRESCENT

This milestone in the history of community action should never be forgotten! It occured in 1966, just prior to amalgamation with East York, scheduled for the following year.

The Cadillac Development Corporation Ltd. and Belmont Construction Ltd. applied to rezone ten half acres, south of Moore Avenue and east of Bayview, on both sides of Mallory Crescent. The new zoning was to permit high-rise apartments. The developers proposed building three 22-storey and two 29-storey apartments on the site, for a total of 1384 suites in an area no larger than 500 square feet. The population density increase would have been 25-fold. To accommodate their proposal, the developers wanted to demolish 50 bungalows and storey-and-a-half homes.

At the time, Mallory Crescent was apart of the Township of East York, but situated on the border with the Town of Leaside.

The battle began in November 1965 when the proposal first came to the East York Planning Board. In December, it was approved by East York, but the Leaside Council pased a resolution opposing it. This act, however, did not stop East York Council from approving the rezoning in February, 1966.

The residents within 400 feet of the proposed development were sent notices. Immediately, they organized the Leaside-Bennington Heights Association, to fight the project. In early March, while the residents collected petitions and letters, the Reeve of East York True Davidson, sent out a letter explaining the benefits of such a development. As a result, the scheme won the approval of the Metro Planning Board. Hundreds of letters in opposition were sent to East York.

On March 30, a public meeting was held at East York Collegiate. Seven hundred homeowners were in attendance, packing the auditorium. A stormy meeting ensued, but nothing was accomplished. By this time, the residents had retained the services of Robert W. Macauley, Q.C. to represent them.

On May 10, the Leaside-Bennington Heights Association met with four hundred people in attendance. By now, they were also supported in their efforts by the Leaside Property Owners Association (LPOA).

The OMB hearing held in June lasted ten days. Mr. Macauley appeared on behalf of the LPOA, the Leaside-Bennington Heights Association, one ratepayer from Leaside (Donald Anderson) and one ratepayer from East York (Eric Moore).

After the lengthy hearing, the Board ruled in favour of the residents. The rezoning application was dismissed and legal costs were awarded against the Township and the developers. Upset at the results, the East York Council and the developers appealed the decision. It would not be until February 1967 that the Mallory Crescent development came to a final end when the cabinet formally rejected the appeal, one month after the amalgamation of Leaside and East York.

The Leaside community has retained its quality residential character because the homeowners like the Leaside-Bennington Heights Association were prepared to give of their time and money to keep it that way. The present residents of Leaside owe them a tremendous debt of gratitude!

AMALGAMATION OF LEASIDE TO EAST YORK

While amalgamation with East York was not embraced by all residents, it was considered to be a more favoured position than the proposed merger with Toronto. There were, however, many transitions requiring thoughtful solutions. East York's mill rate for Township purposes (excluding levies for school boards and Metro) at that time was 19.65. Leaside had enjoyed a lower mill rate (10.32) and hence lower taxes because of its high tax base from the industrial area. Leasiders were concerned about their taxes increasing with amalgamation.

The tax gap between the two municipalities, was something that could not be closed in one year; the adverse financial impact of the consolidation was to be spread over a four year period.

When True Davidson became Mayor, defeating Leaside's Beth Nealson at the polls, Leasiders' had many additional concerns to express.

What would Leaside become? Jack Christie (an East York resident and former Hydro Commissioner who served with True Davidson) revealed the following: True Davidson made an informal edict, although this never appeared in print, "that any building or organization with the name Leaside should remain as such and not be changed to East York." She wanted a friendly and satisfactory amalgamation. True also wrote a song at the time of amalgamation to the tune of "There'll Always be An England."

> "There will always be a Leaside
> With four-way traffic signs
> Where sport and scholarship and grit
> And youth and age combine."

Only one plaque was erected as a result of amalgamation with East York. It was a small ten-inch square plaque on the Parkhurst Transformer Station. This is now the site of a home at Sutherland Drive and Parkhurst Boulevard.

East York Hydro took over Leaside Hydro from Toronto at a cost of one million eight hundred thousand dollars. East York needed to borrow money to do this.

At the time of amalgamation, some of Leaside's historical records were destroyed. Fortunately, the Council meeting minutes can still be found in the Records Office of the East York Civic Centre.

THE LESLIE STREET EXTENSION

The engineering firm of Maksymec and Associates completed a detailed study of a proposed Leslie Street Extension in the early seventies. They recommended that Leslie Street be continued south of Eglinton Avenue over the Don Valley parkland into the Leaside industrial area. From there, it would run parallel with the railway tracks, then cross Millwood Road and cut along the Don Valley heights through Redway Road and the old Crothers site. Access to the Bayview Extension would be by means of a cloverleaf between Nesbitt Drive and Pottery Road.

The intention of this scheme was to alleviate the pressure of traffic by providing a route to downtown Toronto for the residents of Don Mills, eastern North York and Scarborough. It was believed that this would reduce the traffic infiltration through Leaside and Governor's Bridge. As well, it was to lighten the traffic on Southvale, Millwood, McRae Drive and Parkhurst Boulevard.

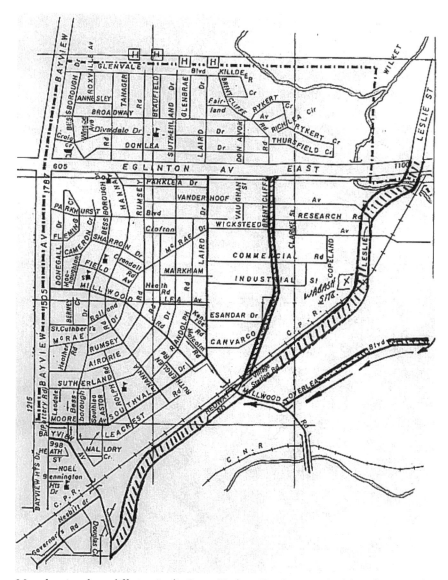

Map showing three differing Leslie Street/Redway Road proposals: (1) Redway Road extended to the Bayview Extension; (2) Brentcliffe Road extended through the industrial area to Redway Road and on to the Bayview Extension; (3) Leslie Street extended along the CPR tracks to Redway Road and on to the Bayview Extension. *Map redrawn, courtesy Jim Hannah.*

The proposal raised extensive concerns about destruction of parkland and detrimental impact on the already fragile ecology of the Don Valley. Many meetings and much press coverage ensued. The whole project, however, was abandoned at Metro Council in the 1980s due to the enormous cost—the last estimate being over 200 million dollars.

Altogether three plans have been proposed which are designed to draw traffic from Eglinton Avenue and divert it south around Leaside onto the Bayview Extension.

The intersection with Bayview below Nesbitt Drive would prevent traffic from flowing into the Governor's Bridge area.

1. Redway Road extended to the Bayview Extension, fed by traffic from Millwood, Overlea and Don Mills Road (least costly).
2. Brentcliffe Road extended through the industrial area to Redway Road (medium cost)
3. Leslie Street extended along the CPR tracks to Redway Road (most costly).[1]

Of these proposals, it would seem that only the Redway Road may have some potential. Currently, a study is being conducted to consider the viability of a "Redway Road" extension which would continue the Redway Road from Millwood over to Bayview Avenue. Included in this study is Brentcliffe. If the conclusions of the study indicate that the present Leaside traffic infiltration has a destination of downtown, then this project may have some value. Certainly, the reduced in scope project would be more economical and should result in substantially reducing traffic on Leaside's residential streets.

20

PROFILES OF PEOPLE AND BUILDINGS OF HISTORIC INTEREST

THE BUILT heritage of a community stands as a testimony to the past. Increasingly, historic homes and buildings are being recognized and preserved, and most importantly, becoming a valued part of the community. By honouring achievements of the past, the community builds pride in its present and confidence in its future. There are some people whose lives touch many and whose legacy is the foundation for that which follows.

ROBERT ELGIE—262 BESSBOROUGH DRIVE:

Although this house was believed to have been built in the early 1880s, the present owners, Sven and Mary Linholm, believe it was originally built in 1847. It was the home of Robert Elgie of the Elgie family who were part of the original settlers of this part of South Leaside. Thomas Elgie, Robert's father, came from England in 1841 and for several years managed a hotel in the Toronto area.

Later, Thomas Elgie purchased 200 acres in Leaside, including this lot. He cultivated this land until he died in 1880. It is believed that his son Robert built 262 Bessborough Drive. The property's original house stood on the present site of Leaside High School, where Wendell Lawson, the artist, lived.

The original home and property was left to Robert's mother, Elizabeth Beckwith Elgie.

One day, Mary Linholm noticed a large well on the property, one that they had almost fallen into. Apparently, there used to be a large vegetable garden behind the home.

After the Elgies, 262 Bessborough was owned by the Bell family. Ernie Bell, born in this home, became Leaside's Fire Chief. The hill sloping down to Talbot Park was known as Bell's Hill and skiing lessons were taught there. It still remains a favorite tobogganing hill.

The Elgie house, believed to be built in 1847, as it looked prior to additions. *Courtesy the Linholm family.*

Cooper purchased the property in the late 40s. In turn, in 1950, Mr. and Mrs. Syme bought the home. Mary Syme Linholm still owns the home with her husband Sven, who works in the construction business. Together, they significantly altered and enlarged the home, done so beautifully that it all looks "original."

In 1991, they severed the north part of the property and built another home which was sold to the present owners.

Mary Syme is an accomplished musician and writer. She is a world-renowned concert pianist and still writes a new Christmas pageant every year which is performed at their church, Leaside United.

Today, their home is often used for film productions and the gardens are magnificent with the circular driveway and fountain in the middle.[1]

JOHN E. LEA HOME—33 HEATHER ROAD

The home at 33 Heather Road was built in 1902 by John Edmund Lea, grandson of John Lea who settled the area in 1819. When John Lea Sr. passed away, he left his son John Jr., 110 acres of land. Later, John Jr. married Sarah Charles and had three children, Mary, James and John Edmund. While John Edmond never married, he did build his own brick house in 1902 on Lea's Lane, a street which no longer exists.

When the Town of Leaside was designed, little consideration was given to this home, one of the original dwellings in the area. The new organization of streets left the house with its front door facing its back yard. Aside from the home's disorientation from Heather Road, the building's exterior (except for the addition of a small room) remains basically unchanged.

The home is presently owned by the Le Brun family.[2]

PERREM AND KNIGHT—322 SUTHERLAND DRIVE:

Originally, this red brick building was built in 1929, the first store in Leaside on the southwest corner of Sutherland and McRae. Mrs. Perrem of Perrem and Knight had a general store, known for its long counter. As was the custom, she lived above the store. The store would also become Leaside's first post office. Everyone knew Mrs. Perrem and she knew them.

The first telephone in Leaside was in her store. When emergency calls came in for someone, she would leave the store and find the individual.

The building, now owned by the Miller family, is a photography studio called Ronald Miller Photography.

If you look carefully (from the side) at the glass window closest to McRae but facing Sutherland, you can still see the name "Perrem and Knight."

AGNES CAMPBELL MACPHAIL—2 DONEGALL DRIVE:

Agnes Campbell MacPhail, born on March 24, 1890, was an exceptional woman, breaking new ground for women in politics. The first woman member to be elected to the House of Commons (1921-1940), she represented the rural riding of South East Grey (later Grey-Bruce) for the United Farmers of Ontario. She was the first Canadian woman to be a delegate to the League of Nations (1929). Upon retiring from federal politics, she moved to East York and resumed her political life. Between the years of 1943–1945 and 1948–1951, she was one of the first two women to sit in the Ontario legislature, representing the riding of York East for the Co-operative Commonwealth Federation Party (CCF).

Born in a log cabin, near Hopeville, Grey County (located south of Owen Sound, Ontario), Agnes MacPhail was the eldest of three daughters. Her father, Dougal MacPhail, was first a farmer and then an auctioneer known for his ability at persuasion and wit. Her mother, Henrietta Campbell MacPhail was strong-willed and compassionate towards the pioneer spirit, especially in times of adversity.

Agnes' first exposure to politics was in the family living room where she would listen to farmers discussing agriculture and politics. It was here that her sympathy towards and understanding of the farmer first grew. This empathetic awareness would last throughout her life.

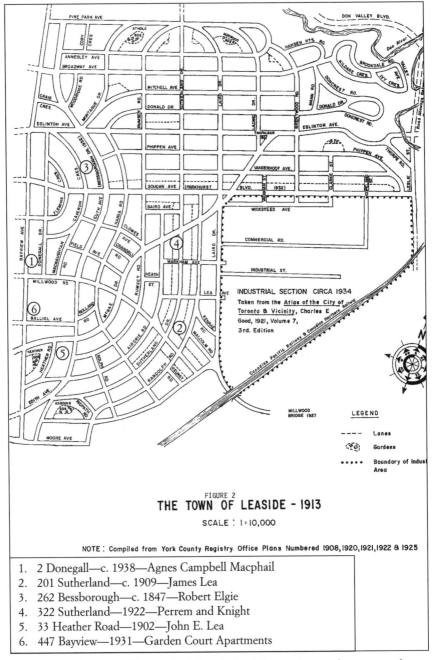

FIGURE 2
THE TOWN OF LEASIDE - 1913
SCALE : 1:10,000

NOTE : Compiled from York County Registry Office Plans Numbered 1908,1920,1921,1922 & 1925

1. 2 Donegall—c. 1938—Agnes Campbell Macphail
2. 201 Sutherland—c. 1909—James Lea
3. 262 Bessborough—c. 1847—Robert Elgie
4. 322 Sutherland—1922—Perrem and Knight
5. 33 Heather Road—1902—John E. Lea
6. 447 Bayview—1931—Garden Court Apartments

Map showing location of historic buildings in Leaside superimposed on a map of 1913, the original plan for Leaside. *Taken from* Atlas of the City of Toronto and Vicinity, *Charles E. Good, 1921, Vol.7, 3rd Ed.*

Agnes MacPhail started her career as a teacher in rural Ontario and Alberta. Surprisingly, she did not participate in the suffragette movement, although most certainly she would have been aware of their issues. In 1918, women were granted the right to vote in the federal election and in the provincial elections of the western provinces, Ontario and Nova Scotia.

In 1921, Agnes Campbell MacPhail became the first woman elected to the House of Commons. For the next fourteen years she was the *only* woman in parliament. Her first term in office was particularly difficult, as daily she had to face much hostility from the male members, as well as from reporters of both genders. It was during this period she changed her name to Macphail.

During her first term in office the party fell apart. The Liberals offered her a cabinet position, but she chose to run as an Independent. Throughout her career, Agnes Macphail remained a supporter of the United Farmers Co-operative movement. She fought for social reforms such as old-age pensions and pay equity for women. A pacifist, she spoke out against the glorification of war in school textbooks and compulsory military cadet training for boys in elementary and high school. Her strong support of the League of Nations, formed following WWI, earned her a seat as the first female delegate from Canada in 1929.

Her greatest achievement was prison reform. She protested against the filthy rat-infested jail conditions, the flogging and the use of untrained prison guards, and the neglect of the imprisoned insane.

In 1940, running federally for the fifth time, Agnes was defeated. She decided, in 1943, to turn to provincial politics, this time running as a CCF candidate for York East. She was defeated the following term but was elected again in 1948. Throughout those years, Agnes Macphail continued to fight for the cause of the underprivileged and to argue for the support of public education, old-age pensions, equal pay for equal work, universal health care and prison reform. During the latter years of her life, not in possession of much income, she lived on the upper floor of a duplex at 2 Donegall Drive in Leaside.

This duplex on the northwest corner of Donegall Drive and Millwood has been constructed with Yorkville brick. It was built in the late 1930s. Very few duplexes of this style were built at this time.

Agnes Macphail lived in the upper half for many years. Discussions are ongoing as to recognition being given to this building because of its prominence as her home in Leaside.

In 1954, without a pension and having been in poor health for some time, she suffered her third heart attack and passed away.[3] Agnes Campbell Macphail is honoured annually on March 24, her birthdate.

OTHER HISTORIC HOMES

Robert Cook House located on the east side of Bayview north of Eglinton. *From* The Story of Leaside *by John Scott.*

Residence of Major Hearne on the southwest corner of Bessborough and Craig Crescent. *Toronto Reference Library, J.V. Salmon Collection.*

Home of R.P. Ormsby from 1914 to 1923. Purchased from Major Hearne. The wind-mill and coachhouse are in the right background. The home was later known as the "Beatty House." *S. Walter Stewart Library, Elmore Gray Collection.*

The George Murray home on Bayview Avenue between Moore Avenue and Sutherland Drive. The photograph was taken on May 19, 1956. The house has been torn down and replaced by an apartment building. *Toronto Reference Library, J.V. Salmon Collection.*

201 Sutherland Drive was built circa 1909 for James Lea, son of John Lea Jr., grand-son of John Lea Sr. Top photograph taken in 1920. *Toronto Reference Library, J.V. Salmon Collection.* Bottom photograph taken in 1974. *S. Walter Stewart Library, Elmore Gray Library*

HISTORIC APARTMENTS

The Strathavon Apartments on Bayview Avenue at the northeast corner of Airdrie Road, July 1939. *Toronto Reference Library, J.V. Salmon Collection.*

The Leacrest Apartments located near Mallory Crescent, 1967. *Leaside Camera Club, Courtesy of Herb Horwood.*

GARDEN COURT

Garden Court was created and designed for Toronto people with means who had long desired a finer quality apartment, who would enjoy the added pleasure of the garden court setting and who would appreciate the attractive rental schedule. The property of five and a half acres with a frontage of 350 feet on Bayview Avenue, offered a prestigious setting.

The architects, Forsey Page and Steele came with outstanding reputation, built up over twenty-five years prior to this project. They had also designed the Whitehall Apartments, St. Clements Church, North Toronto Collegiate Institute, John Fisher School, Bedford Park School and Forest Hill Village School. The Jackson-Lewis Company Ltd., a very competent construction company, was the contractor. This company had also built the East Block Parliament Buildings, Queen's Park, the Imperial Theatre, the Coca-Cola Company building and the Automotive Building at the CNE, just to name a few. The owners, the Berney Realty Corporation, completed the team. They, too, had an excellent reputation of managing upscale apartments.

Built in 1931, Garden Court was in a class by itself because of its superb location. It had a beautiful garden plan and building layout and offered a modern and efficient floor plan. It also offered an attractive rent schedule. The suites ranged in price from $49.50 to $69.50 per

The Garden Court Apartments at 477 Bayview, built in 1931. *Leaside Camera Club, courtesy Herb Horwood.*

month. Some of the suites included wood-burning fireplaces. Separate private garages were offered at $3.00 per month.

The layout of the site and buildings embodied a revolutionary departure from conventional apartment house design. Less than twenty-three per cent of the available property is utilized by the sixteen buildings. There are large court areas which ensure plenty of light and air for each apartment. The large centre court, with its one and a half acres, provided a more formal lawn and garden. The adjacent courts are play areas. Plans included a tennis court (removed in 1995) and several winter recreation rooms with ping-pong tables.

Today, Garden Court is still considered a unique design and is studied in architecture. When originally completed, the design won much acclaim and was awarded the Massey medal. Any upgrades or changes must conform to certain qualifications to maintain the original style established by Forsey Page and Steele. Most of the residents have lived there for a considerable length of time and any vacancies are filled immediately, a testament to the quality of the building.[4]

21

MEMORIES OF LEASIDE

EASIDE HOLDS many memories for many people, each representing part of the past, embedded with all the hopes and dreams for the future. The following excerpts are taken from interviews, conversations and sometimes written copy. Each is a nugget of Leaside's past.

ISABEL ALLEN

About 1936, Gerry and I parked our car at the corner of Donegall and Fleming Crescent and looked at the house on the southeast corner. I said "Oh, that's such a happy little house." We rented it for two or three years and then bought it. The people before us had "gone in the night!" The house had been built in 1928. Donegall was one of the oldest and narrowest streets in Leaside.

The cellar was waist-high full of clinkers from the coal furnace. We couldn't fit them through the basement window so Gerry had to chop them up. It took us months to dispose of them!

Matthews Grocery Store (where Black's Camera is now) was too expensive for us to shop at. We would walk to a Chinese food store on Mt. Pleasant. My daughter played with a Chinese girl out front—" 'what was the matter with her,' she asked?" She had never seen a Chinese person before.

We would walk up Bayview (which was a dirt road) to the woods of Sunnybrook (where the plaza is) for lunch. Mrs. Allen Sr. from England loved to walk. A creek ran through Talbot Park and there were bulrushes, wildflowers and watercress—a great delicacy.

Parkhurst Boulevard which was known as Soudan Avenue was also unpaved. All along the north side were fruit trees, consisting of pear, apple and crabapple. These were wild so the fruit was small and not very juicy, but we would pick a few of them every year.

The house beside us on Fleming Crescent was being built in 1941. Every night Gerry and I and another couple would walk down to see what progress had been made. We would walk all around it inside. Harry Heidman was the builder.

One of my neighbours invited me one day for high tea at 5:00 p.m. It was very formal and she was dressed up like Queen Victoria!

My husband taught at Jarvis Collegiate. He used to drive Leaside kids to his school as there was no high school in Leaside.

We had an old Buick. We would drive up the dirt road of Bayview to Broadway. On the west side was the Kilgour Estate and on the east side was the Robert Cook House, both at the top of the hill. I believe the Kilgour and Divadale estates donated land for Sunnybrook grounds.

We used to go over to Leaside Station and take our children. We knew when to expect the train and the engineers called them by name. Our son could climb up and ride from the east to the North Toronto Station at Yonge Street below St. Clair.

Between 1938 and 1950, we would attend the races at Thorncliffe Park. Gerry would get home just after four, I'd have a babysitter come in and we'd drive over and park in the fields and climb over a fence and we'd arrive just in time for the last three races. We would buy a racing form and place our bets!

I remember Elgie House as a small home on Eglinton where Leaside High School is now. At one point you could take afternoon art classes there. The backyards used to extend farther, but they were graded to create Talbot Park. The creek was too wide to jump across and it had moving water.

I remember the first spring that Leaside High School was built, the basement flooded because of the high water table.

My husband was an avid curler at the Leaside Rink and he stopped finally at 85 years of age! I was very involved at Leaside Lawn Bowling. We would play bridge at the Lawn Bowling every Saturday from October to May.

I used to shop at Loblaws (where the old Bruno's was) across from Belsize. There was a moving picture theatre on Bayview. One night a week I would go with my girlfriend Mary. They changed the show each week. We paid 25 cents each. You would receive a blue glass plate and I collected twelve of them. Where the Valumart is now was a bowling alley called the "Leaside Bowl." I bowled there for three years. I also

The Bayview Playhouse, originally a "moving
picture"theatre—a favourite memory of many
Leasiders. Today, the premises are occupied by
Bruno's. *Leaside Camera Club, courtesy Herb
Horwood.*

used to go to Hopkins Meat Store. The fellow who waited on me took
a fancy to me and he would give me free sausages. I had them coming
out my ears! One day he was caught—it was very embarrassing!

Mr. Burgess was a farmer and was on the Council. He lived across the
street on Donegall. His son ran the farm and came once a week with
eggs and vegetables on a wagon. In the fall he sold apples.

I used to collect for the Red Feather and I knew everybody on the
street. They all invited me in and it took forever! The library on Bayview
was wonderful. The librarian lived on Donegall. We would go twice a
week. My mother-in-law went every day!

I remember watching Jim Smith go off the ski jump at Thorncliffe. I
was so nervous watching him. At the airfield you could go for a ride in
a small plane for $5.00. While we went up my mother-in-law prayed!

"I have had such a happy life in Leaside and my heart will always be
here."

EDNA BEANGE

We visited my brother-in-law on Leacrest Avenue in August of 1948. We had just married in June and had paid three months in advance for a flat on Milverton Boulevard. My husband had a cartage business on Eastern Avenue.

We were impressed with the Leacrest homes and noticed that every fourth house had a bay window! We decided to put in an offer and on October 23, 1948 we moved in! The purchase price was $10,700.00 and with CMHC we arranged a 4% mortgage. Our taxes and mortgage totalled $63.00. Our home was built by Bill Frazer. In 1960, he built a large apartment building on the east side of Bayview Avenue, north of Moore. He also built the apartment buildings on Leacrest.

It was after the war and only the front yard was sod. The backyard was hard-packed Leaside clay. We would all take bushel baskets to fill with loam from the sewage plant to bring back to our backyards. There were all kinds of rogue tomato plants as the sewage had spared the seeds! My husband would work on the clay, one row at a time, and I remember him jumping on the pitchfork to try to break up the ground!

The homes had been built by the Lawrence Construction Company. There was an oak bush at the end of the street before the road was cut through.

The Cadillac Developers wanted to build high-rises on the cliff on Mallory Crescent. They attempted to take options on the Leaside properties. The people there did not want to move. The lots were 40 feet wide and very deep. Stewart Angel formed an organization to fight this. He hired Robert Macauley for legal assistance. These high-rises would have overshadowed the Leaside homes and blocked the view.

I remember that the sidewalk at Rolph and Leacrest was not built for a long time because East York and Leaside could not decide who would finance it. The south side of Leacrest and down the hill belonged to East York. Governor's Bridge and Bennington Heights were always part of East York—not Leaside.

A meeting was held at East York Collegiate. The Mayor of East York at the time was True Davidson. She was very abrupt to the Leaside residents. It eventually went to the OMB and the Chair—a Mr. Kennedy—ruled in favour of the Leaside ratepayers. He rapped the Cadillac Development Company for interfering with Leaside's well-being.

I did not drive a car and so most shopping was achieved by walking to Bayview Avenue. The first Loblaws store opened at Laird and Eglinton where a bagel store is now located. At the time it seemed to have a generous parking lot! I also remember the Kresge's Store, with its oiled floor, where Shoppers Drug Mart now is.

My community involvement began in 1969 when, with the assistance of Llewella Monroe, we began East York Meals on Wheels in Leaside as we realized many seniors were living on tea and toast. We spoke to the churches in Leaside and East York and began deliveries of meals three days a week. On March 6, 1969 we had hampers for four routes. The first day we delivered three meals and soon were up to forty meals.

I decided to seek the position as a Ward Four Councillor and, after attending fourteen coffee parties, I won the election.

When we first moved to Leacrest, there were not many homes with cars—eggs, milk, ice, baked goods, vegetables and even tulip bulbs were delivered to the door. When the Korean War started, we were concerned that ice deliveries might dwindle and so we purchased a refrigerator.

I have always felt that Leaside represented a compact neighbourhood which offered every convenience. Through my experiences on the East York Council, I broadened my involvement in the community, but I have always felt that Leaside retained its special identity and played an important part in the growth of East York.

DR. ROBERT BERTRAM

Rita and I were married in 1940 and first lived in the Kingsway. I was employed by Honeywell on Vanderhoof Avenue. Leaside was underdeveloped at the time, but we had a "good feeling about it,"— still, it felt like a remote and distant spot. Honeywell manufactured small electric motors for aircraft. It was a fully-staffed plant. By the end of 1945, there was a need for manufacturing devices, presses, and screw machines and they decided to buy the factory complete and hired employees.

In 1947, we purchased a new bungalow at 502 Broadway Avenue. It had been built by Reuben Dennis.

Around the corner at 90 Bessborough Drive was a property owned by Gawn Graham and his family. The property, formerly part of a farm, extended 200 feet to where Joe Banigan lived. One day I approached the Grahams to see if they would like to sell some of their property but they did not want to give it up. I continued to ask. Finally, Mr. Graham posed this question to me—"Do you drink or have parties?" I said, "No." He said, "Come back in a week—we've had twelve offers, maybe your offer will be the lucky 13th."

In 1950 we made an agreement. I purchased 45 feet of frontage for $3,000.00 for a building lot. I had met a contractor who built an extension at Honeywell and he became the one who built our home.

The Graham farmhouse caught fire in 1955, but fortunately no one was at home. They were able to save some of the house. Mr. G. Graham then sold 20 feet of his remaining frontage to his neighbour, Mr. Banigan. This still left the Grahams with 135 feet. He considered building two homes, but before he could, they moved away, north of Leaside, as he and his wife felt Leaside was becoming too "built up!" The house was torn down by the Graham brothers who pushed the stone foundation in and covered it with earth. Mr. G. Graham sold the property to a builder.

Mr. Banigan (who was on the Council) informed me that the builder planned to build an apartment, and so I went to Charlie Hiscott (Mayor) and his Council and obtained an agreement that the bylaw would be tightened up to prevent apartments and 30 foot lots. They were in full agreement. Eventually, three homes were built, each with 45 foot frontage.

It is interesting to note that Mr. Graham's home actually faced south as does the home behind where it stood—33 Heather Road. They had both faced Lea's Lane which ran from Bayview to 201 Sutherland and on to Laird.

The Graham farmhouse at 90 Bessborough Drive, between Airdrie and McRae had twelve rooms. The photograph was taken January 1, 1955. *Toronto Reference Library, J. V. Salmon Collection.*

The Graham house caught fire and was so badly damaged on March 14, 1955, that the building had to be razed. The loss was estimated at $15,000. *Toronto Reference Library J, V. Salmon Collection.*

About 1947, Bayview Avenue was paved with sidewalks and many stores had opened and were thriving. For that year, I remember that the property north of 90 Bessborough was farmland. I recall the sweet odour of black locust trees in bloom and wild choke cherries and maple trees springing up naturally. They were not planted in pattern or for reasons of shade.

We enjoyed the Bayview Theatre and one evening saw Nora McClelland performing in "A Flea in Her Ear." On the 24th of May we would attend the town fireworks at Talbot Park. In 1950 or so, a child was burnt by one of the fireworks and so this ended the annual displays, as it was felt to be risky and potentially dangerous.

I was employed at Honeywell from 1931 to 1976, one of six employees who began with Honeywell at 107 Vanderhoof Avenue. The buildings are still standing. Honeywell used to host wonderful Christmas parties for approximately fifteen years. The parties were held at Leaside High School.

I was a member of the Toronto Flying Club and one year, in 1936, we flew six planes into the racetrack at Thorncliffe. I flew a Gypsy Moth from Dufferin and Wilson to the racetrack, over high tension wires, slipped in and taxied to the front of the grandstand. The PA system announced that Lord and Lady Fairburn would inspect the planes. As Lady Fairburn was standing close to one of the planes, a DeHavilland Pussmoth, the mechanic in the plane revved the engine which caused her dress to blow off and leave her standing in her "frillies." It was in the newspapers and it was considered "very risqué," but it had been a set-up prank as Lord and Lady Fairburn were actually actors!

We were members of St. Anselm's Church. This church began at 1609 Bayview in a bankrupt meat market. Then a church was built on Millwood and finally replaced by the existing church.

In 1947, the industrial area was booming with companies such as Philips, Sangamo, Schlumberger, Corning and Research Enterprises. When Eglinton was extended, it brought a lot of extra traffic to Bayview and Leaside. By 1950, Bessborough Drive had become rather dangerous as there was fast-moving traffic from Millwood to Moore Avenue. I approached Council and was successful in obtaining a stop sign at Airdrie and Bessborough to slow the cars.

For at least ten years in the 1950s, Leaside held a Halloween Party at Rolph Road School. It was sponsored by the service clubs and families to keep kids off the streets. Frank Mahovolich was the special guest one year.

I served on the school board for twenty-one years. I began as the Separate School representative and replaced Ed Brisbois who went to the Metro Toronto School Board.

In summing up, "I can't think of a better place to live or a finer community and I have always felt completely at home. Even with amalgamation, it still feels like a small town. People who move here don't remain strangers for very long. I have watched rebirth as people who have moved away or passed on are replaced by younger people and it is a delight to see children on the street again."

ROBERT BUTCHER

I was born in 1921 on Woodycrest Avenue in East York and lived there until 1933. My parents met Herb Bundock who was a builder. He had three lots on Cameron Crescent which he showed to them. They bought #36 for $6,500.00. My father worked at Parkers Cleaners where the Metro Library now stands. It was a cleaning and dyeing business.

I attended Bessborough School for two years. I remember our Principal Miss Pepper who had carrot-red hair. The auditorium was in the centre with eight classrooms around the outside. I used to pay my parents' taxes in the municipal offices in the basement of the school.

Children on an outing near the Don River swimming hole, in 1949. Sitting on the log, from the top: Ted McGovern, unidentified, Norman Hendricks, Warren Hendricks, unidentified, Eleanor Christie, Patrica Reed, Marion Conroy, Linda Mae Keyser. In front, from the left, are John Harris and Gary Reed. The third boy is not identified. *Collection of the Reed family.*

Sandy Bruce, our policeman, used to drive a motorcycle which had a sidecar attached although we never saw him carry a passenger.

I enjoyed riding my bicycle everywhere! I had a wagon which we would pull up to the top of the hill on the dirt road of Bayview and then ride down. We played ball hockey with roller skates on. At the top of Talbot Park there was an empty field on which we rode our bikes, up and down the pathways.

At the bottom was a creek which was fresh water and not stagnant. Watercress was growing in such plenteous supply that my friend, Lloyd Tilley, and I collected it and sold it in bunches, door to door for 5 cents a bundle. Sam Hing's Fruit Market on Bayview gathered it and sold it too!

There was a swimming hole just north of Eglinton in Serena Gundy

Park. The mounties would patrol it and if they caught you without clothes, they would take your name. It was sandy and we would hang our clothes from a hickory tree. There was a path down to it and we would hop across the stones in the river.

Some of the first stores on Bayview were Frey's Pharmacy, Hopkins Meats and Machems Shoe Repair. These were the first stores built on the east side of Bayview at Fleming Crescent. The yellow and brown brick building was Caufield's Dairy.

We belonged to Leaside United Church and would attend two services each Sunday. The Superintendent of the Sunday School was Daisy Keith Page who lived on Donegall. She knew everyone by name. The "Young Peoples" group had fifty teenagers in it. Jack Pember led this. Today, eight of us still get together—we call ourselves the "Leaside Old Young People's Society!"

I attended Jarvis Collegiate for Grade 9. Lloyd Tilley and I would ride our bikes there from Leaside. I then switched to Northern Vocational for the rest of high school.

At the age of seventeen I began to work for CP Express and worked there for twelve years. When World War II began I was stationed in Tar Bay, Newfoundland; Yarmouth, Nova Scotia and Moncton, New Brunswick. The Town and our church sent cigarettes, candy, hand-knit socks and sweaters.

I was married in 1944 where we lived in Yarmouth still and, in 1945, we moved to 36 Cameron Crescent with my parents. I began with Rumble Chevrolet Oldsmobile when it started in 1951.

Pogue's Stables were on the southwest corner of Bayview. At the end of Bayview Heights in Bennington was "Lover's Nook." Along Leacrest, before the apartments were built, were market gardens where people could work their plots yielding fruit and vegetables during the war.

When the Fire Hall was at the northeast corner of Hanna and Sharron, Hanna ended there. If there was a fire, you had to run to the firehall to pull the alarm. There was a siren and light on the top of the hall. Mr. Gilbert Bird of 8 Cameron Crescent was the head of the Volunteer Fire Brigade.

Back in 1934, when 38 Cameron Crescent was built, a sledge hammer and steel wedges were used to dig the frozen ground and the earth was taken away by horse and bucket! I remember hearing that the men who installed and polished the gumwood received only 25 cents per hour. They sat on nail kegs and polished! For quite a while there were only poured basements behind our home over on Fleming Crescent.

When you stood on Clowes Avenue (later named Sharron) you could see the Dome on the Seminary at Kingston Road!

Young families chose Leaside for its location. We were proud to say that we lived in Leaside. We never thought that we could live anywhere else.

MRS. EDITH DAVIES

We were regularly treated to the sight of equestrians from Pogue's Stables on Bayview Avenue below Moore Avenue. There were fields of sweet clover except for where some homes had been built north of McRae Drive. A magnificent cherry orchard from the Lea home at 201 Sutherland went all the way to Millwood Road.

Around Sutherland Drive and Markham Avenue were many cellar excavations that were left during the war 1914–1918 while the men were overseas. Children played in them.

Homes had been built on Laird to McRae and some were scattered on Randolph. The semi-detached bungalows from the Canada Wire and Cable employees were on Airdrie, Rumsey and Sutherland. Some larger farm-type homes could be seen. One still stands at the corner of Rumsey, Sharron and McRae.

Eglinton Avenue ceased at Hoyle and wasn't used much. To go through east or west, one went north on Mount Pleasant to Lawrence. Sunnybrook Plaza did not exist—it was a marsh where people took loam for their gardens. In 1938, the fire reel was a hose on a two-wheel reel staffed by volunteers who would be called by a siren.

The second stage of building homes began south of Millwood Road and, at the time, the closest high school was Jarvis Street Collegiate.[1]

WILLIAM ARTHUR DEACON

I have had the privilege of being a Leasider for more than twenty years, and I like it. Nobody kicks about putting up money for a library, for expensive instruments for the High School band, for playgrounds and rinks and tennis courts. We regard these things as insurance against teenage gangs: we are almost crime-free. The town is not fashionable. Our boast is that we are decent, middle-class folk who hold our jobs and pay our debts. We have no millionaires and no paupers. In the Great Depression, never more than three families were on relief, sometimes only one. But we are the sort of people who see economy in keeping things up, fixing the little hole in the road for $5.00 rather than a big hole for $50.00."[2]

KENNETH FARROWS

I was born in 1915. I remember the wooden church which was St. Cuthbert's. It was set in the woods amidst buttercups, butterflies, birds and a big oak tree. Reverend Lamb baptized me—he was a nice gentleman. We used to play "cowboys and indians" in the Mt. Pleasant Cemetery; we would climb trees and collect beechnuts.

One of our pleasures was to walk to Yonge Street and watch the blacksmith shoe the horses. All the delivery people had horses in those days: Ocean Blend Tea; Naismith's Bakery; Eaton's; Simpson's; the ice man and the coal man. Two or three times a summer there would be a runaway. I can remember a fellow coming around selling Javell water which I suppose developed into our present day Javex. I suppose it is still just chloride and lime in water.

One of the big things in those days was when some of the mothers made Root Beer.

I remember some pretty good weekends walking to various parks and valleys in the neighbourhood. Waterworks Park was one of my favourites. We used to go over to the Don Valley—at that time it was a pretty wild place. And, of course, we spent a lot of time over on the old airport or flying field as it was known in those days. We were able to walk right out on the runways which were only grass—old farm fields, I guess.

My father was a labourer at Canada Wire and Cable. We picked mushrooms in the nearby abandoned field which was the airport. There were still some old military planes there. Another person from Canada Wire, a Mr. Geary, used to sell eggs.

I remember Pogue's Stables at Bayview and Moore Avenue. There was a pony and wicker pony cart that I rode in.

George Phillips had a team of horses and a scoop. He had a hoosier wagon which was a box on four wheels that was pulled by two horses. When a lever on the side was pulled, the bottom would open up. The teamster would lower the bucket to scoop dirt. The bucket had two handles and, with harnesses, the dirt would be pulled in by the scoop. This was how many foundations were dug out for the first homes which were built.

As boys, we used to throw red hot pennies onto the road near Davis' Grocery Store on Davisville Avenue.

BILL FLEMING

I can remember one particular football game at Leaside High School. It was approximately 1954 or so, and I believe it was Hurricane Hazel that

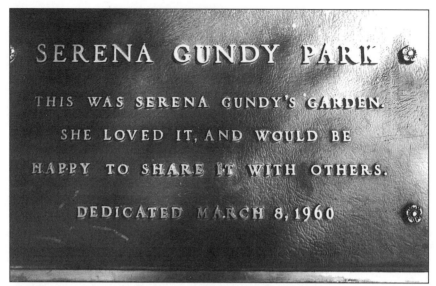

SERENA GUNDY PARK

THIS WAS SERENA GUNDY'S GARDEN.

SHE LOVED IT, AND WOULD BE

HAPPY TO SHARE IT WITH OTHERS.

DEDICATED MARCH 8, 1960

The plaque dedicated to Serena Gundy, March 8, 1960, near the entrance to the park. *Leaside Camera Club, courtesy Herb Horwood.*

brought torrential rains. The refs finally called the end of the game because at that point eight inches of rain had fallen. Players who were at the bottom of the pile in a tackle were drowning! Leaside High School was winning the game quite handily. When we entered the locker room the wooden benches were floating. The gym had flooded. Apparently, the storm sewers had flooded, and it was an awful mess!

I also remember playing many hours on the Gundy Estate. J. H. Gundy had planted many trees and there was a riding path that Mr. Gundy's daughter Serena rode upon. There is a plaque dedicated to her at the entrance of Serena Gundy Park on Rykert Crescent in North Leaside.[3] Many years later we dug up some riding spurs in the area.

RIC HILL

I first came to Leaside in 1936 and lived there, in various places, until 1959. In 1936, my family bought a house at 95 Donegall Drive. The price was $5,000.00 and a deposit of $200.00 was required. In 1938, we moved to 27 Rumsey Road and lived there for 6 years. This house was built by Slightham.

I returned to Leaside in 1961 to live on Thursfield Crescent. In 1969, we purchased a home on Cameron Crescent that had been built by Brockington in 1938.

As a child I remember there were no houses north of Parkhurst or south of Millwood. Many lots were cleared and basement foundations were poured, but they sat there for two or three years because of the Depression.

Why did we choose Leaside? From growing up here you realize that from a convenience and services standpoint nothing can really beat it.

There was a range of value. A semi-detached on Thursfield was a lower cost by 20%. The top 20% of homes were a far better value than those in Rosedale or Lawrence Park. Leaside also offered a complete community. Bayview was paved, but there were big stretches where there were no stores built yet. Some of the first stores were Frey's, Hopkins and Machems. We used to go to the Bayview Movie Theatre every week as there was always a new feature.

I remember bowling in 1950 at the alley where Valumart is now. Loblaws was where the old Brunos was (now a designer outlet and art gallery). There was a car dealership called "Studebakers" on Millwood Road. The owner lived in the Bell's home at 262 Bessborough Drive.

The Lions Club Carnival was the biggest event of the year for kids at Trace Manes Park. The Drum and Bugle marching band wore blue and gold uniforms. Every young guy who had musical ability joined.

In the 1950s, there was a large skating rink at Trace Manes. There was a field house. Music was played from speakers and it was lit at night. It began as a pleasure rink and later a hockey rink was built. There were also a pleasure rink and hockey rink at Talbot Park. While I was at university, I played badminton at Leaside High School.

I later served on the Leaside School Board. There was a school review committee and we would devote one evening to each school to determine what its needs were. I began as a volunteer and later was paid $50.00 per month. We met in the Principal's office. The board table and chairs are still there.

After the Second World War, Leaside was the most industrialized municipality in North America. The ratio of assessments were 85% industrial and 15% residential.

The milk was delivered by horse and wagon. The milk companies were Acme, Borden and Silverwood. Ice was also delivered as refrigerators were uncommon and expensive so ice boxes were the norm. Bread was delivered by Canada Bread.

There was a Chinese laundry on the west side of Bayview south of Manor Road. Large linen tablecloths were washed and pressed for 75 cents. Sam Hing's grocery store was on the east side of Bayview.

An apple orchard was by the stream at one end of Talbot Park where the ground sloped. To grade the park, they removed 20 feet of the hill. There was also a cherry orchard. There were only three houses on the hill north of Eglinton, surrounding them were fields.

Boys would meet after school in Sunnybrook property and have "wars." It was usually the public school boys versus St. Anselm's School. There was a hill and the winner would be the first to fight their way up the hill.

The police had an office in the basement of Bessborough School. Sandy Bruce was the policeman. On Halloween night, 1939, a stone was thrown at a light and it broke. Sandy Bruce was out trying to discover who was pushing over outdoor privies. He ignored the broken street light. He was very understanding. The safe for municipal records is still in Bessborough's basement. It was too heavy to remove so they bricked it over with a wall.

I joined the Air Cadets during the war (1939–1945). It met one night a week at Rolph Road School. There were 150 kids involved. We marched in special parades and wore uniforms. The leader lived at number 6 or 8 Rumsey Road. It was an excellent program.

Dr. John (Jack) McCarthy

We began our married life living in an apartment at Yonge and Sheppard. When our daughter was born, my wife wanted to find a nice community to live in. I was working at Queen's Park and I wanted to lessen the commuting distance. Leaside was close to downtown and had good schools and churches.

In 1957, we purchased 19 Parkhurst. One of the first issues that I became involved in was to fight the two parking lots that were proposed on Donegall Drive. One was to be at Millwood and the other at Fleming Crescent. It would have meant removing seventeen homes on the west side of Donegall. They had wanted to create a shopping district making use of the back entrances of the Bayview stores! The residents of Donegall, Parkhurst and Fleming Crescent strongly opposed this. Fortunately, we were able to defeat the proposal as there had been no previous public consultation. After this, the Leaside Property Owners Association (LPOA) set up a Block Captain System in Leaside.

I was a Director on the LPOA and later became the President. I next decided to run for the School Board. I was instrumental in establishing a more open process and access to the Board's decisions.

In 1967, when Leaside amalgamated with East York, Leaside lost its strong voice as we became one of four wards and only had two representatives of eight. Leaside had been a wealthy, well-run town where people had their say. Leaside had had an excellent police and fire service and our taxes were low for the service we received, due to the high rate of assessment through taxes paid by our industrial businesses.

We had always felt that we made a wise decision in choosing Leaside. Everything that you could need in your life was provided. It had and still has a strong sense of a small town where everyone feels a responsibility for each other.

DR. TOM PASHBY

My parents moved into Leaside from the Broadview and Danforth area in November 1941. At that time, I left my internship at St. Michael and All Angels Hospital, married my wife, whom I had met at Riverdale High School, and joined the Royal Canadian Air Force—all in the space of ten days.

I was a medical officer stationed in Ottawa and Toronto until 1946. When I came back, we lived in an aparment across from Traces Manes Park where I coached a softball team. We won the championship that year.

I had taken a year off for a course in optometry and opened up my own practice at 1050 Avenue Road. I also joined the Hospital For Sick Children and Western Hospital in 1948, retiring at age 65. However, I was asked to come over to Centenary Hospital and organize their optometry department. I moved my private practice over to Wynford Drive and I've been there ever since. I'm there two days a week with my son. It's a chance to see my patients again.

I remember we once had to fundraise for a new roof for the Leaside Memorial Gardens in 1979. The province told us they would contribute two dollars for every one dollar we raised. We needed $450,000 total. We organised a Homecoming which included two oldtimers games with names like George Armstrong and Frank Mahovolich. What we wanted was $10,000, but we aimed for $15,000. We charged $10 per person and some were throwing in $50. In the end we raised $19,000 at that one function. Needless to say, we did raise our required amount.

I still sponsor a ball team at Trace Manes and a hockey team at Leaside Memorial Gardens. I made sure they used the fund insignia on the hockey team to raise the profile. So far, with eight gold tournaments, which have been well represented, and five fundraising dinners, we've raised over $400,000. The next one is on March 23, on my 85 birthday.

Why Leaside? Well, my wife's parents live here and my parents lived here. We just liked the place and it had a lot of sports. I guess it was really because of the people. We have three children and six grandchildren—all in Leaside. It's a home for the kids. My parents lived and died here. It's much like a town in the big city.

I have more years behind me than in front of me, so it's nice to relive them in the comfort of familiar surroundings.

JOAN PARK

What I have loved most about Leaside is simply that it was such a nice place when I came and it had a large number of young families. Originally, I opened the nursery at St. Augustine's on Bayview, with four children, in October 1961. At the time I was living over on Sherwood at Mt. Pleasant Boulevard.

By the end of the year there were 17 children. It just kind of snowballed from there. We now have about 100 a year. In 1970, I moved to Leaside and the nursery moved to Leaside United Church where I sang in the choir as a soloist.

What I loved most about the nursery was the children—and the music. I really loved the music. It was also that the nursery was my own doing. I had children coming from Lawrence Park, Moore Park and North Toronto. There were also some from across the bridge in East York. I never needed to advertise—all has been through word of mouth.

There was a retirement party for me and many, many of the "children" came. It was wonderful to see so many familiar faces—"I always love to see how well everyone grows up and turns out."

Although the nursery school was called Bayview Nursery School, most people know it as "Mrs. Park's." My husband and Mother were also involved for many years and most of the teachers have been there for over ten years. Before Junior Kindergarten began, we had the children for two years. We also had arts and crafts classes for graduates to come back to in the afternoons.

JOHN PAXTON

Thorncliffe is now a market place surrounded by high-rise apartments. I often go there with my wife. Sometimes I find a comfortable seat while she looks for bargains.

As I sit alone, some may wonder how I sit for such a long time and what I would be thinking about. Well, far across the years as memory takes me, I see Thorncliffe Racetrack and hear the crowds cheering for a horse they had $2.00 on. There were some great races and great horses—worthy to be called the "sport of kings."

The area wasn't East York then, but Leaside. Leaside was a thriving town with not only the racetrack, but also an airport which seemed to have planes coming and going all the time. They were small planes and on a Sunday afternoon for $5.00 you could get a ride up in the blue. I know that on Sundays my mother thought I was safe in Sunday School, but most of the times I was at the Leaside Airport. I even had a couple of rides and it sure was "uplifting." But of course, it's all changed now—just a memory—but a great one!

ALAN REDWAY

When I was born, we lived in a quadraplex on Redpath Avenue. We then moved to Thorncliffe Avenue. In early September 1939, when I was four years old, we moved to 110 Bessborough Drive, into a house built by Mr. Whittaker. My father worked at Canada Life.

I remember our winters had a lot of snow and people would rent a horse and cutter from a stable on Bayview Avenue. I began kindergarten at Rolph Road School and Miss Milburn was my teacher. At that time Leaside High School occupied the top floor of Rolph Road School and the football games were held in the Rolph field. The high school students would rotate classes to the various churches—St. Cuthbert's, Leaside United and Leaside Presbyterian. The Rolph gym was used for classrooms, but when a sport activity took place there were folding doors behind which the spectators sat.

It was Ernie Frey from Frey's Pharmacy who sat on the Board of Education who made the motion to build a high school. It was a major decision for them to make as they had all lived through the Depression and there were no guarantees where their next dollar would come from.

Many people living in Leaside had migrated from the Riverdale area. Every couple of weeks there was the threat that we would be going to war. During the war there were wartime gardens. Most homes grew their own vegetables in the backyards. Gasoline was rationed. We swam in the Don River near Serena Gundy Park where there was blue clay.

As young boys we were certainly influenced by the war. We would play military games on "the cliffs" at Leacrest and Mallory Crescent overlooking the valley. The first Leaside Dump was below, near Pottery Road. Later there was one at Brentcliffe where Eglinton ended.

All of the homes had coal furnaces and people would spread the cinders on the ice for traction. I skinned by knees many a time on those cinders. We would go to the Bayview Theatre to see a double bill. There would be a yo-yo contest at intermission. We couldn't afford to buy popcorn, however, a man with a pushcart would sell popcorn all over Leaside. You could buy bags of peanuts. It was about 5 cents. For 1 cent you could buy a B.B. bat which was a candy stick. If you had "big bucks" you could go to Kerr's Drug Store at McRae and Bayview (now Bosley's Real Estate) and buy a "mello roll" which was a roll of ice cream pushed into a cone. At Bayview and Millwood, Murray Simons had a pharmacy with a soda fountain. On Sunday morning the clergy would gather, such as Father Caulfield (St. Anselm's) and Canon Lamb (St. Cuthbert's), to chat together. I remember that beside where the Valumart is now was Wilkinson's Appliances and Art Frost's Florist shop.

We attended St. Cuthbert's Church. One day my mother was in the kitchen with Mrs. Lamb (the minister's wife). She said to my mother, "My dear, this is the way we dry the dishes." It was the last time my mother volunteered!

We used to listen to a wonderful radio program on CBC/CBL called "The Happy Gang." Many of the key people who made up the cast lived in Leaside! It was on the radio at noon. Bert Pearl lived on Millwood between Bayview and Bessborough. Kay Stokes who had two chow-chow, dogs lived at Bessborough and Sutherland, and Blain Mathe, who was a violinist, lived on Bessborough between Airdrie and Sutherland. The announcer, Hugh Bartlett, lived in Garden Court on Bayview

Well-known band leaders across Canada also lived in Leaside. Mart Kenney had a "big band" and his lead singer was his wife, Norma Locke.

In 1962, I married and lived at 36 Thorncliffe Park Drive. It was a new building and there were no high-rises, in fact it was an open field to Grandstand Place. It was a new community and was made up of many young people who had grown up in Leaside. Leaside had won the battle with East York to gain Thorncliffe as part of Leaside.

In 1965, we moved to 38 Vanderhoof Avenue (built by A. B. Cairns) and in 1969 purchased our present home at Hanna and McRae Drive. It was built by Ron Balsdon.

Five years later, I became the President of the Leaside Lions Club and, in 1971, was elected Alderman Ward 4 East York. I served four years as an Alderman and was elected Mayor of East York and served six years. I then was elected federally. My political involvement has spanned approximately twenty years.

Leaside is a very special place. I consider myself very lucky to have grown up here. It has offered a wonderful quality of life.

"But Leaside has always been much more than merely a physical environment. It has had and it continues to have (even after amalgamation) a tremendous community spirit and because of this it is still a great place to live and to raise one's family. There are those who say that change is inevitable and we are foolish to fight it. To those people I would say that the present residents of Leaside have had the good fortune to inherit a truly unique and model community and, rather than accepting its decline as inevitable, we should dedicate ourselves to preserving and improving it."[3]

PAT COLE-SAYLISS

We first arrived from Montreal in 1941, and moved to a home on Airdrie which we rented for one year. It took 24 hours to drive the distance since the tires on our car kept blowing—the quality of rubber during the war was poor. My father had told us that we were coming to a house with mud floors. It was difficult to find a home that could be rented to a family with children. We brought nine rooms of heavy, large furniture to a small bungalow on Rumsey Road.

There was a fire hall on Millwood and McRae and I remember the volunteer firemen running to pull their pants over their pyjamas as they ran across Millwood Park (now Trace Manes).

The Town Hall at the time was in the basement of Bessborough School and I would pay bills for my parents there. The girls' schoolyard and entrance was to the north and the boys' yard and entrance was to the south.

Kresge's was one of my favourite stores on Bayview (where Shoppers Drug Mart is now). It was a five and dime store and I would buy Christmas presents and Mother and Father's Day gifts there. We could walk up there unescorted.

We lived across from Millwood Park. There was a huge tree with a flat mound of earth around it called "the island." Where the library now stands were shrubs and trees in a half-moon shape. We played hide and seek there. Nearby was a flat grassy area.

My father was Matt Sayliss. He was British and an avid tennis player. One day he said, "Gee I'd like to play tennis." He got a net and strung it up and played with three of his friends—Al Ogue, Norm Lamport and Norm Ramsey.

From this point, my father decided he would like to build a public tennis club with a private atmosphere. He approached the Leaside Council and Recreation Committee. It took some convincing, but he finally got the approval. He felt if it was "pay as you play" people would respect it. He felt strongly that the gates should not open before 1:00 p.m. on Sundays to respect churchgoers and those who wanted to sleep in. He insisted on white tennis attire and felt that children under 14 years should not play in the evenings.

Initially, two courts were built and the others followed later. A brick field house with cement steps was built. There were separate girls and boys entrances. It also had two big empty rooms with washrooms. In the winter you could put your skates on inside. When the winter finished, a gang of us went in, painted it and found some old couches to make it our clubhouse.

We wanted to open the two tennis courts with fanfare! We had a stand with hot dogs and coca-cola. There were spectators on the hill. In the evening we had square dancing on the courts and people were lined up to get on!

We loved the Lions Carnival in the park each June, even though it was the same week as the high school exams! One of my father's dearest friends was Bill Morgan. He was a wonderful man who lived on Airdrie, north of Hanna Road. He was President of Leaside Lions and was involved with everything in Leaside. William Morgan Drive in Thorncliffe is named for him.

Unfortunately, my father died at a very young age, but he will be remembered as the founder of the Tennis Club and a promoter of recreational activities in Leaside.

CHILTON SELKE

My personal interest in Thorncliffe goes back to 1933 when my father, Frank J. Selke, the well-known hockey executive with the Toronto Maple Leafs and the Montreal Canadians, purchased a thoroughbred stallion in Kentucky with the intention of improving the breed in Canada. Because of the Depression in the 30s, and the slowdown in racing in Canada and the States, he was able to buy an excellent horse at a reasonable price. "Ladder" was a grandson of the famous "Fair Play." He had finished third in the Preakness behind the renowned "Mate" and "Twenty Grand." He had been injured in a railway unloading accident in Chicago and was retired from racing. My father rented the old Davies barn, located at the Forks of the Don, from the racetrack and set up a modest breeding establishment with the fancy name of "Merrie Maple Court."

The Christmas card greetings sent, in 1934, by the Selke family, owners of Merrie Maple Court. *Courtesy Chilton Selke.*

The rest of the story could take a whole book to tell, but here are the basic details. It seems that with the low ebb of racing in the "dirty thirties," some of the racing establishment weren't too keen on having a "new kid on the block." Early one Sunday morning before Christmas, 1934, the huge barn was set on fire. Nineteen horses were destroyed in the blaze, including "Ladder," my father's broodmares, "Showery" and "Sphere of Beauty," our yearling, "Merrie Prancer," and our Welsh pony, "Patsy." Among the horses belonging to others was a Kentucky-bred yearling of the fledgling and ill-fated "Three Cs Stable," owned by three eminent stars of the Toronto Maple Leaf hockey team, Charlie Conacher, Frank "King" Clancy and Harold "Baldy" Cotton. From our home two and a half miles away in North Toronto, we six children watched, in horror, the demise of Merrie Maple Court, as a fiery glow soared above the eastern horizon. However, I do not want to dwell on the devastating effects of the disaster. I will conclude by revealing our "Phoenix" from the ashes of Merrie Maple Court. One of Ladder's three offspring was "Bunty Lawless" whose dam was Willie Morrissey's good mare, "Mintwina." Morrissey, who was probably pretty busy with his well-known hotel at Yonge and Davenport, undoubtedly did not realize we had adopted his fine colt. "Bunty Lawless," of course, after a distinguished career in racing and breeding, was voted the outstanding Canadian thoroughbred of the first half of the century. The eminent sportswriter, Jim Coleman, authored a well-known book about racing, *Hoofprints on My Heart.* I think my title would be "Thorncliffe on My Heart."

In the summer of 1934, three of my Hillsdale Avenue chums (Bob Bevington, Ernie Woolford and Eddie Cornes) and I spent several weeks "camping" at the Forks. Our "camp" was a box stall in the old Davies' broodmare stable across the barnyard from the main barn. Our beds were flat springs with thick winter horse blankets for mattresses. They definitely didn't have the aroma of pine needles or cedar branches about them. We shared the otherwise unused barn with numerous families of field mice which didn't seem at all bothered by our intrusion. Eddie was alarmed at the prospect of having little rodents travelling across his bed at night so he set up a hammock in the passageway outside our stall. At night we would hear the stomping and snorting of the horses grazing in the orchard pasture outside our window, and the mournful whistle of the steam engines. We would listen to their far-off wails and try to decide if they were CNR or CPR. The CPR trains would eventually rumble hollowly across the quarter mile trestle up the west valley of the Don, or the CNR trains would shake, rattle and roll as they swept around the curve at the Forks, hardly more than a stone's throw from our barn.

The barn, as I recall, had seven box stalls with dirt floors and a single stall with a brick floor. The outer wall of the single stall had been removed, and it served as our kitchen. We had a two-burner hot plate for cooking, but there was also a small cookhouse across the lane with a wood stove used for cooking the hot mashes for the horses. The cook-

Frank Donald Selke, five years old, astride "Patsy." This photograph was taken in 1934 in front of the main barn at the Thorncliffe farm, located at the Forks of the Don. The barn was burned just before Christmas 1934, with the loss of 19 horses, including the pony, "Patsy." Arson was suspected. *Courtesy Chilton Selke.*

house was a comfortable spot on cool mornings or evenings. One evening I had heated water on the hot plate to make a pitcher full of Vi-tone, a chocolate drink advertised in the Maple Leaf Gardens program, for our bedtime snack. Unfortunately, the glass pitcher wasn't pyrex and the bottom fell out. I learned that hot Vi-tone wasn't good for bare feet!

There was still a small swimming hole by the ruins of the old paper mill dam where we were able to perform our morning ablutions. The river was really only a stone's throw from our barn, just a quick dash down for a skinny dip. The hole would have been quite a bit bigger if the deepest part hadn't been used, for years apparently, as a dumping place for the small discarded bundles of used baling wire. On a religious note, we once witnessed a baptismal party there when the Don symbolically became the River Jordan.

Memories of our Welsh pony, "Patsy," could also provide some interesting stories. We city slickers were very inexperienced in horseback riding, being more at home on bicycles. Ernie's first and only attempt ended quite abruptly when he pulled back too hard on the reins before even getting going. Patsy reared up on her hind legs and dumped him. Our Irish Setter got into the act, barking excitedly at Patsy's heels and got a kick on the head for her interference. My turn for being brought down to earth happened when I took Patsy for a gallop around the racetrack. We came around the final turn and into the home stretch with me "Dude Foden," a popular jockey at the time, hearing the roar of the crowd in the grandstand as I led the charge for the finish line. Patsy, however, had a different plan in mind. She suddenly swerved and darted for the opening to the track, leaving me airborne for a brief moment. Fortunately, the invisible thundering herd behind me were forgotten, and I was left feeling somewhat winded and disillusioned. "Dude Foden" was just a patsy, just a dude from North Toronto. I later became a veterinarian, but I never got over the feeling that when it came to horse sense, the horse usually had more than I did.

ARTHUR H. SMITH

For me, Leaside holds many valued memories, presented here as they occur to me:

Clowes Avenue was renamed Sharron around 1940-41. The Post Office requested that it be changed because it was being confused with Close Avenue in Toronto.

Tadpole fishing at the swamp in the spring.

Learning to ski on Bell's Hill, the hill of Talbot Park which was named for the Bell family who lived at 262 Bessborough.

Watching the new houses being built in 1938, '39 and '40 to the north of us on Bessborough.

Eglinton Avenue East and Bayview Avenue North ending at the intersection of Bayview and Eglinton—the pavement just stopped.

Skiing in the Gundy Estate, also watching "home guards" train for warfare there.

Winter hikes to the Don Valley and cooking over an open fire. (The food never really got that hot.)

Seeing the *Wizard of Oz* at the Bayview Theatre. All of the classes at Bessborough School got to see it at a matinee.

Riding in the engines of the trains northbound out of Leaside Station. We'd ride up to Oriole Station and catch the next one back.

Watching Leaside grow from a little village-type atmosphere to a bustling energetic wartime factory town.

1944 Christmas—the worst of my young life—Don Rae's brother Clifford was reported killed in action 10 days before Christmas Day. Cliff

The record snow fall of 1944 brought hardship for some but fun for others. Standing in the middle of Fleming Crescent are Marion Conroy (left) and Patrica Reed. *Collection of the Reed family.*

was on HMCS *Shawinigan* and was sunk November 1944 in the Cabot Straits. Don was one of the guys I hung out with, along with Bill Johns, Alan McDonald and Alex Potter.

The snowstorm of 1944 which brought Toronto to its knees. I would have to ski to Frey's Drug Store (on Bayview) to get milk and bread with ration coupons.

The long walk to Belsize Drive to get the bus to anywhere else.

Rasmussen Bakery on a Saturday morning—m-m-m-m-m-m-good.

Frey's Drug Store for sodas, sundaes and coke floats and more.

Clair's (on Bayview)—where we bought grab bags for the theatre matinee (5 cents each, 15 cents for the show, also cigarettes 5 for 5 cents).

The haunted house which belonged to the Colonel and his sister where Leaside High School now stands.

MARY (DEMKO) THOMPSON

When we moved to Leaside in 1932, I was ten years old. My father was with the CPR and we lived in a large 2-storey frame house across from the Leaside Station platform. It was a railway house owned by the CPR and had a large verandah across the front and seven bedrooms.

My father was transferred to Leaside from the Lampton Yard (West Toronto Station). The house was provided at a small rental fee. Dad was a "section foreman" and he worked six days a week. He would get out of bed in the middle of the night in winter to thaw the switches for the approaching trains. The road master was a Mr. Francis and the station master was Mr. Wansborough.

Our house had no electricity. My mother used a scrubbing board and would boil our clothes on top of a wood stove. We had a well for our water. My father would dig a hole each year to move our outhouse. Many of my friends had modern plumbing and toilets. We did not have a telephone and when a call came for me, the station master would call me to the station to use the telephone!

During the "dirty thirties" many "hobos" would ride the empty boxcars or sit on the top of the train. There were CPR police at the station and so the hobos would jump off a mile or so before Leaside so they would not be caught. Although my father asked her not to—whenever hobos knocked on the back door my mother gave them sandwiches and water to drink. To repay her, they would chop our wood.

We were one of five Catholic families in Leaside. There was initially no Catholic church in Leaside so we would attend Holy Cross on the Donlands. We eventually attended St. Anselm's. My father was Polish and my mother Ukranian. Most families in Leaside were English, Irish or Scottish and so I received a lot of teasing.

I had attended a two-room school in Saskatchewan and when I came to Ontario I had to be put back one grade. I attended Leaside Public School with Mr. Leonard G. Hill as the Principal. Mr. W. W. Wright was the Vice-Principal. Mr. Hill was always very kind to me—he was a warm person and he would always choose me to answer questions. The school consisted of an auditorium and a few classrooms. Miss Milburn taught kindergarten.

For high school I could have attended either North Toronto or Northern Vocational. My best friend chose East York Collegiate Institute. We usually walked all the way to Coxwell Avenue since we didn't have the money to take the bus. We would walk across the Woodbine Golf Club which had no houses on it. If we did take the bus, it only went to Pape and Cosburn and then we would have to walk! When I graduated from high school, I attended the Shaw Business School on the Danforth which was above the United Cigar Store.

There was one Native Indian family who lived on Laird Drive. Mrs. Massingbird would make dresses for my mother and me.

Behind our house was the Dominion Box Company which manufactured cardboard boxes. My mother would hang our clothes on the line, but when a train was coming she would have to take everything down or it would get very dirty. The Canada Varnish Company would also send dirty smoke from its chimney and my mother would often have to wash our clothes a second time.

The nurse and dentist would visit our school. The dentist practised on Belsize and the service was free to school children. I never saw a doctor except once when I needed to get a tight ring cut off.

For leisure activities we would skate at the outdoor rink at a park which is now Trace Manes. In the summer we would play tennis. On Sundays when my dad had a day off, we would walk across the Don River on the railway trestle. It had no sides but there were empty barrels which you could jump into if a train came. My father would caution me not to look down at the water because boys were swimming in the nude!

We had sweeping lawns from our house to the "subway" which was the road under the railway bridge at Laird and Millwood. The lawns were immaculate and the railway men worked on the lawns and the flower beds. The oldest brick homes were on Airdrie, Rumsey and Randolph.

We picked up our mail at Perrem and Knight's store on McRae at Sutherland Drive. Mrs. Perrem had a large English bulldog which would sleep and still look ferocious. Mrs. Perrem would feed him ice cream. Some days my father would give us twenty cents and we would go to "Osmond's Lunch" on Laird Drive. We would buy a box lunch which consisted of a sandwich, fruit, a piece of cake and a stick of chewing gum. On the weekends we would go to the Bayview Theatre to see western serials.

We could always hear the Hydro station hum at night and you could feel a spray of water from it. During the Second World War, there were sentry boxes around the Hydro to protect it from any terrorist activity.

We used to carry bushel baskets down to the Waterworks and fill them with loam or manure for our gardens. My mother grew all of our fruit and vegetables. In the spring there were lovely wildflowers at the Waterworks, such as jack-in-the-pulpit and dogwood. Leeks also were in plenteous supply!

One of my best friends lived at the Thorncliffe Racetrack. Her father was Roddy McArthur and he was the superintendent of the Racetrack. They lived near the paddock. The Clubhouse was at the entrance to what is now the East York Town Centre. While the races were on we used to sneak into the kitchens and eat roast beef. Doug McQuarrie worked for a newspaper and wrote about the races.

There was an Italian family living on Sutherland Drive. The father was Sam DeMarco. He built the first walkup apartments on Millwood. They are still there. He wanted my dad to purchase part of the old airfield. My father could not afford it. Instead Sangamo purchased it and built their plant there.

I remember the Thorncliffe Ski Jump. It was thrilling to watch the ski jumpers. The Donalda Farm was at the bottom of the jump. The Campbells lived there and looked after the farm. I remember the chickens running around. The Campbells were friends of the MacArthurs.

Girls could not get jobs. Boys usually worked delivering newspapers and groceries. We shopped for what we needed at the grocery store on Millwood. My mother would ride the train from Leaside to the Don Station and would go to shop on Queen Street.

There was a taxi kiosk at Pape and Danforth, but it closed in the early evening. The last bus left to return to Leaside at 11:30 p.m. Many times my dates would walk me home from East York and hitchhike home again.

When King George V died, Bessborough School was draped in black and purple. We had a service in the auditorium which was very sombre, and we cried for our King who had died. A commemorative medal was issued to all of us.

We were the last family to live in this Railway house. When the old station was torn down and the new one built, we left Leaside. The house was demolished in 1948. My parents moved to Beeton. I married in 1945 and moved to Mortimer Avenue.

Harry Weston and son Bob Weston

Talbot Park was a pond with bulrushes. Over by Sunnybrook was a swamp containing pollywogs. Bayview Avenue was unpaved north of Eglinton. There was a big argument between Leaside and Toronto about Millwood and Bayview being paved, and so it was delayed for a few months.

We first bought 72 Hanna Road for $4,600.00. Then I bought my lot at 71 Hanna and gave the town $500.00. I was a contractor and, to save money, I did the plumbing and heating. When I went to pay my taxes in 1943, Dick Burgess, the Treasurer at the Town Hall, apologized profusely and said it was $75.00 to pay for pavement and sewers in Leaside.

During the war everyone was encouraged to have a "victory garden" where you would grow your own food. For one year the corn and tomatoes were beautiful, then the bugs devoured them and that was the end of that! There were two Italian families living on our street, however they moved away as they did not feel welcome.

In the 1930s, I did the plumbing for the bungalows on Randolph, Sutherland and Airdrie. It was the middle of winter and the houses were surrounded by fields and there were no trees to break the wind! I was paid $25.00 for each house. It was hard work, but through the Depression I thought that it was better than nothing.

Pogue's Stables were at Moore and Bayview. Eric Pogue went to Leaside High School.

Bob Weston, my son, would often get lost returning from Rolph Road School and the garbage truck would bring him home. He used to work setting up the pins at the bowling alley. He also delivered milk for Acme Farmers Dairy (from Dupont). On Saturdays he would go with the driver in the truck and collect the bottles. The driver would go in and have a drink with his customers and Bob would do the work! For payment the driver would buy him lunch, a roast beef sandwich, at the Garden Court Restaurant (beside Canada Trust), plus giving him $2.00. The driver was eventually fired for delivering milk before 7:00 a.m.

Harry and Bob Weston also helped build the 10-storey apartment building on the east side of Bayview north of Moore Avenue in 1960. It was the biggest at the time.

Harry Weston owned a 1924 Durant Star from the Durant factory in Leaside.

A young Harry Weston showing off his 1924 Durant Star made in Leaside. *Courtesy Harry Weston.*

BRUCE WHITEHEAD

When I was a child in the late 40s, I was so fortunate to be living in Leaside because I could ride my CCM or walk to the end of Eglinton just
past Laird to start my hikes through the Don. Hiking was the single
greatest adventure we could imagine; it cost us nothing, yet it rewarded
us greatly.

Our chums on Parkhurst, (the two Rogers) Allan, Tony, Grant (my
brothers) and I, built branch-covered lean-tos, collected rocks and
bones, snail shells, butterflies and other insects. Wading through the
shallow areas in the bend of the river, we looked for turtles and tadpoles.
Once in a while we caught a glimpse of the odd larger fish.

Over a small campfire in the early spring or fall, we roasted marshmal-
lows or weiners bought at Jeffrey's Meat Market on Bayview, and experimented with crumpled dried oak leaves to make foul tasting cigars.

On the south side of the gully, near the foot of Eglinton, I often
climbed a giant spruce tree which served as a look-out. Sometimes I collected the sap, thinking that it repelled mosquitoes, because once up the
tree, with the wind blowing, I never seemed to notice any bites.

Perhaps fishing on the Don is better when you wear your Sunday best! Circa 1920. *City
of Toronto Archives, William James Collection.*

We could walk for miles along the riverbanks, cross over on logs and large rocks, climb the steepest cliffs if we gathered enough courage, get soaked in the rain and chilled in the wind. Allan even fell through the ice in the winter of '52, right over his head. The small fire we started with damp wood didn't provide much heat so we bicycled home, his clothes stiffening as the water froze.

In our innocence, we did not understand that there was industrial waste in the river. We had no idea how plentiful wildlife used to be a century earlier. A single fish over 6-inches long, spotted on a hike, was a great thrill for us.

We were lucky to be born in the 40s, not hearing the whine of traffic on the Parkway, nor smelling the fumes of the city. The grass was not cut, the fallen limbs not gathered up, and there were no paved walkways. For us, this second or third growth forest was primitive.[4]

APPENDIX A

THE LEA FAMILY TREE—JOHN SR.*

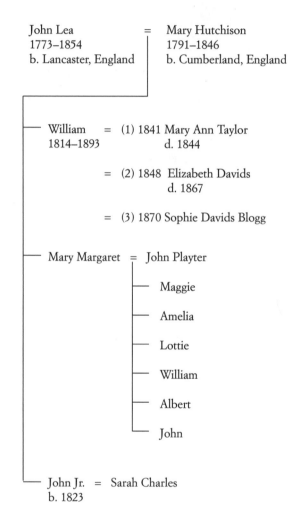

John Lea   =   Mary Hutchison
1773–1854   1791–1846
b. Lancaster, England   b. Cumberland, England

    William   =   (1) 1841 Mary Ann Taylor
    1814–1893   d. 1844

            =   (2) 1848   Elizabeth Davids
                  d. 1867

            =   (3) 1870 Sophie Davids Blogg

    Mary Margaret   =   John Playter

            Maggie

            Amelia

            Lottie

            William

            Albert

            John

    John Jr.   =   Sarah Charles
    b. 1823

* Information on the Lea Family from "The Lea (Leigh) Family Tree" March 1975, *courtesy Edgar Lea (1919–1993).*

LEA FAMILY TREE—WILLIAM*

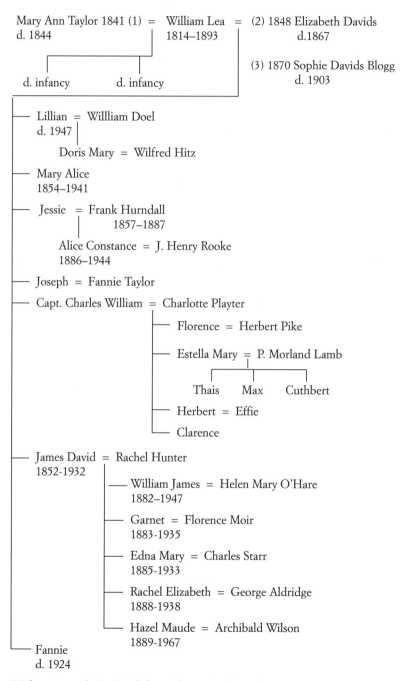

Mary Ann Taylor 1841 (1) = William Lea = (2) 1848 Elizabeth Davids
d. 1844   1814–1893   d.1867

(3) 1870 Sophie Davids Blogg
d. 1903

d. infancy   d. infancy

Lillian = Willliam Doel
d. 1947

    Doris Mary = Wilfred Hitz

Mary Alice
1854–1941

Jessie = Frank Hurndall
          1857–1887

    Alice Constance = J. Henry Rooke
    1886–1944

Joseph = Fannie Taylor

Capt. Charles William = Charlotte Playter

        Florence = Herbert Pike

        Estella Mary = P. Morland Lamb

            Thais   Max   Cuthbert

        Herbert = Effie

        Clarence

James David = Rachel Hunter
1852-1932

       William James = Helen Mary O'Hare
       1882–1947

       Garnet = Florence Moir
       1883-1935

       Edna Mary = Charles Starr
       1885-1933

       Rachel Elizabeth = George Aldridge
       1888-1938

       Hazel Maude = Archibald Wilson
       1889-1967

Fannie
d. 1924

* Information on the Lea Family from "The Lea (Leigh) Family Tree" March 1975,
courtesy Edgar Lea (1919–1993).

The Lea Family Tree—John Jr.*

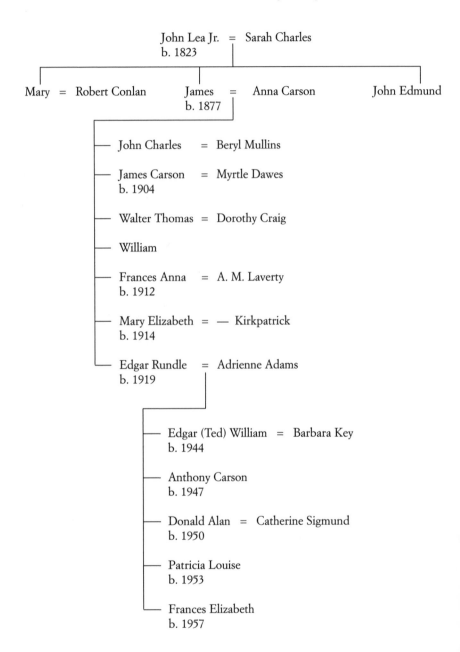

APPENDIX B

LEASIDE TOWN COUNCILS 1913–1967

1913 Mayor—Randolph McRae; Councillors—L. C. Boulton, A. G. McRae, H. Fitzsimmons, G.W. Saunders.

1914 Mayor—Randolph McRae; Councillors—L. C. Boulton, A. G. McRae, H. Fitzsimmons, G. W. Saunders.

1915 Mayor—R. P. Ormsby; Councillors—G. W. Saunders, H. Fitzsimmons, L. W. Mitchell.

1916 Mayor—R. P. Ormsby; Reeve—Jas. Lea; Councillors—R. L. Fairbairn, D. R. Stevenson, F. F. Clarke, L. W. Mitchell.

1917 Mayor—R. P. Ormsby; Reeve—Jas. Lea; Councillors—R. L. Fairbairn, R. J. Conlon, D. R. Stevenson, G. Wilkinson, F. McCready.

1918 Mayor—R. P. Ormsby; Reeve—R. L. Fairbairn; Councillors—Jas. Lea, R. J. Conlon, D. R. Stevenson, G. Wilkinson, F. McCready, LW. Mitchell.

1919 Mayor—R. P. Ormsby; Reeve—R. L. Fairbairn; Councillors—Jas. Lea, R. J. Conlon, D. R. Stevenson, G. Wilkinson, F. McCready, D. J.Bell.

1920 Mayor—R. P. Ormsby; Reeve—Jas. Lea; Councillors—H. Horsfall, R. J. Conlon, J. A. Beatty, G. Wilkinson, P. M. Lamb, J. Cooper.

1921 Mayor—R. P. Ormsby; Reeve—Jas. Lea; Councillors—H. Horsfall, R. J. Conlon, J. A. Beatty, P. M. Lamb, A. E. Stuart.

1922 Mayor—R. P. Ormsby; Reeve—Jas. Lea; Councillors—H. Horsfall, W. Workman, J. A. Beatty, G. Wilkinson, J. A. Woodard. A. E. Stuart.

1923 Mayor—R. P. Ormsby; Reeve—Jas. Lea; Councillors—H. Horsfall, W. Workman, J. A. Beatty, G. Wilkinson, J. A. Woodard, R. Cook.

1924 Mayor—H. Horsfall; Reeve—Jas. Lea; Councillors—J. W. Muirhead, F. G. Hearne, T. Dunsmore, G. Wilkinson, J. A. Woodard, A. E. Stuart.

1925 Mayor—H. Horsfall; Reeve—Jas. Lea; Councillors—J. W. Muirhead, J. Osmond, T. Dunsmore, G. Wilkinson, J. A. Woodard, A. E. Stuart.

1926 Mayor—H. Horsfall; Reeve—Jas. Lea; Councillors—J. M. Muirhead, J. W. Dorkin, J. A. Beatty, G. Wilkinson, J. A. Woodard, A. E. Stuart.

1927 Mayor—H. Horsfall; Reeve—Jas. Lea; Councillors—J. W. Muirhead, F. G. Hearne, J. A. Beatty, G. Wilkinson, J. A. Woodard, A. E. Stuart.

1928 Mayor—H. Horsfall; Reeve—Jas. Lea; Councillors—A. A. Johnson, J. W. Dorkin, F. Perrem, G. Wilkinson, J. A. Woodard, A. E. Stuart.

1929 Mayor—H. Horsfall; Reeve—Jas. Lea; Councillors—J. MacDonald, F. G. Hearne, W. P. Henderson, G. Wilkinson, J. A. Woodard, J. Scott.

1930 Mayor—H. Horsfall; Reeve—Jas. Lea; Councillors—J. MacDonald, F. G. Hearne, W. P. Henderson, G. Wilkinson, F. Perrem, J. Scott.

1931 Mayor—G. Wilkinson; Reeve—F. G. Hearne; Councillors—J.MacDonald, S. Hobbs, W. P. Henderson, R. Clark, J. A. Woodard, J. Scott.

1932 Mayor—G. Wilkinson; Reeve—F. G. Hearne; Councillors—J. MacDonald, S. Hobbs, A. T. Lawson, R. Clark, C. Petteplace, J. Scott.

1933 Mayor—G. Wilkinson; Reeve—A. Johnson; Councillors—J. MacDonald, S. Hobbs, A. T. Lawson, R. Clark, F. Perrem, J. Scott.

1934 Mayor—G. Wilkinson; Reeve—A. Johnson; Councillors—J. MacDonald, J. Garlick, A. T. Lawson, Wm. Page, F. Perrem, J. Scott.

1935 Mayor—G. Wilkinson; Reeve—A. Johnson; Councillors—R. Clark, J. Garlick, A. T. Lawson, Wm. Page, F. Perrem, J. Scott.

1936 Mayor—J. Scott; Reeve—R. Clark; Councillors—H. Talbot, G. Dickson, F. Brimicombe, Wm. Page, E. Bartholomew, F. Perrem.

1937 Mayor—J. Scott; Reeve—R. Clark; Councillors—H. Talbot, G. Crothers, F. Brimicombe, Wm. Page, E. Bartholomew, F. Perrem.

1938 Mayor—H. Talbot; Reeve—R. Clark; Councillors—G. Crothers, F. Brimicombe, C. Gardner, P. Bedford, E. Bartholomew.

1939 Mayor—H. Talbot; Reeve—R. Clark; Deputy Reeve—A. Johnson; Councillors—R. J. Hibbs, G. T. Manes, C. Gardner, P. Bedford.

1940 Mayor—H. Talbot; Reeve—R. Clark; Deputy Reeve—A. Johnson; Councillors—R. J. Hibbs, G. T. Manes, C. Gardner, P. Bedford.

1941 Mayor—H. Talbot; Reeve—R. Clark; Deputy Reeve—A. Johnson; Councillors—R. J. Hibbs, G. T. Manes, C. Gardner, P. Bedford.

1942 Mayor—H. Talbot; Reeve—R. Clark; Deputy Reeve—A. Johnson; Councillors—R. J. Hibbs, G. T. Manes, C. Gardner, P. Bedford.

1943 Mayor—H. Talbot; Reeve—A. Johnson; Deputy Reeve—G. T. Manes; Councillors—W. S. Morgan, Wm. Page, C. Gardner, D. D. Martin.

1944 Mayor—H. Talbot; Reeve—R. Clark; Deputy Reeve—G. T. Manes; Councillors—W. S. Morgan, Wm. Page, C. Gardner, A. A. Outram.

1945 Mayor—H. Talbot; Reeve—G. T. Manes; Deputy Reeve—W. S. Morgan; Councillors—Wm. F. Page, E. Harding, C. Gardner, A. A. Outram.

1946 Mayor—H. Talbot; Reeve—G. T. Manes; Deputy Reeve—W. S. Morgan; Councillors—K. Bryant, E. Harding, C. Gardner, A. A. Outram.

1947 Mayor—H. Talbot; Reeve—G. T. Manes; Deputy Reeve—W. S. Morgan; Councillors—K. E. Bryant, H. Burrell, C. Gardner, A. A. Outram.

1948 Mayor—G. T. Manes; Reeve—W. S. Morgan; Deputy Reeve—K. E. Bryant; Councillors—H.T. Burrell, E.F. Frey, C. H. Hiscott, A. A. Outram.

1949 Mayor—G. T. Manes; Reeve—W. S. Morgan; Deputy Reeve—K. E. Bryant; Councillors—H.T. Burrell, E.F. Frey, C. H. Hiscott, D. G. R. Brown.

1950 Mayor—G. T. Manes; Reeve—W. S. Morgan; Deputy Reeve—D. G. R. Brown; Councillors—H. T. Burrell, E. F. Frey, C. H. Hiscott, R. Clark.

1951 Mayor—H. T. Burrell; Reeve—D. G. R. Brown; Deputy Reeve—E. F. Frey; Councillors—R. Clark, R. H. Frith, C. H. Hiscott, J. Banigan.

1952 Mayor—H. T. Burrell; Reeve—D. G. R. Brown; Deputy Reeve—E. F. Frey; Councillors—R. Clark, R. H. Frith, C. H. Hiscott, A. E. Donahue.

1953 Mayor—H. T. Burrell; Reeve—D. G. R. Brown; Deputy Reeve—R. H. Frith; Councillors—R. L. Clarke, J. Banigan, C. H. Hiscott, A. E. Donahue.

1954 Mayor—H. T. Burrell; Councillors—R. L. Clarke, J. Banigan, C. H. Hiscott, L. M. Dickinson.

1955 Mayor—H. T. Burrell; Councillors—R. L. Clarke, J. Banigan, C. H. Hiscott, L. M. Dickinson.

1956   Mayor—C. H. Hiscott; Councillors—R. L. Clarke, M. A. Bews, E. S. Birrell, L. M. Dickinson, G. S. Flagler, V. H. Page.

1957–58   Mayor—C. H. Hiscott; Councillors—R. L. Clarke, Lenore Sibbald, E. S. Birrell, L. M. Dickinson, G. S. Flagler, V. H. Page.

1959–60   Mayor—C. H. Hiscott; Councillors—E. S. Birrell, Wm. Colvin, L. M. Dickinson, G. S. Flagler, Beth Nealson, Lenore Sibbald.

1961–62   Mayor—C. H. Hiscott; Reeve—L. M. Dickinson; Deputy Reeve -Wm. Colvin; Councillors—G. S. Flagler, Colin McMechan, David Jagger, Beth Nealson.

1962   Mayor—C. H. Hiscott (resigned); Mayor—L. M. Dickinson; Reeve -Wm. Colvin; Deputy Reeve—G. S. Flagler; Councillors—David Jagger, Colin McMechan, Gilbert Bird, Beth Nealson.

1963–64   Mayor—Beth Nealson; Reeve—Vern Page; Deputy Reeve—G. S. Flagler; Councillors—E. S. Birrell, Gilbert Bird, Jame Nottingham, Keith Stainton.

1965–66   Mayor—Beth Nealson; V. H. Page, G. S. Flagler, J. D. Jagger, R. Peringer, G. D. Bird, R. K. Stainton.

APPENDIX C

MEMBERS OF PROVINCIAL PARLIAMENT FOR YORK EAST 1913–1967

GEORGE STEWART HENRY (CONSERVATIVE)

1 September 8, 1913 by-election
2 June 29, 1914 general election: until May 21, 1918
3 August 19, 1918 by-election
4 October 20, 1919 general election
5 June 25, 1923 general election: until July 16, 1923
6 August 16, 1923 by-election
7 December 1, 1926 general election
8 October 30, 1929 general election
9 June 19, 1934 general election
10 October 6, 1937 general election

AGNES MACPHAIL (COOPERATIVE COMMONWEALTH)

1 August 6, 1943 general election: until March 24, 1945

JOHN A. LESLIE (PROGRESSIVE CONSERVATIVE)

1 June 4, 1945 general election

AGNES MACPHAIL (COOPERATIVE COMMONWEALTH)

1 June 7, 1948 general election

HOLLIS EDWARD BECKETT (PROGRESSIVE CONSERVATIVE)

1 June 9, 1955 general election
2 June 11, 1959 general election
3 September 25, 1963 general election

ARTHUR KENNETH MEEN (PROGRESSIVE CONSERVATIVE)

1 October 17, 1967 (until general election April 29, 1977)

APPENDIX D

POPULATION OF LEASIDE: 1913–1967

Prior to incorporation in 1913, Leaside was expected to attract a population of 10,000 within four or five years (*The Globe.*March 28, 1913).

Twenty-eight years later, Leaside's population had not yet reached this level.

Leaside grew from a population of 43 in 1913, to 325 in 1921, to 605 in 1929, to 938 in 1931. Leaside experienced rapid growth in the Depression reaching 6,131 in 1941.

Throughout the period 1921-1941, over 90 per cent of Leaside's population was made up of people with British origins. Leaside was home to a handful of French, German, Italian and Dutch.

In 1921, 52 per cent were members of the Anglican Church, 17.8 per cent were Presbyterian and 9.8 per cent Roman Catholic.

In 1924, the highest concentration of houses were found near the industrial section. By 1934, the houses were concentrated close to Bayview Avenue. Leaside grew from east to west and from south to north. The number of residences rose from 52 in 1924, to 68 in 1929, to 324 in 1934 and 1,832 by 1939.

Population of Leaside: 1913-1967

1913–23	under 500	1939	4,001	1955	16,779
1924	500	1940	5,493	1956	16,590
1925	500	1941	6,687	1957	16,418
1926	500	1942	7,750	1958	16,409
1927	500	1943	8,310	1959	16,416
1928	500	1944	9,227	1960	16,645
1929	605	1945	9,800	1961	18,271
1930	860	1946	10,959	1962	18,850
1931	1,005	1947	11,681	1963	18,453
1932	1,217	1948	13,568	1964	18,404
1933	1,304	1949	14,807	1965	19,418
1934	1,428	1950	15,255	1966	20,972
1935	1,670	1951	15,686	1967	23,548
1936	1,965	1952	15,829		(including 8,792 for
1937	2,612	1953	15,910		Thorncliffe Park)
1938	3,309	1954	16,873		

APPENDIX E

Residents of Leaside Killed in World War II

A silver plaque is mounted by the outside entrance to the William Lea Room at Leaside Memorial Community Gardens dedicated to the Leaside residents who died in the Second World War, 1939-1945.

The plaque reads: "In memory of the men of the Town of Leaside who gave their lives for their country in the Second World War 1939–45."

This plaque was dedicated on the occasion of the Golden Anniversary of the Town of Leaside, 1963.

Trueman William Albert Anderson
Douglas Stewart Brown
Conrad Cromer Evans
Richard Charles Holmes
Vernon John Lazier
William Clothier Leaming
William Robert Merrall
Archibald Allen Muirhead
Walter David Newel

James George Gordon Peterkin
Robert Eric Bonman Pike
Clifford Laureano Rea
Willard Hugh Rowland
Leonard Ogilvy Stalker
Richard John Walton
William Milton Wilbur
James Edward Wilkes

APPENDIX F

LEASIDE PUBLIC SCHOOL BOARD: 1920–1966
(from the Ontario Archives)

1920   J. A. Woodward (Chair), H. Wilson, Thos. Dunsmore, Wm. Craven, F. C. Irwin, C. A. Rundle.

1922   Harding Wilson, Thomas Johnson, John McClement, F. C. Irwin (Chair), Wm. Craven, C. A. Rundle.

1923   F. C. Irwin (Chair), Harding Wilson, J. McClement, J. Rundle, Rev. P. M. Lamb, F. Humphreys.

1924   ———

1925   Harding Wilson, J. McClement, F. Humphreys, T. Turner, T. Johnson (Chair), Rev. P. M. Lamb.

1926/27   R. Hancock, A. Sims, Rev. Lamb, F. Humphreys, T. Johnson (Chair), T. Turner.

1928   T. Johnson (Chair), Rev. Lamb, F. C. Irwin, R. Hancock, H. Wilson, J. McClement.

1929   F. C. Irwin (Chair), J. McClement, R. Hancock, T. Turner, G. Bird, Rev. Lamb.

1930/31   F. C. Irwin (Chair), Rev. Lamb, T. Turner, A. Sims, R. Hancock, C. McWeaver.

1932   F. C. Irwin (Chair), Rev. Lamb, T. Turner, A. Sims, R. Hancock, J. H. Garlick.

1933   F. C. Irwin (Chair), Rev. Lamb, T. Turner, A. Sims, R. Hancock, C. Rayner, J. H. Garlick.

1934   H. T. Turner (Chair), A. Sims, L. G. Wrinch, W. H. Holmwood, H. Spanton, Rev. Lamb.

1936   A. Sims (Chair), L. G. Wrinch, W. H. Holmwood, H. Spanton, Geo. Mackness, Rev. Lamb.

1937/38   Geo. Mackness (Chair), Rev. Lamb, L. G. Wrinch, A. Sims, J. H. Pember, T. Turner.

1939   Geo. Mackness (Chair), Rev. Lamb, A. Sims, L. G. Wrinch, D. G. Brown, T. Turner.

1940   L. G. Wrinch (Chair), Rev. Lamb, Geo. Mackness, D. G. Brown, Chas. Mason, M. Henry.

1941   D. G. Brown (Chair), A. Sims, M. Henry, Chas. Mason, L. G. Wrinch, Geo. Mackness.

1942   D. G. Brown (Chair), K. M. Henry, Chas. Mason, L. G. Wrinch, Geo. Mackness.

1943   D. G. Brown (Chair), L. G. Wrinch, B. Barnum, Mrs. Gertrude Jones, Paul Mclelland, A. Sims.

1944   D. G. Brown, B. Barnum, G. Jones, J. J. Knights, D. A. Sinclair.

1945 P. A. McClelland, P. G. Turner, D. G. Brown, Mrs. N. F. Jones, J. J. Knights, Mrs. H. V. Shaw, E. F. Frey, M. McGee.

1946 P. A. McClelland (Chair), D. G. Brown, E. F. Frey, Mrs. G. Jones, J. J. Knights, Mrs. H. V. Shaw, P. G. Turner, Mr. Leonard, M. Wiertz.

1947 E. Bancroft, D. G. Brown, W. R. Coulter, E. F. Frey, J. J. Knights (Chair), P. A. McClelland, P. G. Turner, L. M. Wiertz.

1948 S. D. Simpson, E. Bancroft, D. G. Brown, J. J. Knights (Chair), P. A. McClelland, P. G. Turner, L. M. Wiertz, A. A. Buckley.

1949 P. A. McClelland (Chair), A. A. Buckley, R. L. Clarke, S. D. Simpson, L. M. Wiertz, P. G. Turner, E. Bancroft, E. Scott.

1950 P. A. McClelland, O. Wainwright, G. Harlow, W. Rogers, S. C. Dean, Mrs. M. Towers, R. L. Clarke (Chair).

1951 Mrs. M. Towers, P. A. McClelland, G. Harlow, O. Wainwright, W. Rogers, H. Eve, R. L. Clarke (Chair), L. M. Wiertz.

1952 R. L. Clarke, Mrs. M. Towers, Mrs. B. Nealson, L. M. Wiertz, O. Wainwright, Wm. Rogers (Chair), P. A. McClelland, H. Eve.

1953 Wm. Rogers (Chair), Mrs. B. Nealson, Mrs. L. Bleeker, J. E. Huggins, O. Wainwright, L. M. Wiertz, H. Eve, S. C. Dean.

1954 Mrs. L. Bleeker, H. Eve, S. C. Dean, Mrs. B. Nealson, Wm. Rogers, S. D. Simpson, O. Wainwright (Chair), L. M. Wiertz.

1955 Mrs. D. F. Bleeker (Louella), Mr. Brisbois, H. Eve, J. W. M. Dixon, Mrs. B. Nealson, Wm. Rogers, H. W. Simpson, O. Wainwright (Chair).

1956 T. Beckett, Mrs. D. F. Bleeker, Mr. Brisbois, D. W. Brown, H. Eve (Chair), Mr. Dixon, Wm. Rogers, H. W. Simpson.

1957 H. Robert Bertram, Mrs. D. F. Bleeker, Wm. Rogers, D. W. Brown, Dr. Rupert Warren, T. Matthew Daglish, John W. M. Dixon, H. Eve (Chair).

1958 H. Robert Bertram, Mrs. D. F. Bleeker, D. W. Brown, T. Matthew Daglish, H. Eve, Wm. Rogers, Dr. Rupert Warren, John W. M. Dixon (Chair).

1959 H. Robert Bertram, D. W. Brown, T. Matthew Daglish, John W. M. Dixon (Chair), H. Eve, Wm. Rogers, Dr. Rupert Warren, Gordon B. Hodgins.

1960 H. Robert Bertram, D. W. Brown (Chair), T. Matthew Daglish, H. Eve, Gordon B. Hodgins, Wm. Rogers, Dr. Rupert Warren, John W. M. Dixon.

1961 H. Robert Bertram, D. W. Brown (Chair), John W. M. Dixon, H. Eve, Chas. F. Mist, Wm. Rogers, R. Keith Stainton, Betty J. Strang.

1962 H. Robert Bertram (Chair), T. Matthew Daglish, John W. M. Dixon, H. Eve, Chas. F. Mist, Wm. Rogers, R. Keith Stainton, Betty J. Strang, D. W. Brown.

1963 H. Robert Bertram (Chair), D. W. Brown, John W. M. Dixon, H. Eve, John W. Huether, Chas. F. Mist, Douglas G. Pittet, Wm. Rogers, Betty J. Strang.

1964 H. Robert Bertram, D. W. Brown, H. Eve, Frederick C. Hill, John H. Huether, Chas. F. Mist (Chair), Douglas G. Pittet, Wm. Rogers, Betty J. Strang.

1965 Chas. F. Mist (Chair), Betty J. Strang, Douglas G. Pittet, H. Eve, Frederick C. Hill, D. W. Brown, H. Robert Bertram, Wm. Rogers, Dr. Robert J. Murray.

1966 Betty J. Strang (Chair), Douglas G. Pittet, H. Eve, Wm. Rogers, H. Robert Bertram, D. W. Brown, Dr. Robert J. Murray, Chas. F. Mist, Frederick C. Hill.

APPENDIX G

ADDITIONAL CLUBS AND OTHER ACTIVITIES IN LEASIDE

Leaside continues to support a number of active clubs and organizations:
Aerobee's Flying Club (model planes)
Art Gallery Group of Leaside
Bayview Businessmen's Association
Boy Scouts Association
Canadian Girl Guides Association
Canadian Red Cross
Foremen's Club of Leaside
Leaside Atom Baseball Association (boys 9–11) (began in 1952 with John Kennedy
   as President)
Leaside Badminton Club
Leaside Baseball Association (junior teams)
Leaside Bridge Club
Leaside Camera Club
Leaside Chapter IODE
Leaside Gyro Club
Leaside Hockey Association (Peewee to Minor Midget)
Leaside Horticultural Society
Leaside Lawn Bowling
Leaside Personnel Discussion Group (Industrial Plants)
Leaside Rifle and Revolver Club
Leaside Shriner's Club
New Horizons Club (seniors over 60) (began in 1954 with Frank Leonard as
   President)
Square Dance Club

Sports, Arts and Hobbies at Leaside Memorial Gardens:
Bingo (Wednesday nights, May to August)
Free Skating
Leaside Curling Club (formed in 1962)
Leaside Hockey Association for Boys
Toronto Hockey League

APPENDIX H

LEASIDE BASEBALL HONOUR ROLL METRO TORONTO CHAMPIONS

1947   Leaside Electric Peewees (Eastern Ontario Champions)
1950   Leaside Rotary Peewees*
1951   Canada Wire Peewees
1953   Metropolitan Motors Juveniles
1954   Metropolitan Motors Juveniles
      Rumble Motors Midgets
      Doug Lauries Bantams
1955   Metropolitan Motors Juniors
1956   Metropolitan Motors Juniors
1959   Moores Drugs Midgets
1968   Doug Lauries Juveniles
1969   Rumble Motors Midgets
1971   Richardson Sports Juniors*
1972   Leaside All-Star Bantams
1975   Leaside All-Star Bantams*
1977   Leaside All-Star Bantams
      Pitts Construction Juniors*
1983   Richardson Sports Juniors
1986   Leaside All-Star Peewees*
1987   TRL Tigers Midgets
      Leaside All-Star Peewees
1990   Richardson Sports Juniors
1991   Leaside Lightning Midgets
      Richardson Sports Juniors
1992   Leaside Lightning Bantams
1993   Leaside Lightning Bantams
      Leaside Lightning Juveniles (Leaside Midgets Ontario Champions)
1995   Leaside Lightning Bantams
      Leaside Lightning Midgets*
1997   Leaside Lightning Bantams
      Leaside Lightning Juniors
1998   Leaside Lightning Peewees
      Leaside Lightning Juveniles

* = Ontario Champions

PLAYERS

Terry Adams*	Frank Glionna	George Deratney*
Tim Ampleford*	Derek Bienasz*	John Munn
Phil Anderson	Don Graham*	Ian O'Grady
Ted Baylis	Billy Graham	Brian Osborne
Marv Berbeck*	Greg Hales	Paul Papadopoulos
Ron Blackmore	Gerry Hillsdon	Alf Payne*
Steve Breitner*	Tom Irwin	Dave Peyman
Charlie Burns*	Bob Johnstone*	Terry Porter
Brian Canning	Bill Kennedy	Ron Purdy
Ken Chambers	Mike Kilkenny*	Brian Quinlan
Gary Collins*	Cec Kozloski*	Bill Reade*
John Cronk	Dick Krol*	Brian Revin
Colin Cummins	Brian Labute	Alf Riverso*
Clint Dadswell	Ken Lawrence*	John Ryan*
Ryan Davey	Doug McBryde	Pete Slezak
Ron Dominico*	Bob McClelland	Roger Speller
Mike Du Maresq	Ross McDonnell	Robbie Stevens*
Jim Eliopoulos	Mike McEwen	Jim Stevenson
Paul Evans	Bob McKillop*	Dave Sullivan*
John Fallis*	Shawn O'Sullivan	Pete Mahovolich
Remo Cardinale*	Frank Sidey	Mark Zwolinski*
Bob Campbell	Ted Campbell	Roger Lippert
Joe Balazovic*	Bernie Nisker*	John Lightfoot
Barry Jakeman	Jim Parr	Butch McGee

More

Ron Taylor*
Ron Thomas
Mike Thompson
Wayne Thompson
Rick Traugott
Chris Volpe
Bill Weedon
Fred White
Jim Wilson
Peter Wilson
Cliff Wooder*
Duncan Wood*

Brother Acts

Fred/Brian Armstrong
Don/*Jack/Terry Caffery
Tom/Andy Edur
Adrian/Hillary/Leo Ferreira
Johnus/Jim/Peter/George Georgiadis
Bruce/Rae Godbold
John/Brian/Kevin Marks
Paul/Peter/Dan McCann
Marty/Scott McGeown
Peter/Steve/Paul Morris
Don/Barry/Ken Norri
Adam/Jordie Pettle
Ron/Bill/Peter Woods
Rich/John/David Evans

*Signed to professional contracts

NOTES

PRE-SETTLEMENT HISTORY

1 Robert R. Bonis, "A History of Scarborough," 1968, referred to in Don Ritchie's book, *North Toronto*. See Don Ritchie, *North Toronto*. (Erin; Boston Mills Press 1992) 16.
2 Bill Ivy, *A Little Wilderness*. (Toronto: Oxford University Press) 1983, 10, 11.
3 Don Ritchie, *North Toronto*. (Erin: Boston Mills Press, 1992) 19.
4 Elizabeth Simcoe, "Life at York", (January 14, 1974), in *Mrs. Simcoe's Diary*. (Toronto: MacMillan of Canada 1971) 115.
5 Michael Hanlon, *Toronto Star*, January 3, 1998.
6 John Scott, *The Story of the Town of Leaside*. (The Publicity and Industrial Committee of Leaside Town Council, 1931) 5.

THE LEA FAMILY

1 Based on "The Lea (Leigh) Family Tree," March 1975.
2 Edith G. Firth, *The Town of York, 1815-1834. A Further Collection of Documents on Early Toronto,* Toronto: University of Toronto Press, 1966. (The Champlain Society for the Province of Ontario).
3 Scott, The *Story of the Town of Leaside*, 23.
4 John I. Rempel, *The Town of Leaside—A Brief History*. (The East York Historical Society, 1982) 3.
5 *History of Toronto and County of York, Ontario; Vol. 2*. (Toronto: C. Blackett Robinson, Publisher 1885) 195.
6 Ibid.
7 "Inside Leaside," speech given by Percy Turner, Rolph Road School to Rolph Road Home and School, January 13, 1953. (Leaside Library Collection).
8 Editor's note: It is interesting to note that although John Lea Sr.'s tombstone records his death as 1851, it states that he died at 81 years of age. The Lea Family Tree shows his birthdate (as does the *History of Toronto and County of York, Ontario)* as 1773. To have lived 81 years, he would have died in 1854. Upon checking with York Mills Church where the cemetery is, the burial registry confirms it as being December 21, 1851. However, in six other sources, it is said he died in 1854.
9 Rempel, 3–4.

10 *Yore Lore.* The Newsletter of (East York Historical Society, 1983).

11 Orson Fowler, *The Octogonal House, a home for all.* (New York: Dover Publications Inc. 1973).

12 Speech by Percy Turner, Rolph Road School, (1953). (Leaside Library Collection).

13 William Frankling, "The Lea's of Leaside," in *Down Memory Lane.* (March 25).

14 Charles Sauriol, *Remembering the Don.* (Toronto: Consolidated Amethyst Communications Inc., 1981), 144.

15 Percy Turner's speech (1953).

16 Ibid.

17 *York Lore,* East York Historical Society, Saturday December 17, 1983, No.15.

THE RAILWAYS OF LEASIDE JUNCTION

1 Gordon Lightfoot—"A Railway Trilogy," 1965.

2 J.I. Rempel, *The Town of Leaside—A Brief History.* (The East York Historical Society, 1982) 16.

3 In October 1998, Canadian Pacific Ltd. was granted permission by the courts to buy out the shareholders of the dormant Ontario and Quebec Railway Co. The $9.97 million buyout gave CP sole ownership of railway lines to downtown Toronto, through Leaside and North Toronto, lines on which Canadian Pacific trains have travelled for over 100 years.

4 Today, the Don branch continues to give rail access to downtown Toronto. The branch leaves the CPR mainline (Leaside Junction) opposite the Leaside Curling Club, begins its southwesterly path and curves beneath the Bayview Extension just south of Nesbitt Drive. The high steel trestle at the old brick works carries the line above the Bayview Extension as the branch drops steadily towards the floor of the valley on its way to Union Station.

5 The Canadian Northern was a major transcontinental railway.

6 The Duncan Spur, constructed in 1917, runs south from CN Oriole (York Mills) and connects with the CP line into Leaside just north of Eglinton Avenue (behind the Inn on the Park). The Spur continues to serve as a major connection between the Canadian Pacific and Canadian National railways. GO service from the north into Leaside would use the Duncan Spur.

7 The saga of Donald Mann and William Mackenzie, the daring Canadian railway pioneers, began in 1896 when the partners purchased the charter of the Lake Manitoba Railway and Canal Company to build a 125 mile pioneer railway in northern Manitoba.

Mackenzie was born in Kirkfield, Ontario, and Mann in Acton, Ontario. Both had worked for the Canadian Pacific Railway in the 1880s when that company pushed its track westward across the prairies towards Calgary.

Seeing the tremendous potential of the prairies as the region was opened to settlement and knowing of the huge profits made by the Canadian Pacific, Mackenzie and Mann formed a partnership to build a railway of their own to compete ultimately with the Canadian Pacific.

From their humble railway beginnings in northern Manitoba—a line leading nowhere in particular—(Keith McKenzie, *The History of the Canadian National.* [Bison Books 1988] 44)by 1915, just 19 years later, Mackenzie and Mann's railway, the Canadian Northern, had become Canada's second transcontinental line and possessed 10,000 miles of track, along with steamship lines, hotels, mines, express services, grain elevators, irrigation and land development projects! It was an astonishing success story for these two enterprising men from Ontario.

For their work in building the Canadian Northern Railway, Mackenzie and Mann were knighted. However, by now, the Canadian Northern's financial foundation was a fragile and complex web of municipal and provincial loans, land-grant sales, federal tax concessions and federal loans. In 1914, cracks had begun to appear in that financial foundation. With the outbreak of the First World War, British investment money stopped as did the profitable flow of European immigrants. Throughout its feverish continental expansion from Quebec City to Vancouver, the Canadian Northern had accumulated massive debts (as had 14 other railway companies). The Canadian Pacific continued to operate as a healthy and profitable railway.

Faced with the urgent transportation demands of the War, Prime Minister Robert Borden reasoned that the 15 indebted companies were almost 90% publically funded and for another 10% their facilities could be owned and controlled by the government to produce a national railway system.

In 1917, the Canadian Northern passed into full federal ownership—its name and corporate logo disappeared but, shed no tears for Mackenzie and Mann. They walked away with at least $8.5 million in compensation—a princely sum for the time.

In 1919, the huge new federal railway system was named the Canadian National Railways. David B. Hanna, a Vice President with Canadian Northern, was named the first president of the new Canadian National Railways. Leaside's gently curving Hanna Road is named for D. B. Hanna.

8   The early part of the 20th century was the height of the power and profit of the railways—they ruled the transportation world, totally and with some arrogance. The period from 1895 to 1930 saw the construction of some of North America's grandest railway sations—Montreal, Ottawa, Quebec City and the magnificent columned stations in Vancouver, Winnipeg and Toronto.

In the early 1900s in Toronto, there were four competing railway companies. Canadian Pacific decided to withdraw its passenger trains form the old Union Station (near the waterfront) which the four railways had shared.

To retain its corporate distinctiveness, Canadian Pacific would run its passenger service from a new, prestigious station in North Toronto where CP's Leaside line crosses Yonge Street (Summerhill Avenue).

In 1916, Canadian Pacific's grand North Toronto station opened to enthusiastic crowds. The 167 foot clock tower, fashioned after the campanile of St. Mark's Square in Venice crowned the building. The marble walls soared to the 33 feet high ceiling in the elegant concourse which gathered its light from three south-facing graceful arched windows. For the succeeding 10 years the North Toronto station was in its busy heyday.

In 1927, Toronto's splendid new Union Station opened on Front Street. It could accommodate greater crowds and offered more trains to more places. At the North Toronto station, the number of travellers fell off precipitously. Canadian Pacific closed North Toronto in 1930.

THE YORK LAND COMPANY

1   *The Toronto World*, April 8, 1912.
2   Frederick Todd had planned the successful Vancouver and Montreal residential projects.

3   J.I. Rempel, *The Town of Leaside,* 16

4   Frederick Todd had become the town planner of choice of Mackenzie and Mann. They had commissioned Todd earlier to lay out the new towns of Port Mann (Vancouver) and Mount Royal (Montreal). The Mount Royal plan had been a highly popular one and a very profitable development. Assigned to the Leaside project, Todd was expected to incorporate many features of Mount Royal into his plan for Leaside. He was not given a totally free hand, but worked under the direction of Col. F. F. Clarke, the manager of planning for the Canadian Northern Railway. Trained as a landscape architect, Frederick G. Todd was a successful town and garden planner. He was a member of the Garden Beautiful group and a respected landscape painter. Born in New Hampshire, Todd moved to Montreal in 1900 where he established his practice. His commissions included drives and parks for the Ottawa Improvement Commission, site plans for the Parliament Buildings, parkland around the legislatures in Saskatchewan and Alberta, as well as projects in British Columbia and Newfoundland. In Quebec, he worked on Montreal's St. Joseph's Oratory, Quebec City's National Battlefield's Park and the Montebello's Seigniory Club. Thus, Leaside's plan was in the hands of a true professional.

5   By 1929, the date of this photo, these repair facilities were owned by the Canadian National Railway. The bankrupt Canadian Northern Railway had been absorbed by Canadian National in 1917. The repair shops were closed in the 1930s. Today, from Escandar Drive in the Leaside Business Park, two vestiges of the old Canadian Northern shops can be seen. The locomotive house with its 12 doors each high enough to admit a locomotive, serves as a warehouse for WinPak Co. Ltd. On the opposite side, the small red brick yard office which housed the superintendent, still stands.

6   Mackenzie and Mann recognized the importance of a high level bridge across the Don Valley to give easy access to Leaside's open land. They had planned such a project as early as 1911. Their York Land Company shared the cost of the bridge in 1927 with the Township of East York. The bridge was designed to carry both a streetcar line and automobile traffic into Leaside.

7   *The Toronto World*, May 8, 1912 and March 6, 1913.

8   Ibid, March 14, 1913.

9   *The Globe,* July 8, 1912.

10 Leaside Council Minutes, 1913.

11 *The Toronto World*, October 4, 1912.

12 This aerial view is taken above North Leaside, looking east. The prominent building in mid photo is the newly built Northlea School.

FACTORIES COME TO LEASIDE

1   J. Harry Pryce, *The Red Reel, The Story of Canada Wire.* (Toronto: Canada Wire and Cable 1978) 3.

2   Ibid, 6.

3   "The Town of Leaside," (Issued by the Publicity and Industrial Committee of the Town Council 1993) 2. PAO.

4   Excerpt of letter from Kenneth Farrows to his children, 1920. A former employee of CWC who wrote a collection of his memoirs to his children and re-typed it in 1992.

5   Pryce, 25.

6   Pryce, 26-27.
7   Hugh Durnford and Glenn Baechler (eds.), *Cars of Canada,* (Toronto: McClelland and Stewart Ltd., 1973) 181.
8   Ibid, 182.
9   Durnford et al (eds), 181.
10 Ibid, 181.
11 Ibid, 184.
12 Ibid, 187.

THE WAR EFFORT: WORLD WAR I AND WORLD WAR II

1   *Canada Wire and Cable Yearbook,* June 1975, 92.
2   Erin Hawkins, "Remembering the Leaside Aerodromes" *The Observer,* February 21, 1992.
3   J.I. Rempel, *The Town of Leaside.,* 2.
4   P. Turner's speech (1953).
5   Ibid.
6   Donald Jones, *Fifty Tales of Toronto.* (Toronto: University of Toronto Press 1923) 18–19.
7   Donald Jones, "First Mail Flight: No High Flying Adventure," *Toronto Star,* Saturday, October 26, 1985.
8   Jeanne Hopkins, "Looking Back," *Post Newspapers,* June 2, 1995.
9   There appears to be much discrepancy in the spelling of Peck's first name. Some sources use "Brian," some use "Bryan." For consistency in this book, "Brian" has been used.

INDUSTRIAL AND BUSINESS AREAS EXPAND

1   John Scott, *The Story of the Town of Leaside,* 16.
2   Newsletter published by the Lincoln Electric Co. of Canada Ltd. Reprinted from *Canadian Machinery and Manufacturing News,* April, 1958.
3   From notes prepared by Mike Vuchnick, Lincoln Electric Co. January 7, 1998.
4   *Leaside Advertiser,* "Golden Anniversary Issue," May 1963.
5   Ibid.
6   Researched by Art de Waald of Tremco Ltd.
7   *Leaside Advertiser,* "Golden Anniversary Issue."
8   Regal Greetings and Gifts Inc., Merchandising and Communications Department, 1999.
9   Information on Apco taken from *Coatings Magazine,* 1985, 3 & 7; & American *Society of Metals,* October 1931.
10 Researched by Paul Beatt (Winpak Technologies).
11 Researched by Barbara Kalb of Corning Canada.
12 Information on Valvoline prepared by Karen Rout.
13 Hugh Durnford and Glenn Baechler (eds.), *Cars of Canada.* (Toronto: McClelland and Stewart Ltd., 1973)
14 Researched by Rolland Jerry.
15 Contributed by Paul Martin of DEL.
16 Interview with Mr. Borsook by Allan Swinton, October, 1999.
17 From *Ontario: A Celebration of our Heritage.,* 37.

18 Researched by Rolland Jerry.
19 Ibid.
20 Ibid.
21 Ibid.
22 Ibid.
23 Information adapted from Research Enterprises Limited: (Leaside's Secret Little Company) by Bruce Whitehead.
24 *"Church of St. Augustine of Canterbury, Memoir and Appreciation."* Published by a Committee of Parishioners, April 1966, 11.
25 John Scott, *The Story of the Town of Leaside*, 1931, 11.

MERCHANTS OF BAYVIEW, MILLWOOD AND SUNNYBROOK

1 Conversation with Dr. R. Warren, now deceased.
2 Information taken from the "Sunnybrook Anniversary Flyer."
3 Interview with M. Cuzzolino and F. Fusco, owner of Stanley Cleaners.
4 Interview (1999) with Mr. Photi Philos, owner of Bell Jewellers.
5 Interview with Irene Quibell (34 years an employee) October 1999.
6 Interview with Sal Badali at Badali's Fruit Market, October 1999.
7 Extracts from Leaside Council minutes compiled by John Naulles. The minutes are stored in the Record Room at the East York Civic Centre.

A PLACE TO WORSHIP

1 Information from P. Turner's speech (1953) and literature from St. Cuthbert's Church.
2 From Leaside United Church publications.
3 Ibid.
4 *The War Cry*. The Salvation Army Printing House, Nov. 15, 1930, 8.
5 *Leaside Advertiser*, "Golden Anniversary Issue."
6 St. Anselm's Parish Celebrates 50 Years of Faith, 1938–1988. (Toronto: Golla Graphics Ltd.)
7 Ibid plus Editor's research at St. Anselm's School.
8 *Church of St. Augustine of Canterbury: Memoir and Appreciation,* April 1996 (Co-ordinated by a committee of the Parishioners), 12.
9 Ibid, 7.
10 Ibid, 11.
11 Ibid.
12 Ibid, 6.
13 "40th Anniversary Pictorial Directory and History 1950–1990," Published by Northlea United Church.
14 Interview with Moira McNab (longtime member of the congregation), 1998.

EDUCATION FOR OUR YOUTH

1 ___, *The Establishment of Schools and Colleges in Ontario, 1792–1910,* 257.
2 Patricia W. Hart, "Pioneering in North York," in *A History of the Borough.* (Toronto: General Publishing Co.) 103.
3 Audrie J. Baldwin, A written paper (1956) in the Leaside Library Archives.
4 From "Rolph Road School, Wisdom, With Purpose: Our History," School History Committee, 1974, 1.

5   Ibid, 2.
6   Ibid, 2.
7   St. Anselm's Parish Celebrates 50 Years of Faith, 1938-1988 (Toronto: Golla Graphics Inc.)
8   Ibid, 43.
9   From Percy Turner's speech to Rolph Road Home and School (1953), 8.
10 *Clan Call,*" Leaside High School Yearbook, Anniversary Issue, 1975.
11 Ibid.

THE LEASIDE LIBRARY: A COMMUNITY RESOURCE

1   Leaside Library Archives, Book 1
2   Information on Leaside Library from the Leaside Library Archives, Books I, II and III. Compiled by Gail Culligan.

THORNCLIFFE PARK: FROM RACETRACK TO RESIDENTIAL

1   This section on Thorncliffe is adapted from Alan Redway, "Redway's Remarks," *Leaside Advertiser.*
2   Information on Thorncliffe Racetrack researched and written by Chilton Selke of Leaside.
3   Fred Hall (ed.), *"50 Years of Skiing in Southern Ontario with the Toronto Ski Club 1924–1974."* (Toronto Ski Club, 1974).
4   General information on the Thorncliffe Ski Jump taken from *50 Years of Skiing in Southern Ontario.*

THE ORIGINS OF STREET NAMES

1   From Leaside Property Owner's Association 25th Anniversary Special, *Leaside Advertiser*, February 17, 1972.
2   Information from Jeanne Hopkins of North York Public Library, Summer, 1998..
3   Unless indicated otherwise, the information presented here is from: Mary Hoskin Jarvis, "Historical Street Names of Toronto" in *Transactions.* No. 28, 1931–1933 & 1933–34, (Women's Historical Society of Canada) 16–44.

COMMUNITY INVOLVEMENT: SERVICE CLUBS AND LOCAL GROUPS

1   Interview in 1998 with David Thamer, Leaside resident, past Governor of Kiwanis Club.
2   Alan Redway, "Redway's Remarks" *Leaside Advertiser*, (1974), 4.
3   *Leaside Lions Club Carnival Newspaper.* June 10, 1954, 1.
4   Alan Redway, "Redway's Remarks" (1974).
5   Ibid, 4.
6   Researched and written by Ed Barnett, Leaside resident.
7   *Leaside Advertiser*, "Golden Anniversary Issue."
8   Ibid
9   Information on Leaside—East York University Women's Club from Joan Neilson, a member.
10 Information on Leaside Garden Society, June Murdock.

The Parks of Leaside

1   Alan Redway, "Talbot, Mayor We'd Turf Out Today," *Leaside Villager,* May 28, 1982.

Leisure Time in Leaside: Sports and Recreation

1   Interview with Elsie Boyd November, 1999
2   "The Leaside Tennis Club, a Chronicle" by Ann Leach and Stan Goldsmith, 1973.
3   Information on Leaside Aquatic Club from Richard Van Dine, November 1999.
4   Information on baseball in Leaside researched and written by Howard Birnie.
5   Information on Leaside Skating Club researched and written by Yvonne Butorach.
6   *Leaside Advertiser*, "Golden Anniversary Issue."
7   Information for this section was received from: Henry Stachelback (Manager, 199 to the present); Peter Oyler (Chair 1979-1999 and long time Director); Tim Willis (former Chair and Board member); and the Leaside Memorial Community Gardens Archives. Researched and written by long-time resident and Board member, Peter McMurtry.

Safety and Security: Police and Fire Protection

1. Information of the Leaside Police Force researched and written by John Naulls (Leaside resident).
2   Information on Leaside Fire Department as told to John Naulls by John McLean (retired fire fighter).

SELECTED HIGHLIGHTS OF LEASIDE COUNCIL MEETINGS

1   Mike Filey, "Mr. Lea's New Town," in "The Way We Were," *Sunday Sun*, Nov. 24, 1985.
2   Ibid, "Happy 75th, Leaside," May 29, 1988.

RALLYING TO THE CAUSE: ISSUES TO BE RESOLVED

1   Based on "Redway's Remarks".

Profiles of People and Buildings of Historic Interest

1   Interview with Mary (Syme) and Sven Linholm.
1   *Leaside Advertiser*, "Golden Anniversary Issue."
3   Interview with Agnes Vermes.
4   Garden Court promotional materials (12 pages), undated.

Memories of Leaside

1   Taken from recollections prepared by that late Mrs. Edith Davies in February, 1974.
2   Taken from Charles Clay, *The Leaside Story*. 1958, 25.
3   Alan Redway, "Redway's Remarks."
4. All other "Memories" are from interviews by the editor with the individuals, either in their homes or by telephone, between 1997 and 1999.

SELECTED BIBLIOGRAPHY

LEASIDE HISTORY

Charles Clay, *The Leaside Story*. Leaside Council Brochure Committee for Leaside's 45th Anniversary, 1958.*

John I. Rempel, *The Town of Leaside: a brief history*. East York Historical Society, 1982.*

Kathleen Rennick, *The Town Of Leaside: Origins and Development, 1913–1939.* Geography 491 Research Project, University of Toronto, 1986.‡

John Scott, *The Story of Leaside*. Leaside Town Council, 1931.*

OTHER RELATED TITLES

Eleanor Darke, *A Mill Should Be Build Thereon: An Early History of the Todmorden Mills*. Toronto: Natural Heritage Books, 1995.

Eleanor Darke, *Call Me True: A Biography of True Davidson*. Toronto: Natural Heritage Books, 1997.

Edith G. Firth, *The Town of York, Vol. 1. 1793–1815; Vol. 2. 1815–1834*. Toronto: University of Toronto Press, 1966.

Ann Guthrie, *Don Valley Legacy: A Pioneer History*. Erin: Boston Mills Press, 1985.

Donald Jones, *Fifty Tales of Toronto*. Toronto: University of Toronto Press, 1992.

Charles Sauriol, *Remembering the Don*. Toronto: Amethyst Communications Inc., 1981.

Charles Sauriol, *Tales of the Don*. Toronto: Natural History Books, 1984.

Alan Rayburn, *Place Names of Ontario*. Toronto: University of Toronto Press, 1997.

Don Ritchie, *North Toronto*. Erin: Boston Mills Press, 1992.

* These books are out of print. They may be available through a library or from a rare book store.
‡ Available through the Leaside Library.

INDEX

ACKNOWLEDGMENTS

The making and completion of *Leaside* has been a labour of love, one that has brought me even closer to my community. This book, however, is the result of work by many people who generously contributed their time and expertise. In addition to acknowledging the contributors as listed below, special thanks goes to Rosemary White who volunteered to input the original version of the manuscript, many hours of work, and to John Naulls who conscientiously went through every page of the Leaside Council Minutes and extracted copy for this project. Also, appreciation goes to the publishers, Natural Heritage Books (Barry Penhale and Jane Gibson), for their commitment to this publication and to the designers, Norton Hamill Design, for their extraordinary effort in keeping to a deadline. And most importantly, I thank my family for their support, encouragement and patience.

CONTRIBUTORS TO THE DEVELOPMENT OF THE MANUSCRIPT

The publication, *Leaside*, was developed over a span of two years. Thank you to the following:

Isabel Allen	interview
Mr. & Mrs. William Aitken	interview
Sal & Dom Badali	interview; photographs
Donald Bailey	visuals of Canadian Wire and Cable
Mary Bailey	information, Leaside 432 Squadron
Ed Barnett	information, Leaside Rotary
Edna Beange	interview
Paul Beatt, Winpak Ltd.	photograph
Paul Bennedetto	articles
Hilda Berlis	interview
Dr. Robert Bertram	interview; photograph
Bessborough Public School	photographs
Bill & Vito's	interview; photograph
Howard Birnie	information, Leaside baseball
Elsie Boyd	interview
Phyllis & Horace Brockington*	interview

Mariette Brosseau	photograph
Mitch Bubulj	information, Leaside High School
Robert Butcher	interview; photograph
Yvonne Butorach	information, Leaside Skating Club
Canadian Imperial Bank of Commerce	photograph
Wendy Canney	interview
Bernadine Carroll	slides
Jack Christie	interview
Burny Clark	took Editor to site of Thorncliffe Ski Jump
Paul Clough	photographs
Pat Cole-Sayliss	interview; photograph
H. O. Coish	interview; photographs, Canada Wire and Cable
Beryl Ruth Corneil	interview
Gail Culligan	information and photographs, Leaside Library
Mr. Cuzzolino & Mr. F. Fusco	interview, Stanley Cleaners
Ray and Rick Dade	written information, CWC, Roll of Honour
Edith Davies	written memories
Art de Waald	information, Tremco
William Arthur Deacon	interview
Bruce Dowdell*	written information, Millwood Merchants
Jack Doody	interview
Anne Farrows	photograph; written material by Kenneth Farrows (deceased)
Bill Fleming*	interview
Ed Freeman	pre-settlement map
Liz French	information, Leaside skating
Craig Fuller	telephone interview
Gary's Fast Photo	photographic reproduction
George Scott Railton Heritage Centre	photograph
Dave Grierson	information, APCO
Stuart Halliday	photograph
Jim D. Hannah*	research and written information, the railways of Leaside, the York Land Co. and Frederick Todd
Jim Henderson	loan of book, *The Red Reel*
Ric Hill	interview
Carol Hillsdon	photograph, Bessborough School class with names
Corrine & Ted Hiltz	interview (Lea descendants)
John Hoffman	interview
Peg Holloway	interview; photograph
Jeanne Hopkins	information, street names
Herb Horwood	slides from Leaside Camera Club
Susan Hughes	Todmorden Mills Museum and Archives
Bruce Humphrey	interview
Rolland Jerry*	interview; written material, Durant Motors
Dorothy Lamb	made available *Leaside Advertiser*, (50th) Golden Anniversary Issue, 1963

Judy Lauzon	interview
Edgar Lea (deceased)	family tree; photographs
Ted & Barbara Lea	Lea family archival materials (Lea descendants); photograph
Leaside Advertiser	photograph
Bernice Lester	computer input
Sven & Mary (Symes) Linholm	interview; photographs
Paul Martin	information, DEL
Jack McCarthy	interview
Peter McMurtry	information, Leaside Memorial Gardens
Moira McNab	infomation, Leaside Bible Chapel
Ted Mills*	maps; photographs
Anne Morgan	interview (Lea descendant)
Dalton A. Morrison	information, School Board
June Murdoch	information, Leaside Garden Society
John Naulls*	interview; written material on Leaside Council Minutes, Police and Fire Department
Pam Newall	information, Bessborough School
Eric Olson	background, Tennis Club
Pat Osborne	photographs of Leaside schools
Anne Page (deceased)	interview
Joan Park	interview
Parkhurst Auto	interview
Audrey Parr	interview
Dr. Tom Pashby	interview
Doris & John Paxton	interview
Raymond Perringer	interview; photograph
Charles Perry	photograph
Photi Philos	interview
Irene Quibell	interview
Alan Redway	access to "Redway's Remarks" articles; interview
Reed family	photographs
John Ridout	East York Historical Society
Chris Russy	photographs
S. Walter Stewart Library	photographs
St. Anselm's School	photographs
Chilton Selke*	interview; written material, Thorncliffe Racetrack
Arthur Sellers*	interview, historical background
Bill Sherk	slides on Durant Motors
Art Smith	interview
Lorne Smith	telephone interview
Stanley Cleaners	photographs
Alan Swinton	research
David Thamer	information, Leaside Kiwanis
Mary Thompson	interview
Stuart L. Thompson (deceased)	photograph
Albert Turner	photograph

Agnes Vermes*	information, Agnes Campbell MacPhail
Richard Van Dine	information, Aquatic Club
Dr. Warren	interview
Harry & Bob Weston	interview; photograph
Mr. Wilkinson	interview
Harry Wilsher*	interview
Rosemary White	computer input; distribution
Bruce Whitehead	interview; photograph; written information, Pre-settlement, Research Enterprises
Leonard Whitworth	photograph
Mike Vuchnick	information, Lincoln Electric Co.

* denotes members of original Leaside Book Committee

APCO Industries Co. Ltd.
Badali's Fruit Market
Bayview Clipper
Bell Jewellers Ltd.
Bill and Vito Auto Service Ltd.
Bonnie Byford Real Estate Ltd.
Brennan Pontiac Buick GMC Ltd.
Canadian Imperial Bank of Commerce (CIBC), Laird Dr.
Canadian Tire Store, Leaside
Coca-Cola Beverages Ltd.
Diesel Equipment Ltd.
Dorothea Knitting Mills Ltd.
East York Kiwanis Club
First Professional Management Inc.
Future Shop Ltd.
Garthwood Homes
Goldlist Properties Inc.
Humphrey Funeral Home and Chapel Ltd.
Interior Care Ltd.
James Graham Paving
JOV bistro
Kosmor Construction Ltd.
Leaside Autobody
Leaside Rotary Club
Leonard Linton
Linda Lundstrom

Lincoln Electric Co. of Canada Ltd.
Loblaws Ltd.
Merchant of Tennis Ltd.
Dr. Paul S. Monczka
Monterra Capital Corp.
Paradox
Parkhurst Auto Centre
Peaches and Green
Pet Smart
PSInet Ltd.
Revenue Properties Co. Ltd.
Patrick Rocca (Bosley Real Estate)
Scotia Bank, Leaside
Shoppers Drug Mart
Stanley Cleaners
Sunnybrook Home Hardware
The Country Store
The East York Mirror
The Second Cup
The Smokin' Cigar
Tremco (Canada) Ltd.
Wenday Publishing Ltd., *Leaside Advertiser*
W. H. Bosley and Co. Ltd.
Whimsical House
Winpak Technologies Inc.
Richard Wolfe

ABOUT THE EDITOR

Jane Pitfield has been a resident of Leaside since 1984. She is married to Rob and has four children—Elizabeth, Stephanie, Alison and Hartland. She has been active in Leaside as a director on the Leaside Property Owners Association and the Bessborough After-Four program. She represented the Leaside/Thorncliffe Community as a School Trustee for three years and currently is one of the three Councillors representing East York on the Toronto City Council.

Her interest in heritage is reflected by her membership on the East York Historical Society and Todmorden Mills Museum Board.